Date Due

FEB 2 8 196			

STUDIES IN PHILOSOPHY

X

THE PSYCHOLOGICAL BASIS

OF

HERDER'S
AESTHETICS

by

JOE K. FUGATE

Kalamazoo College

1966

MOUTON & CO.

THE HAGUE · PARIS

424

ACKNOWLEDGEMENTS

The author wishes to express his indebtedness to those whose help and encouragement have made this work possible: to my former teacher and long-time friend Prof. H. A. Hartwig, who first introduced me to Herder and awakened my interest in him; to Prof. Konrad Schaum, who directed this work as a doctoral dissertation, made innumerable valuable suggestions, read and corrected all the drafts and evaluated the finished product; to my wife, who was ever ready with words of encouragement and who helped me prepare the final manuscript; to Miss Kathleen Young, who assisted me with the proofing and in the preparation of the index; to Kalamazoo College, whose generous grant has made the publication of this work possible.

Kalamazoo College
Kalamazoo, Mich.
August 1965

JOE K. FUGATE

TABLE OF CONTENTS

INTRODUCTION

Although even a perfunctory survey of a list of Herder's works, which would contain such titles as *Vom Erkennen und Empfinden der Menschlichen Seele,* and *Ist die Schönheit des Körpers ein Bote von der Schönheit der Seele?,* cannot but help to indicate to some degree Herder's interest in a psychological approach to aesthetic questions, the full scope of this interest becomes apparent only upon careful examination of the texts themselves. It is of considerable significance, then, when in the *Viertes Wäldchen* Herder refers to aesthetics as an "innere Plastik des Geistes" (IV, 97),[1] as a "Seelenlehre des Schönen" (IV, 97). There can be little doubt of the importance which Herder assigns to an understanding of the human soul as a prerequisite to an understanding of any of man's endeavours when he writes in the *Journal meiner Reise im Jahre 1769*, "Die Menschliche Seele, an sich und in ihrer Erscheinung auf dieser Erde, ihre sinnlichen Werkezeuge und Geschichte und Hoffnung (en) und Vergnügen, und Charaktere und Pflichten, und alles was Menschen hier glücklich machen kann, sei meine erste Aussicht" (IV, 364). Nor can there be any doubt regarding Herder's concept of the power of the soul when we read in the *Viertes Wäldchen*: ". . . die Menschliche Seele [hat] mehr gewürkt, und entwickelt, gefehlt und gefunden, als der Philosoph im ganzen Leben seiner Abstraktionen" (IV, 29f).

Mere recognition of the fact, however, that Herder has consistently worked with concepts of the soul hardly does justice to

---

[1] Johann Gottfried v. Herder, *Sämmtliche Werke,* ed. B. Suphan *et al.* (Berlin, 1877f). Cited in the text by volume and page without further identification.

the importance of these concepts for his aesthetic. Why he chooses the soul as an avenue of approach and how he applies this choice are of equal importance. In the *Viertes Wäldchen* Herder postulates his concept of the soul as a composite whole, where all of man's powers and faculties work together in harmonious unity. Although an integral part of this whole, each of man's powers and faculties nevertheless maintains its own identity, thus illustrating the basic principle of universality in individuality. Since the soul itself, its organization and operation, remain hidden to the view of man, it can be said that Herder's concept of the soul is more functional in nature than concrete-objective. The existence of the soul and its powers can never be proved in the same sense that one proves the dimensions of an object, but must be accepted on the basis of certain perceptible manifestations which point to its existence.

Herder says in one of the drafts of *Vom Erkennen und Empfinden der Menschlichen Seele:* "Wir leben immer in einer Welt, die wir uns selbst bilden" (VIII, 252). With this statement Herder points to the tremendous creative power of the human soul. The soul itself is a creation of God, and as such is man's link with the Creator, with things which are eternal, divine, and heavenly, rather than mortal, human, and earthly. But from the moment of its inception on it is a dynamic entity. The first task which faces the soul is to create some means of communication with the rest of creation, and this it does by creating a body. "Alsdenn wirds offenbar werden, dass die Seele sich einen Körper durchs Gefühl und zum Gefühl von aussen bilde, oder sich fühlend in die Welt hineinbilde!' (VIII, 104) This body Herder describes as: ". . . Werkzeug der Seele . . . Phänomenon, Begrif der Ordnung" (VIII, 249). Even more important, however, is the significance of the body for the function of the soul. "Kurz, der Körper ist Symbol, Phänomenon der Seele in Beziehung auf's Universum" (VIII, 250). Thus through the body which it creates the soul enters into a relationship with the world roundabout it, i.e. the material, while at the same time by its very nature it maintains its original relationship with that which transcends the material, i.e. the spiritual. The soul therefore occupies a medial position, even as man is referred to by Herder as the *Mittelgeschöpf*, and becomes the arbiter between the material and the spiritual, both as the means of this union, and as the exact point of transition between the two realms. As Herder expresses this in one of his poems never published in his lifetime (XXIX, 258), man is the beginning and end of a process which finally unites the antitheses darkness and light, nothing and everything, the material and the spiritual, being and non-existence, and the origins of this process, indeed of man himself, are to be found within the soul of man.

As soon as the soul has created its body, the body begins to perform its function as the soul's medium of contact with the universe about it. In other words, the body is created as an organ of and for feeling, that omnipresent concept in Herder's writings which will frequently be discussed in this study. As Herder puts it: "So muss alles Körper werden, um schön fürs Gefühl zu seyn und zwar insonderheit Menschlicher Körper . . . Schöner Körper ist sinnliche Idee von Vollkommenheit; dies in uns Idee von unserer Vollkommenheit, erinnert also die Seele an das Bild, das sie hatte, da sie sich ihren Körper schuf." (VIII, 101) According to Herder there is no perception without feeling, nor for that matter is there feeling and sensation without a certain perception. Lest there be any doubt that in spite of the important function of the body as a medium for the soul it is the soul which is of prime importance in this process, Herder says: "Die innere Kraft gibt dem ganzen Symbol von Empfindung, von sich selbst aus Richtung, Dauer, Zweck, Fortleitung: denn nicht der äussere Körper ists, der in meine Seele kommt (er bleibt immer auf seiner Stelle) sondern der Geist, das Bild von ihm, das vermittelst meines Organs mir analog war" (VIII, 252). Herder's concept of the body as the soul-created medium of the soul, this "Psychologische Physiologie" (VIII, 250) as he terms it, of the soul as a unified, dynamic entity, of a process which permits no perception without feeling and sensation, are all parts of a divine plan which points to the unique function of the soul within the whole of creation. "Und das es nun der natürliche Fortschritt ist von Dunkeln zum Hellern, vom Unvollständigen zur Vollständigkeit, welch ein schöner Weg ist jeder Seele bestimmt im Universum" (VIII, 242). The way designated the soul is one which is constantly changing and developing through the influence of the feelings channeled into it, it is a way which recognizes the spirit as more important than mere ideas, the universal human condition as more important than theoretical norms, development as more important than momentary perfection. Herder recognizes the functional principles revealed so clearly in the operation of the soul as basic to the production and understanding of art. The soul is the seat of man's creative powers, and it is through them that man is able to emulate the Great Creator. Only the soul has the power to perceive the essence of art, and to make this essence a part of man's being. Only the soul has the power to create visible evidence of its existence, first in the form of its own body, later in the work of art.

Thus the concept of the soul, and its functional principles gain importance in every facet of Herder's aesthetic, and can be traced throughout the whole corpus of his writings. In his first major work, the *Fragmente*, where Herder deals primarily with the problem of language, and offers numerous suggestions for the improvement of German, it is clear that the emphasis here is on the internal, rather than the external aspects of language. He points to the relationship of thought and expression and says that the purpose of language, insofar as this is possible, is to allow the poet to present his "ganze lebendige Seele" (I, 395) through the medium of language and to speak to the soul of another that he might feel it. The task of the critic, also sketched in the *Fragmente*, is: ". . . dass der Kunstrichter sich in den Gedankenkreis seines Schriftstellers versezze und aus seinem Geist lese" (I, 247). In another later work Herder described this as: ". . . im Geist eines Autors zu *wohnen*, seine Sprachweise sich eigen gemacht zu haben, vom Plan und Zweck seines Werks aus dessen eigner Seele gleichsam unterrichtet zu seyn . . ." (XXIV, 182). Author and critic must concern themselves with the spirit of the work because: "Wahre Poesie steht nicht in Büchern, schwebt nicht auf Lippen allein; sie denkt und dichtet in der Seele, sie ordnet und regiert das Leben" (XVIII, 156), Poetry is "Abdruck der Seele" (VIII, 339), "Ueberbringer der Natur in die Seele" (VIII, 340). As such, literature exerts a profound effect upon man, and more than any

other art furthers the development of his soul. Herder gives special
attention to these formative functions of art in the prize essay of
1778, *Ueber die Würkung der Dichtkunst auf die Sitten der Völker
in alten und neuen Zeiten.*

Even in the plastic arts, which are usually considered to be
static and inorganic, the soul of the work of art is the most important consideration. In the *Plastik* Herder writes: "Die Bildnerei arbeitet *in einander. Ein* lebendes, Ein *Werk* voll Seele, das
da sei und daure" (VIII, 16). The plastic arts, indeed all arts, have
only one purpose: ". . . *Seele* im *Körper* darzustellen, Götter,
Menschen und edle Thiere, das bilde die Kunst und das hat sie
gebildet" (VIII, 17). Beauty does not exist in form alone, but in a
combination of form and content. Without an inner perfection of
the spirit to complement the outer form there can be no beauty.
"Nur die *Bedeutung innerer Vollkommenheit* ist Schönheit"
(VIII, 56). If this is true for the work of art, it must also be true of
man himself, whom Herder considers the measure of the rest of
God's creation. He refers to the countenance of man as "Tafel
Gottes und der Seele" (VIII, 45), as a "heilige Decke" behind
which "Menschheit" (VIII, 45) lies concealed. Recognition of
the figure or shape of man is not sufficient. To understand what
man is one must also understand the workings of his spirit. *"Welcher Mensch weiss, was im Menschen ist, ohne der Geist des Menschen, der in ihm ist"* (VIII, 43).

In the *Kalligone* we read the significant lines: "Allem Orga-
nischem schafft der Geist Form, die Er belebet" (XXII, 193). The
important words here are *schafft* und *belebet*, which point to the
soul as a dynamic entity. Not only is the soul alive and ever active,
it possesses definite creative powers. In fact, according to Herder
the soul creates the form through which it is revealed. Herder conceives of the soul as a unified, harmoniously functioning whole,
where each of man's faculties exists with equal rights. This state
of unity and harmony is made possible by the ordering power of
the soul, for the soul, and the soul alone, possesses sufficient power
to mold all of man's faculties into an ordered totality. Already
here in this ordering process the soul has given evidence of its
dynamic creative power. But this power is revealed to an even

greater extent in the production of a work of art, for here it is not from man's form, but from the power of his soul that the work of art emanates. Like the soul itself, the work of art is composed of many elements, all moulded together in harmonious unity by the creative power of the artist's soul. Art for Herder is a synthetic process, a process of making "one from many". This is one of the great themes of the Shakespeare essay, and one to which Herder returns again and again. In the aesthetic experience, which for Herder requires the presence of both subject and object, the subject must apprehend the totality of the work of art if his experience of it is to be vital. Although the subject experiences the work of art through his senses, the senses channel these varied impressions into the soul, where they are then ordered into a unified whole. Thus Herder's concept of the soul assumes prime importance in every aspect of aesthetics. It is *the* most important consideration in the creation of the work of art, and it is *the* most important factor in the experiencing of a work of art. Moreover, the role of the aesthetic experience in the developmental process of the human soul must not be overlooked. As an organic entity, the soul is constantly growing and developing. Internally, the soul is able to grow because of its own innate potential. To a large degree, however, the development of the soul is dependent upon external stimuli. This then is the function of art, to provide the soul with the necessary stimuli and to aid it along on its drive toward perfection, *Humanität*.

This study is an attempt to examine Herder's aesthetic from the perspective of his basic psychological presuppositions and principles, already briefly sketched here, and thereby to reveal hitherto unnoticed vistas within his aesthetic. It must be admitted that much that is said here has already been said elsewhere. Thus any claims which this study has to originality must rest upon its treatment of Herder's approach and the methodological principles of his writings, and not on the treatment of their content alone, which although important, for the purposes of this study must remain something secondary. Haym, for example, whose work continues to be indispensible to the Herder scholar, seems to recognize that there is a relationship between Herder's psychology and his aesthetics, but he never goes beyond the mere observation of this fact. Martin Schütze, who has performed a valuable service by calling attention to the existence of a system of psychology in Herder's writings in his *The Fundamental Ideas in Herder's Thought*, which appeared serially in *Modern Philology* from 1920 until 1924, and even more so in his fine essay "Herder's Psychology" in the October 1925 edition of *The Monist*, remains however more the historian of ideas in both studies than one interested primarily in aesthetics. Clark's article on "Herder's Concept of 'Kraft' " in the September 1942 *PMLA*, and his more recent remarks in his comprehensive study of Herder, are comparable to Schütze's investigations. Both are significant for what they have to say about psychology itself, but nowhere is there an attempt to apply these ideas to Herder's aesthetic. The only place where such an application is made seems to be Spranger's contribution to the Petsch *Festschrift*, "J. G. Herder: Ahnung und Erfüllung". Spranger's essay is important because in it he not only recognizes the significance of Herder's doctrine of the soul, but also sees Herder's own poetic attempts as the best avenue of approach to his own complex personality. The formative aspects of art and the importance of the soul in this process have been admirably presented in Berger's *Menschenbild und Menschenbildung*. But here too the emphasis is more psychological than aesthetical. As this brief survey of the most pertinent literature indicates, nowhere has the role of Herder's psychology as an inner principle and a creative approach to all aesthetic observations been explored and presented in its entirety as this work attempts to do.

I

THE RELATIONSHIP OF PSYCHOLOGY
AND AESTHETICS

A. PHENOMENOLOGY OF THE SOUL

The word "aesthetics" is derived from the Greek verb *aistha-nesthei*, which means to feel or perceive through the senses. In the Latin derivative form *aesthetica* the word was first used by Baumgarten in 1750 in his treatise of the same name to designate a science of sensuous knowledge, whose goal is beauty. As a part of his argument against Riedel in the *Viertes Wäldchen* Herder discusses several of Baumgarten's definitions of aesthetics. Herder was well aware of the significant contribution which Baumgarten had made to the science of aesthetics, and considers him the greatest of the three aestheticians mentioned by Riedel. Yet Herder finds it difficult to accept unconditionally Baumgarten's definition of aesthetics as "die Wissenschaft des Gefühls des Schönen" (IV, 22), or as Baumgarten expresses this in Wolffian language, "die sinnliche Erkenntniss" (IV, 22). Baumgarten also advanced another definition for aesthetics, and this was "die Kunst schön zu denken" (IV, 22). As far as Herder was concerned the latter part of Baumgarten's definition of aesthetics is completely unacceptable, not so much because he could not agree with Baumgarten's assertion that sensuous perception played an important role in aesthetics, but rather because he was convinced that Baumgarten's emphasis of the sensuous excluded other equally important elements which also had a contribution to make to aesthetics. When Herder calls aesthetics a science, then he is in agreement with the first part of Baumgarten's definition. But as a science aesthetics must include analyses, judgements, deductions, and proofs. It must make use of the combined total of man's mental faculties and not restrict itself to any single one. The word which Herder most often uses to designate this sum of man's faculties, that which distinguishes him from every other creature, is the soul. It is of considerable significance, then when in the *Viertes Wäldchen* Herder calls aesthetics "die Seelenlehre des Schönen" (IV, 97). In the *Plastik* aesthetics is referred to as "die Phänomenologie des Schönen und Wahren" (VIII, 11). From still another statement of the *Viertes Wäldchen* it is clear that for Herder beauty is the main concern of aesthetics: *"Schönheit ist das Hauptwort aller Aesthetik"* (IV, 46). Beauty, in turn, is merely the outward expression of truth, for Herder defines beauty as "dies Phänomenon der Wahrheit (IV, 20).

If Herder can call aesthetics "the soul doctrine of the beautiful," then it must be assumed that his own psychology will have an important bearing on his aesthetics, and that an understanding of this psychology is one of the important gateways to an understanding of his aesthetics.

Although Herder was frequently accused of being unorthodox in religious and theological matters, his concept of the creation would undoubtedly satisfy the most fundamental of orthodox thinkers. For Herder God was the creator of the universe and of every creature in it. "Niemand gibt, wie Gott gibt, und niemand kann wie Gott ersetzen und vergelten. Allen Geschöpfen gab er das Daseyn aus freier Liebe" (XV, 295). Since God is the creator and all life owes its existence to Him, Herder sees in every species of animated creation a spark of the divine. "Alles Leben der Natur, alle Arten und Gattungen der beseelten Schöpfung, was sind sie, als Funken der Gottheit ... O Freund, würde uns ein Auge gegeben, den glänzenden Gang dieser Gottesfunken zu sehen: wie Leben zu Leben fliesst ... welch eine neue Stadt Gottes, welche Schöpfung in der Schöpfung würden wir gewahr werden!" (XV, 289). Already in the act of the creation itself the soul, for this is the divine spark, the new city of God that Herder is talking about here, is endowed with divine attributes. In Herder's metaphor the soul is a "creation within a creation", i.e. the soul is a microcosm, bearing all the salient features of the macrocosm – its harmony, order, and completeness. Just as the soul of the

Creator is assumed to be complete within itself, with every one of its imaginable attributes moulded together in a completed, harmonious whole, so too must it be assumed that the same unity is inherent in all of its offspring, especially since the human soul is conceded to be a duplicate in miniature of the Divine Soul. Riedel's disregard of the conclusion reached here, which for Herder was basic to any psychology, was, as we shall see, the main point of Herder's disagreement with him in the *Viertes Wäldchen*.

The basic importance which Herder attaches to a concept of the soul for any understanding of the creation is revealed by his definition of creation as "Fortrückung zu einer Menschlichen Seele" (VIII, 253). The soul therefore represents the culmination of the creative process. But with this statement Herder also seems to be casting doubt on the validity of the creation unless the completing factor of the human soul is attained; or to state this in slightly different terms, there is no creation at all unless the creation process is complete, and the completing factor is the human soul.

The beginnings, indeed the whole habitat, of the human soul are shrouded in a mysterious realm invisible to the eye of man. "Die Menschliche Seele schwebt in einem Reich andrer Kräfte, als das unser Auge sieht" (VIII, 254). This realm of other powers, as Herder terms it, is a spiritual realm of the divine, where the germ of the soul as a dark, amorphous substance awaits the intercessive creative act of divine power to give it identity. Herder describes this process as follows: "Ist Göttliche Kraft da, die aus Zween Eins bilde: warum sollte nicht auch Göttliche Kraft daseyn, die einer dunkler bisher empfindenden Substanz, die gewiss nicht müssig war, sondern auf dem Wege der Continuität fortklimmte, jetzt den Grad Helle, Kraft, Deutlichkeit gebe, dass sie Menschliche Seele werde und über das Aggregat ihrer neuen Organe herrsche" (VIII, 253). In another metaphor Herder sees the beginnings of the soul in a suspended state awaiting the hymn of creation. "Des Träumenden Seele hörte in Allem *Einen* Klang, den Hymnus der Schöpfung" (XXIV, 573). Not until divine thought, which has in it the rule of the creation, is infused into the dark substance awaiting formation into the human soul, does the actual creation take place. "Welten umwandelten mich: mir wars, als empfände ich hier *Gottes Gedanken,* die Regel der Schöpfung" (XXIV, 573).

Immediately, in its first moments of self-sufficiency after the creative process has taken place, the soul possesses all of its basic attributes. Fundamental among these is the ability to act, and to develop and unfold, which according to Herder is the purpose of any organism. "Die innere Thätigkeit des Entwickelns ist aber sein Zweck, sein inneres dunkels Vergnügen, und eine beständige Vervollkommung sein selbst" (IV, 29). But Herder also seems to regard spontaneous action as a capability of the dark substance from which the soul originates even before divine power is infused into it, as the lines above ("gewiss nicht müssig war, sondern auf dem Wege der Continuität fortklimmte" (VIII, 253), from the first version of *Vom Erkennen und Empfinden* indicate. As the soul gradually awakens after its creation the first substance of which it becomes aware is itself, its ego. Yet even before the soul begins to perceive outside of itself, within it is present its full potential, a potential which cannot be increased, but which can be developed, a potential which innately possesses the entire possibility of human ideas. Herder makes this clear in his first excursion into the realm of psychology in the *Viertes Wäldchen.* "Noch scheint ihm [i.e. dem Menschen] keine Empfindung beizuwohnen, als die dunkle Idee seines Ich, so dunkel als sie nur eine Pflanze fühlen kann; in ihr in dessen liegen die Begriffe des ganzen Weltall; aus ihr entwickeln sich alle Ideen des Menschen" (IV, 28f). The process and purpose which the soul is destined to undergo and to strive for must therefore never be construed to mean that the soul is transformed or that its essential character is in any way changed. Rather, it is a question of the development of this character to its fullest possibilities.

Herder's first organized treatment of psychology is found in his *Viertes Wäldchen,* a work which, as Clark has accurately observed, "could have changed the entire course of German aesthetics and hence of German art, which at this period was so closely bound up with aesthetic thought",[1] had it not slumbered in ob-

---

[1] Robert T. Clark, Jr., *Herder: His Life and Thought* (Berkeley-Los Angeles, 1955), p. 88.

scurity in Herder's unpublished papers until nearly a half-century after his death. As was so often the case with his writings, Herder gains an approach to his subject through a polemic, in this instance against Friedrich Justus Riedel, the author of two now forgotten works, *Theorie der schönen Künste und Wissenschaften,* 1767, and *Briefe über das Publicum,* 1768. The crux of Herder's attack against Riedel did not first and foremost have its origins in personal animosity against Riedel, as Richard Wilhelm [2] has stated in his standard work on Riedel, or as Haym [3] had claimed, in Herder's opposition to Riedel's assertion that simple feelings directly convince us of the true, the good, and the beautiful. Instead, as Martin Schütze first observed, Herder's attack was directed against Riedel's tripartite division of the soul. [4]

Riedel's chief concern, in Clark's words, "was the laudable one of establishing aesthetics on a psychological basis". [5] According to Riedel man has three ultimate aims (*Endzwecke*), all of which are subordinate to his intellectual perfection. These three he designates (1) the true, (2) the good, and (3) the beautiful. Each of these has its own fundamental faculty which nature has bestowed upon it: for the true a *sensus communis,* for the good the conscience, and for the beautiful taste. The *sensus communis* is for the true, as are conscience and taste analogously for the good and the beautiful, a sort of inner feeling whereby one is directly convinced of the truth or falseness of a matter without the benefit of reasoning or judgement. Herder sees dire consequences in this line of reasoning. When Riedel says that common sense is always immediately convinced of truth solely by means of a sensation without reasoning or any other psychological activity, then this *sensus communis* is little more than a feeling, which in itself is the assurance of one thing only: "Unmittelbar, durch ein inners Gefühl bin ich eigentlich von nichts in der Welt überzeugt, als dass

---

[2]   Richard Wilhelm, *Friederich Justus Riedel und die Ästhetik der Aufklärung* (Heidelberg, 1933), p. 121.
[3]   Rudolf Haym, *Herder,* ed. Wolfgang Harich (Berlin, 1954), I, 272.
[4]   Martin Schütze, "Herder's Psychology", *The Monist,* XXXV (Oct. 1925), p. 514.
[5]   Clark, *Herder,* p. 89.

ich bin, dass ich mich fühle" (IV, 7). It should be remembered that
for Herder this self-awareness was the state of the soul in the very
first moments of its existence following its awakening by the
creative act. But for the perception of anything outside of the ego
something beyond mere feeling is required, i.e. judgement, distinction in judgement, and deduction. One faculty of the human mind
cannot be divorced from it if the sensitive balance of order and
harmony within its delicate mechanism is to be maintained. Otherwise, the mind would turn into a chaos of unrelated, individual
concepts, or in Herder's language *Inselbegriffe.* "Siehe da eine
Menge Inselbegriffe, ohne Ordnung, ohne Zusammenhang, ohne
Brücken und ohne Dämme. Sie sollen gereihet, sie sollen verbunden
werden – ei! nun würkt mein inneres Gefühl nicht mehr allein,
ich lerne verbinden und trennen, siehe da! eine reflechirte Würkung der Seele: ich urtheile" (IV, 8). The fact that development
of the mind depends upon something more than a group of isolated individual concepts without order or connection is easily ob-
servable in a child. A child does not learn from *one* feeling, but
from many individual feelings, all of which are united into a
composite whole by the mind. "Aber freilich! von der ersten
Kindheit an haben wir uns an Denken, und an die mancherlei
Arten des Denkens, und an alle Arten unter ein ander gewöhnt,
dass, so wie bei allen Gewohnheiten, auch endlich bei dieser, das
Bermerken und Unterscheiden der Theilhandlungen, die wir Ge-
wohnheitsweise verrichten, schwer fällt. Wir haben von der
ersten Lebenszeit an gedacht, geurtheilt, geschlossen, alles dies
oft wechselweise, unter einander, zusammen" (IV, 9). The workings of man's mental process as described by Herder in these lines
already point out at this early date a principle which is basic to
Herder's concept of the soul. "Sie [i.e. the senses] stellen ihr [i.e.
the soul] alle ein Mannigfaltes vor, wo ihr Macht und Amt gegeben
wird, daraus ein Eins zu machen" (VIII, 239). In other words, it
is the function of the soul through its various thought processes to
combine into harmonious unity the infinite perceptions delivered
to it by the senses. As Herder often expresses it, the soul makes
"Eins aus Vielem".

After examining Riedel's statements Herder concluded that

Riedel had erroneously changed the essential concept of the soul as *one* fundamental faculty into one of three fundamental faculties, each of which pursues its own individual course, unmindful of a conception of the mind which presupposes an active bond of interrelation between all of its constituent parts. "Denn eben diese drei Habituelle Anwendungen einer Geisteskraft macht er, und das ist sein Zweck, sein Verdienst, seine Verbesserung der Philosophie, zu *Grundkräften der* Seele" (IV, 11). In the biting ironical tone which he frequently employs in the heat of a polemic, Herder labels Riedel's effort "wahrer Psychologischer Unsinn" (IV, 11). Herder's evaluation of Riedel's psychology is undoubtedly correct, for once established each of these fundamental faculties is thought of as a separate entity, i.e. a man is possible without taste, but with understanding, without understanding, but with conscience, etc. Furthermore, if Riedel builds up a philosophy and a psychology based on each of these faculties, what is to prevent the addition of more faculties, each with its own system?

The remainder of the *Viertes Wäldchen* is devoted to Herder's vindication of his own basic psychological premise that the soul exists as one unified, harmonious whole. As Martin Schütze points out, Herder discusses the unity of the soul from three points of view: the genetic, the functional, and the logical.[6] Of these three the logical is the most important, for its concern is with the processes involved in reaching the ultimate conceptions of the true, the good, and the beautiful. The functional view, which is the subject of the second chapter of the *Viertes Wäldchen* and which deals with the relation between sense impressions and abstract ideas, has no direct bearing on Herder's concept of the unity of the mind, and so can be ignored here. The genetic view, which is one of Herder's hallmarks, can best be seen by turning to what Herder himself has said.

Since Herder sees growth and development exemplified in everything about him, in every aspect of human and cosmic nature, it should hardly be any wonder that he also applied the criteria of growth and development to that most basic of human factors, the

6   Schütze, "Herder's Psychology", p. 515.

human soul. The conditions which determine the development of the soul, the role played by the senses in channeling into it stimuli and feelings, and the effect which the development of the soul exerts upon the course of human events are all questions sufficiently important for an understanding of Herder's psychology to merit individual treatment. Since the second part of this chapter will direct itself to these questions, here we shall restrict ourselves to Herder's treatment of the genetic view within the *Viertes Wäldchen*, which is best summed up in the following quotation:

Vorausgesetzt also nichts als den Unterschied zwischen Empfindung, Urtheil und Schluss; lasset uns in unsere Kindheit zurückgehen: die ersten Begriffe von den Körpern, z.E. ihre Undurchdringlichkeit, Farbe, Figur, wie haben wir sie erlangt? unmittelbar durch ein einzeln Gefühl? Nichts minder! durch viele einzelne Gefühle, durch das lange Gegeneinanderhalten derselben, durch Vergleichung, und Urtheil, blos dadurch lernten wir sie bis zur Ueberzeugung. Der Begrif von Grösse, von Weite, von Entfernung, scheint Empfindung, unmittelbares Gefühl, dass ers aber nicht sey, das zeigen unsre oftmaligen Irrthümer und die kleinsten Versuche mit Reflexion. Sie zeigen, dass alle diese Ideen Urtheile, spätgefasste Urtheile, die Folgesätze aus vielen, anfangs verfehlten, und noch oft fehlenden Schlüssen sind (IV, 8f).

The concepts attained during the first stages of growth of the soul all relate to concrete items. But even to acquire these most rudimentary concepts the soul must call upon all of its faculties working together in a harmonious whole. These processes within the soul can be compared to the workings of a delicate mechanism. Each individual part performs its own specialized function, and yet the combined total of these functions can be seen in the overall operation of the mechanism. Although a proper and orderly operation of the mind is one of its innate potentials, this potential must first be developed by the trial and error method before it can be realized. Even though growth and development involve a process of continuing complexity, whereby more and more of the individual functions of the mind are brought into play, there also develop at the same time a simplification and acceleration of these processes through habit. Consequently, the more the habit is applied, the greater will be the facility of the mind's operational processes and the more harmonious its functioning as a unified whole.

Riedel's second work, *Briefe über das Publicum,* 1768, provided Herder with an approach to his examination of the soul from the logical point of view. In his work Riedel distinguishes between three different roads to aesthetics; Aristotelean (derivation of laws from master's works); Baumgartenean (definition of principles); and Homean (feeling). But after he draws these distinctions, Riedel rejects the ideas of all three of these great thinkers by asserting that aesthetics can be found in none of them, and replaces each of them with one of the fundamental faculties he had already established in his earlier work. Herder quite rightly argues that each of the three aestheticians has a contribution to make to aesthetics, and he fails to see how Riedel can ignore them or how he can replace them with his fundamental faculties. "Ist dies nicht alles Eine Arbeit Einer Seele, und warum denn muthwillig zu verläumden, da doch ohne alle drei zusammengenommen nie eine Aesthetik werden kann?" (IV, 18).

Since beauty was the basic concept of any aesthetic, the problem which confronted Herder here, and indeed which confronts any aesthetician, was to establish criteria to determine the beauty of the object. Seizing upon the three ways to aesthetics rejected by Riedel, Herder finds that each of the mental processes best exemplified by the method of one of the great thinkers is essential to a determination of the beautiful, but that each, in turn, is incomplete unless complemented by the others. Thus Herder finds that all good thinkers make use of the analytic-deductive method of Aristotle to determine basic principles. But since without definition a principle will likely prove useless, Baumgarten's method must be included with that of Aristotle. And finally, since Home had clearly established the important role of feeling and perception for any aesthetic system, his method must be added to the Aristotelean-Baumgartenean approach already in use. Instead of recognizing, as Herder did, that each of these methods is only a part of a composite, harmonious whole, Riedel had sought to reduce each to one of his *Inselbegriffe* in much the same manner that he had attempted a tripartite division of the mind in his *Theorie der schönen Künste und Wissenschaften.* Thus Herder's refutation of Riedel's argument in the *Briefe über das Publicum* both supports his rejection of Riedel's faulty psychology with its tripartite division of the soul and exposes to plain view the errors of Riedel's aesthetic, which in effect is built on the foundation of this faulty psychology. Herder is convinced that without all the mental processes exemplified by the methods of the three thinkers Aristotle, Baumgarten, and Home, there can be no aesthetic.

Und ohne alle drei Wege zu verbinden, ist wahrhaftig keine Aesthetik möglich. Diese wählt sich die Methode der Philosophie, die strenge Analysis: nimmt Produkte der Schönheit, in jeder Art, so viel sie kann, merkt auf den ganzen ungetheilten Eindruck: wirft sich aus der Tiefe dieses Eindrucks auf den Gegenstand zurück: bemerkt seine Theile einzeln und zusammenwürkend: vergibt sich keine leidschöne Halbidee: bringt die Summe der Deutlichgemachten unter Hauptbegriffe, diese unter ihre; endlich vielleicht ein Hauptbegrif, in dem sich das Universum alles Schönen in Kunst und Wissenschaft spiegelt. (IV, 21).

As Martin Schütze has observed, Herder's statement is an excellent summary of the process of inductive analysis applied to art.[7] But stated in the terms which Herder himself so often uses, the process illustrated here is Herder's familiar "Eins aus Vielem".

By rejecting Riedel's tripartite division of the mind and his reduction of the three aesthetic approaches to individual fundamental faculties Herder has not only established the intellectual unity of the mind, but also has shown that the true and the good are of equal importance with the beautiful in any aesthetic system. Riedel had been correct when he recognized that the mind was capable of performing a variety of functions, but he had erred when he tried to partition these off, each into its own separate area. Again and again throughout the *Viertes Wäldchen* Herder emphasizes the unity of the soul and points to this basic unity as the essential factor in its further development toward perfection. "Wie schön wird eben damit die Menschliche Seele! Einheit im Grunde, tausendfache Mannichfaltigkeit in der Ausbildung, Vollkommenheit

---

[7] *Ibid.,* p. 521.

in der Summe des Ganzen! Keine von der Natur zubereitete fertige drei Grundgefühle; alles soll aus Einem gebildet, und zu mannichfaltigen Vollkommenheit erhoben werden" (IV, 34). We see from these lines that Herder conceives of the soul passing through three definite stages: first of all there is the inherent state of unity within the soul which remains constant; second, there is the development of the potential within the soul; and third, there is the ultimate achievement of the highest possible development-perfection.

Indeed, Herder seems to indicate a marked preference for tripartite divisions in his writings. The clearest example of this and the one which is most closely related to his concept of the soul is found in the *Kalligone*. The three divisions of this work correspond exactly with the three stages through which the soul passes. The first part is a phenomenology of the beautiful, the second a discussion of how further to refine and develop the potential of the beautiful and the third a résumé of what constitutes the highest form of the beautiful. When viewed strictly according to thematic structure, other works also evidence this same tripartite division. The first and so tremendously important part of *Über den Ursprung der Sprache* is divided into three *Abschnitte*. Strictly speaking the *Fragmente* has only three main topics: (1) language in general; (2) criticism and the genius; (3) the impact of foreign literatures in Germany. The same may be said of *Auch eine Philosophie*, where historical development is seen falling into three rough periods; (1) antiquity; (2) Rome and its influence on Europe through the Middle Ages; (3) modern time.

Herder's campaign against the evils of a division of the mind into various fundamental faculties did not end with the *Viertes Wäldchen*. In every one of his works where the subject of psychology is broached Herder feels it necessary to reiterate his stand on this concept which was so basic to his own psychology. In the psychology of 1778 (*Vom Erkennen und Empfinden*) he writes: "Man ist gewohnt, der Seele eine Menge Unterkräfte zu geben, *Einbildung* und *Voraussicht, Dichtungsgabe* und *Gedächtniss*" (VIII, 195). But after discussing these so-called subordinate faculties of the soul, Herder arrives at the same conclusions he had already stated in the *Viertes Wäldchen*. "Kurz, alle diese Kräfte sind im Grunde nur eine Kraft, wenn sie menschlich, gut und nützlich seyn sollen, und das ist *Verstand, Anschauung* mit innerem Bewusstseyn. Man nehme ihnen dieses, so ist die Einbildung Blendwerk, der Witz kindisch, das Gedächtniss leer, der Scharfsinn Spinnweb; in dem Maas aber, als sie jenes haben, vereinigen sich, die sonst Feindinnen schienen, und werden mit Wurzeln oder sinnliche Darstellungen Einer und der selben *Energie der Seele"* (VIII, 196).[8]

Also closely related to this concept of a unified soul is Herder's rejection of the main tenet of rationalism. Herder never denied the necessity for or the validity of reason. In fact, according to the essay on the origin of language, reason and rationality (*Besonnenheit*) are those features which distinguish man from all else in creation. But, as the following lines make clear, this is not a "pure" reason which assumes complete dominance over the functioning of the mind, rather it is a characteristic total direction innate in the soul of man which is by no means in conflict with its basic unity. "Ist nemlich die Vernunft keine abgetheilte, einzelnwürkende Kraft, sondern eine seiner Gattung eigner Richtung aller Kräfte: *so muss der Mensch sie im ersten Zustande haben, da er Mensch ist.* Im ersten Gedanken des Kindes muss sich diese Besonnenheit zeigen, wie bei dem Insekt, dass es Insekt war" (V, 31). All efforts of the rationalists to delegate superiority to one of the functions of the soul, in this instance reason, or to restrict any area of human perception to one of these functions is hotly contested by Herder. The latter is the subject of several of his *Provinzialblätter*, where he calls to task those who would ban man's experience of God to the realm of reason and would ignore the value of feeling in man's relation with God. "Aber den Geist Gottes ins *kalte Oberdach* der Seele . . . hinaufzubannen, wer bist du, absondern, was Gott zusammengefügt hat? . . . Alle Stimmen des Worts Gottes . . . zu *welchen Kräften* sprechen sie? In *Psalmen* und *Lobgesängen, Segen* und *Weissagungen, Bildern* und *Gleichnissen,* in *Feuerströmen* der Rede an *Herz* und *Seele* – so sprachen sie! . . . Auf Zeugniss *der Sinne* und nicht der Oberkräfte allein"

8 Cf. also *SWS*, VIII, 201.

(VII, 264f).[9] This is a clear statement of Herder's belief that the unity of the soul is one of its most basic characteristics and is acquired simultaneously with the act of creation itself as a gift from God. Martin Schütze has written concerning the role of reason: "Reason is only one of the functions of the total personality; it is not superior to, not even primarily distinct from, any other faculty or rather, function." [10]

Herder himself had a great deal to say about the individuality of each product of creation. He also frequently points out that man's idea of and reaction to nature's creatures are to a large degree dependent on environmental and psychological factors. A good example of this is what constitutes beauty among different cultures and at different times. Exactly what stands behind Herder's ideas on individuality can be seen from his application of these ideas to the soul. Although the soul consists of a harmonious unity of powers, it must be remembered that these powers are never static. They are constantly in a state of flux, always being developed and sharpened by the myriad of impressions, perceptions, and experiences with which they come into contact. Since no two souls can possibly undergo the same experiences, then no two souls can expand their potentials in exactly the same manner. Herder thus comes to the conclusion that each soul is an individual entity in itself, while at the same time he makes his own unique application of this individuality. "Wenn keine Menschliche Seele mit der ander völlig dieselbe ist: so ist auch bei ihren Wesen vielleicht auch eine unendlich veränderte und modificirte Mischung von Kräften möglich, die noch alle zu ihrer Summe eine gleiche Anzahl von Realität haben können" (IV, 28). Although he acknowledges that each soul is individual, this individuality exists as a part of a universality. A clear statement of this belief of Herder's is found in a fragmentary utterance where Herder wrote: "dass meine Wahrheit auch fremde Wahrheit wird, denn die Formen der Seele sind überall Eins: und die ersten Grundgedanken, die noch solcher Form gemacht werden, auch einerlei Gestalt etc." (VIII, 113). Just as each person has its own individuality, but is never-

---

[9]   Cf. also *SWS*, V, 29.
[10]   Schütze, "Herder's Psychology", p. 510.

theless an essential part of humanity as a whole, so too does each soul possess an individuality, but at the same time never loses its identity as a part of "the universal soul". The goal of mankind does not lie in its individual existence, but rather in its attainment of *Humanität*, which is a universal concept, valid for all people and at all times. Likewise, the individual soul is only a symbol, a reflection of the universal soul. Herder's belief in the fulfillment of definite values and the oneness of the forms of creation is carried over into every aspect of life. "Die allweise Natur, die sich überall gleich ist, hats also so gefügt, das ihr nichts zuströmen kann, was nicht Symbol der Wahrheit, Güte und Vollkommenheit sei" (VIII, 245). "Es gibt also ein Ideal der Schönheit für jede Kunst, für jede Wissenschaft, für den guten Geschmack überhaupt, und es ist in Völkern und Zeiten und Subjekten und Produktionen zu finden. Schwer zu finden freilich" (IV, 41). "Es gibt nur Eine Poesie, nur Einen guten Geschmack auf der Erde; haben wir diesen nicht, so haben wir gar keinen oder einen falschen" (XVIII, 516). What Herder means by this idea of oneness is best illustrated by his comparison of Shakespeare and Sophocles in the Shakespeare essay. Herder freely acknowledges that there are a host of differences between Shakespeare and Sophocles. These must be apparent to the most casual observer. Yet at the same time Herder finds that of all modern dramatists Shakespeare alone can be compared with Sophocles. The differences between the two dramatists are restricted to considerations of form. In questions pertaining to content however, the more important factor in the dichotemy content-form, Herder designates Shakespeare the brother of Sophocles. Herder is able to do this because he finds that the works of both dramatists embody that all important quality of the tragedy, which for convenience we may designate the "tragic" here, and which is limited to neither place nor time, but which is absolutely essential to the purpose of the tragedy. To put this same idea into the language that has been used in our discussion of the soul, Herder finds that Shakespeare has developed the tragic potential to a like degree as that attained by Sophocles. In this respect their dramas are one, despite their external differences.

One basic attribute of the soul still remains to be discussed and to be added to the three that we have already established. So far we have seen that the soul is created by God through a divine spark, that the soul is an indivisible unity with all of its faculties working together in perfect harmony, and that the forms of the soul are universally one. The fourth characteristic of the soul is closely related to the first. Now if the soul is created by a Divine Being, it can rightly be assumed that it will reflect certain of the characteristics of its creator. Herder does just this, for to him the soul is, according to the orthodox Christian view, in the image of Him who created it. The soul, therefore, is a divine likeness of the Great Creator. For the first two drafts of *Vom Erkennen und Empfinden* Herder chooses mottoes from Virgil, "Est Deus in nobis" (VIII, 231) for the first version of 1774, and "Est Deus in nobis, agitante colescimus illo" (VIII, 263) for the second of 1775. The concept inherent within these mottoes is echoed countless times within the text itself. "Mit der Fortdauer der erkennenden Seele ist also such immer Fortstreben verbunden. Sie umfasst mit jedem Schritte ein grösser Theil des Weltalls und wird immer mehr geübt, das Bild Gottes, Wahrheit und Güte in Allem zu entwickeln, immer mehr in wenigeren Zeit auf leichtere Weise in ihr Wesen zu assimiliren, das Eins der Wahrheit und Güte ist, das sie in allem findet" (VIII, 246). Now although in these lines Herder may seem to be saying that the soul is not a likeness of its creator in the beginning, that this characteristic comes only as a result of development and growth of the soul, this is by no means the case. The development which takes place here does not constitute the addition of a new dimension to the soul, but rather the refining of a potential which is already present, much in the same way that the so-called faculties of the soul were developed by habit into a smoothly operating whole.

Herder's use of Virgil's mottoes, which at first glance may seem to raise certain questions of an ambiguous nature, is entirely in keeping with his psychology, and indeed, with his philosophy of religion, even though this philosophy may not be able to lay claim to orthodoxy in the more narrow sense of the word. Herder's identification of the human soul with the Divine rests upon two main premises, both of which had already gained wide acceptance before his time. The first of these was the belief, long a basic tenet of orthodoxy, which was based on the biblical account that God had created man in his image. In time this belief was extended by such thinkers as St. Augustine and St. Thomas Aquinas to mean that man is not only in the likeness of the Divine, but that there is furthermore something of the essence of this divine likeness within him. The second premise upon which Herder's argumentation rests is a more recent one, whose origins lie in the seventeenth century. This was the complex of ideas centered around the concept of the genius and the divinity of the creative in art and science. The similarity of Herder's ideas with those of Leibniz in this area are undeniable, nevertheless they differ in one all important respect. Within the framework of his system of pre-established harmony Leibniz emphasizes that all ideas originate within the soul monad, and that they are innate within this monad. The soul creates and produces within itself, but recongnizes no chance of change from without. While not disagreeing with Leibniz' basic idea of an innate potential, Herder adds the important elements of formation and development which act upon the soul from without and aid it in the development of its potential. In the important area of his psychology Herder's system cannot lay claim to the precision and clarity as that of Leibniz', as Herder's exact position is often extremely difficult to ascertain. But it is precisely these points where his ideas represent an advancement beyond those of Leibniz that were so immensely fruitful in the intellectual clime of the eighteenth and nineteenth centuries.

Man is admittedly a complex being, and precisely this complexity led observers such as Riedel to false conclusions. The reason for this complexity can be found in the characteristic likeness which the soul has in common with its Creator. The soul is not the only product of the Creator, for the same Divine Being who created the soul also created the universe in which the soul moves and has its being. As a creation of God the universe also reflects its Creator, but not to the same extent as the soul which is a likeness of the Divine in miniature. Once it is admitted that the universe reflects in it the power and image of its Creator, then it must follow by analogy that the universe is likewise reflected in the human soul, which of all of creation is most like its Creator. Man in his complexity can thus be likened to a microcosm, to a universe in miniature. "Er [der Mensch] schwimmt in einem Meer von Eindrücken der Gegenstände, wo Eine Welle leiser, die andre fühlbarer ihn berühret, immer aber mancherlei Veränderungen von aussen sein Inneres reizen. Auch in diesem Betracht ist er eine *kleine Welt*, wie ihn Protagoras in einer andern Absicht das *Masz der Dinge* nannte, die ihn umgeben" (XV, 523). And again: "Er [der Mensch] fasst es [das Unendliche] aber doch, denn in ihm liegt ein lebendiger Spiegel des Universum, d.i. die Kraft seines Wesens ist der Kraft der Gottheit ähnlich, was sie sich vorstellt kann sie nur unter dem Bilde der Wahrheit und Güte fassen. Also strebt sie immer, sich nach ihrer Analogie ein Weltall zu bilden, und kann, so fern sie jede Formel treu empfängt und richtig berechnet, nicht irren, und wo sie irrt, rückt sie, wenn der Irrthum überwunden ist, weiter" (VIII, 246f). From this it can clearly be seen that the four basic characteristics of the phenomenology of the soul all support and complement one another. As the creation of God the soul reflects with it His likeness, and is analogous in miniature to the rest of His creation. Since the soul, or better spirit, of the Creator is both one and universal, the same can be said for the soul of the creature which most closely resembles the Creator.

B. DEVELOPMENT AND GROWTH OF THE SOUL

The second stage of Herder's psychology, already alluded to several times previously, concerns itself with the unfolding and development of the soul. It constitutes, in effect, a history of the activity of the soul. As we have already seen, the creation takes place in that moment in which a living, divine spark is breathed into a dark, obscure, unfeeling mass. "Das Gesetz Gottes ist schon mit Flammenschrift in ihr Herz geschrieben: in ihr glühen Kräfte, lebendige Funken, alles in ihr Wesen zu verwandeln, wie sie kann, das Bild der Gottheit in Allen anzuerkennen und als ein

Theil ihres Selbst zu geniessen" (VIII, 248). From that moment on these living sparks, these glowing powers, begin to manifest themselves. "Die Seele . . . kann nichts thun, als dass sie würke, d.i. die Empfindungen auflöse wie sie ihr zuströmen. Ihre Natur ist Eins und sie bringt ein deutliches oder klares Eins in alle das Vielfache im Spiegel ihrer Organe. . . . Sie erkennet, will, handelt" (VIII, 245). Herder terms this activity and movement of the soul "das dunkelste Analogon des Lebens" (VIII, 247). The very fact that the soul is active shows that it is alive, that it possesses the same dynamic powers, and the same ability to perceive, to will, and to act that are undeniable attributes of its creator. When Herder refers to this activity of the soul as "das Phänomenon der Menschlichen Freiheit" (VIII, 245), he calls attention to the fact that man is a free being, and as such can assert his own will and can act in accordance with the dictates of this will.

Yet although the soul may reflect the same characteristics as its creator, although it may have in common with this creator freedom to act, to assert its will, yes even to create, it, like this creator, is still a spirit. The spirit of the creator has revealed itself in the universe which it has created. In order to be perceivable the soul must likewise reveal itself through something tangible. The first manifestation of the creative power of the soul is therefore the living body, which is the visible evidence of the existence of the soul. This idea, which Herder touches upon briefly in the fourth *Wäldchen*, finds its most complete expression in the psychology of 1778 and in the unpublished studies of the same period. Herder writes in the fourth *Wäldchen*: "Als Mensch, nach ihrer Masse von innern Kräften, im Kreise ihres Daseyns, hat sie [die Seele] sich eine Anzahl Organe gebildet, um das, was sie ist, zu empfinden, und gleichsam zum Genusse ihrer selbst, in sich zu ziehen" (IV, 28). The number of organs which the soul creates for itself is, of course, the human body. "So muss alles Körper werden, um schön fürs Gefühl zu seyn und zwar insonderheit Menschlicher Körper. Nun suche man Grund in uns. Schöner Körper ist sinnliche Idee von Vollkommenheit; dies in uns Idee von unserer Vollkommenheit, erinnert die Seele also an das Bild, das sie hatte, da sie sich ihren Körper schuf" (VIII, 101). The occurrence of a number of words in these lines that refer to the senses emphasize that this creation is no mere act of reason. Thus the soul must become corporeal in order to be beautiful for feeling, and a beautiful body is a "sensuous idea of perfection". Herder makes it clear that not only is the body created for feeling, but that it is also through a sensuous act that the soul creates the body. "Alsdenn wirds offenbar werden, dass die Seele sich einen Körper durchs Gefühl und zum Gefühl von aussen bilde, oder sich fühlend in die Welt hineinbilde" (VIII, 100). This statement neatly sums up both Herder's affinity and fundamental disagreement with the psychology of the Enlightenment. The premise that the soul possesses the innate power to derive everything from itself is basic to the psychology of the Enlightenment. But to suggest as Herder did that the soul likewise posesses the power to transcend its own limitations and to project itself by a sensuous act out into the objective world adds an entirely new and exciting dimension to its sphere of activity. The full impact of the significance of this idea that the creation which takes place within the soul is carried out by a sensuous act becomes apparent only when one realizes that this is essentially the same process which Herder ascribes to the creative act of the artist. The basic element of the soul which enables it to create, and to reveal itself sensuously through the body, is its inherent dynamics. "Bewegung ist die sinnliche Ankündigung des Lebens: Leben der Ankündigung der Seele: so und nur so spricht die Seele durch Körper" (VIII, 100).

Although the more important of the two elements body-soul is undoubtedly the soul, this is not to say that the role of the body is minor or of little consequence. Herder defines the relationship of the body to the soul with a variety of metaphors, all of which point to the fact that he considers the body the intermediary between the soul and the universe, much in the same way that he considers light the medium of sight, or sound the medium of hearing. Here are several of the metaphors which Herder uses. "Der Körper stellt also Seele vor: ist Spiegel der Seele" (VIII, 112). "Kurz der Körper . . . ist, Analogon, Spiegel, ausgedrücktes Bild der Seele" (VIII, 239). "Kurz, der Körper ist Symbol, Phänomenon der Seele in Beziehung auf Universum" (VIII, 250).

Since the body is a "Phänomen von Substanzen" (VIII, 249), "ein Phänomenon innerer Kräfte" (VIII, 249), the soul, which itself in an "innige Kraft" (VIII, 249), can act upon this body, which is its agent of revelation. One statement from the first version of the psychology of 1778 draws all the loose ends of Herder's thoughts on the importance of the body-soul relationship together and establishes once and for all the importance which he attaches to this relationship. "So ... ist die Physionomik im weitesten Verstande, d.i. die Psychologische Physiologie der wichtigste Theil der Weltweisheit. Sie allein kann uns ins Heiligthum der Seele führen: denn der Körper ist nur lebendwürkendes Symbol, Formel, Phänomenon der Seele. Ohne alle Mystik und im schärfsten Philosophischen Verstande ist der innern Mensch dem äussern durch und durch einwohnend" (VIII, 250).

There is no place in Herder's psychology for a dualism of body and soul. As the outward symbol of the soul which dwells within it and as the sole medium through which the soul can be approached, the body must exhibit the same unity and harmony of the soul and must also exist in harmony with the soul which dwells within it. In the experience of mortal man the soul is inconceivable without the body, for although he may be convinced that the soul is immortal and has the power to exist in a state separated from the body, this belief is a matter of faith, and not of empirical knowledge. It is true that Herder devotes more effort to calling attention to the importance of spirit, i.e. inner content. But it must be remembered that what might seem like an overemphasis of one aspect was only Herder's way of counteracting the gross imbalance of the prevailing notions of his day and time which placed the greater emphasis on questions of form. These same questions suggested by the form-content relationship in an organic being, in this case men, are likewise applicable by analogy to non-organic objects. Hence Herder distinguishes between the form and content of a word, or a statue, or a poem. Herder's insistence on an approach that encompasses both the spirit and the form is clearly demonstrated when he calls for a "psychological physiology", i.e. a psychology for the spirit, a physiology for the form. The importance of such an approach is further underscored when he writes: "Meines geringen Erachtens ist keine *Psychologie*, die nicht in jedem Schritte bestimmste Physiologie sei, möglich (VIII, 180).

The creative power of the soul, which first manifests itself in the creation of its own body, does not limit itself to this one act, but continues to assert itself throughout the existence of the soul. One of the most important ways in which the soul does this is in the production of its own images. This is the subject of one of the contributions to the *Zerstreute Blätter, Ueber Bild, Dichtung und Fabel*.[11] Herder defines image as any datum of an object connected with some degree of consciousness of the perception. This consciousness is not a passive process of receiving impressions, but rather an active function of the mind whereby the latter transforms sensations into its own images. "In dem Walde sinnlicher Gegenstände, der mich umgiebt, finde ich mich nur dadurch zurecht und werde über das Chaos der auf mich zudringenden Empfindungen Herr und Meister, dass ich Gegenstände von andern trenne, dass ich ihnen Umriss, Maas und Gestalt gebe, mithin im Mannichfaltigen mir Einheit schaffe und sie mit dem Gepräge meines *innern Sinnes*, als ob dieser ein Stempel der Wahrheit wäre, lebhaft und zuversichtlich bezeichne" (XV, 525f). Without this power to actively create images the mind would be overcome by the sheer mass of the impressions which rush in upon it. Chaos would reign supreme and the mind would be unable even to distinguish the source of the impressions, for it would exist only as a passive receptacle. Simultaneous with this active, creative function of the mind is also a process of analysis and synthesis. The details of the perceptions are analysed and at the same time are synthesized into an orderly whole so that they can be recognized by the mind. Herder sees an analogy between the complicated, yet orderly, operation of the soul and the creation of a work of art. "Unser ganzes Leben ist also gewissermaassen eine *Poetik*, wir sehn nicht, sondern wir erschaffen uns Bilder. . . . Denn das Bild, das sich auf der Netzhaut deines Auges zeichnet, ist der Gedanke nicht, den du von seinem Gegenstande dir zueignet; dieser

---

[11]   See also Martin Schütze, "Herder's Concept of 'Bild' ", *GR*, I (1926), pp. 21-35.

ist blos ein Werk deines innern Sinnes, ein Kunstgemählde der Bemerkungskraft deiner Seele" (XV, 526). The use of the word *Poetik* in this analogy assumes added significance when one remembers that its basic meaning is to make or create. Thus, in the words of Martin Schütze, "the essential primary constituent of our experience, of our universe of discourse, is not any external object, is not the image reflected on our retina; but is the image created by our inward sense, the work of a creative artist, which is our "soul" or integral individual self".[12] Despite Schütze's apparent overemphasis of the autonomy of the creative soul, the fact that for Herder the soul cannot exist independent of the body must never be lost sight of. What seems to be a misplaced emphasis on Schütze's part is doubtless the result of his desire to place the function of the soul in its proper perspective, i.e. to stress that without the power of the creative soul the corporeal and sensuous world would be nothing but disorderly chaos and amorphous mass. To be sure, the soul is an active force (*Würkung*), but not an absolutely free force, for it is only through its corporeal form that the soul reveals itself. The form of the image does originate in the soul, but not entirely independent of the possibility or necessity of an outside image-stimulating substance. It must be emphasized again, as was the case when the soul created its own form, that it is the *innere Sinn*, not an act of reason, which is the creating agent. Schütze is correct when he says that the *primary* constituent of our experience is the image created by our inward sense, but it is important to remember that it is not the *only* constituent. Herder himself has written: "Liegt nämlich das, was wir Bild nennen, nicht im Gegenstande, sondern in unserer Seele, in der Natur unsres Organs und geistigen Sinnes . . ."(XV, 532).

Although originality is assumed to be the characteristic of any creation, this factor, already called attention to by Schütze, is especially stressed by Herder. "Dass jeder wahrnehmende Mensch aber seinen Gegenstand *eigen* schildern kann, als ob er noch nie geschildert wäre; darüber, dünkt mich, sollte kein misstrauender Zweifel walten" (XV, 530). Just as each soul is an individual entity, so too are the images created by each soul individual crea-

[12] *Ibid.*, p. 24.

tions, for as Herder's metaphor expresses it, each spirit sees with its own eyes. "Der Geist dichtet: der bemerkende innere Sinn schafft Bilder. Er schafft sich neue Bilder, wenn die Gegenstände auch tausendmal angeschaut und besungen wären, denn er schaut sie mit seinem Auge an" (XV, 530). Thus the individuality of each soul is underscored while at the same time its universality is not lost sight of. Each soul may create its own images, but each creates them in a manner analogous to the process employed by all organic beings. In the mind of man thoughts and images, experiences and happenings, are paired together, and from these, new ones are created through the powers of the soul, through analogies. Although this is a process common to all men to some degree, it reaches its highest development and culmination in the genius-artist, who is wholly deserving of the designation creator. Addressing Homer, Sophocles, Shakespeare and Klopstock, Herder writes: "Ihr Schöpfer und Erreger der Seelen, die ihr alle Triebfedern würkend, alle Züge der Seele sich selbst äussernd, alle Symptome in Handlung zeigt" (II, 174). It is important to remember that the soul does not create images arbitrarily. Rather, by virtue of its divine character the soul has the ability to discover and to fashion according to the essence of the individual objects which it perceives. In this manner the soul proceeds from one essential to another, simultaneously unfolding its own possibility of growth, since it nourishes itself from the essentials which it finds. Thus there arises the uniqueness in style, the husk *(Schlaube)* that Herder talks about in the Shakespeare essay, whose core however remains universally human. The individual character of each situation and every object is not abolished by this soul activity and creative power, only developed and given greater continuity.

When Herder wrote in *Vom Erkennen und Empfinden* (1778) that in his opinion there could be no psychology without an accompanying physiology, he had with one short statement both overthrown all the extant systems of psychology with their multifarious forces,[13] i.e. the *vires* of medieval and Renaissance

---

[13]   S. Clark, *Herder*, p. 218f. S. also Friedrich Berger, *Menschenbild und Menschenbildung* (Stuttgart, 1933), p. 25.

medicine, and at the same time firmly established his claim to the title as "the founder of modern psychology".[14] We have yet to see, however, how Herder was able to support such a statement. We have already seen that feeling plays an important role in the creative process of the soul, that the body is created to be beautiful for feeling, and that it is a sensuous act of the soul that creates the body. So far, although the role of outer feeling has been alluded to, our main concern has been with "inner" feeling. The problem which confronted Herder in the psychology of 1778 was how to coordinate the seemingly independent functions of "outer" and "inner" feeling and to preserve his assumption of the unity of the body and soul. "Outer" feeling, or better feeling outward, is important because it is through the feelings which the senses channel into the soul that man acquires recognition of the world about him. In this capacity feeling is the first sense of man, and the origin of the true, the good, and the beautiful. "Gefühl ist der erste, profondste und fast einzige Sinn der Menschen: die Quelle der meisten unsrer Begriffe und Empfindungen: das wahre, und erste Organum der Seele Vorstellungen von aussen zu sammeln: der Sinn, der die Seele gleichsam ganz umgibt, und die anderen Sinnen als Arten, Theile oder Verkürzungen in sich enthält: die Masse unsrer Sinnlichkeit: der wahre Ursprung des Wahren, Guten, Schönen" (VIII, 104).

As Friedrich Berger has already observed, the concept of feeling (*Gefühl*) comprises much more than is ordinarily understood when used synonymously with the sense of touch (*Tastsinn*).[15] In addition to the sense of touch, whose primary organ is the hand, we speak of specific pressure, heat, cold, and pain sensations, or of muscle, energy, local, and motor sensations. All of these come together under the general concept of feeling for Herder, not only designating the psychological process and all of its vital stimulative components, but above all the inner psychic process of experiencing, which can be accompanied

[14] Martin Schütze, *The Fundamental Ideas in Herder's Thought*. Serially in *Modern Philology*, XXI (1923), p. 120.
[15] Berger, p. 86.

by all these organic sensations, but which nevertheless extends into the sphere of psychic importance. The sense of touch supplies the external contacts, so consequently is called the "outer feeling" (*äussere Gefühl*). But in the broad sense feeling (*Gefühl*) refers to an internal comprehension and ferreting out of a significant content. This is "inner feeling" (*innere Gefühl*). Commenting on the lines above from the psychology of 1778 and Herder's concept of feeling, Berger writes: *"Herder versteht unter 'Gefühl' jenes totale Vermögen der Seele, durch das die unbewusste Berührung von Seele und Welt vor sich geht, ohne dass eine Differensierung im Bereich der äusseren Sinne noch in dem der inneren, geistigen Sinnrichtungen vor sich gegangen ist."* [16] This contact of the soul with the world, whether it be conscious or unconscious, is, it must be remembered, basic to Herder's concept of soul development, for without the contributions of these outside stimuli, there can be no soul growth. Feeling for Herder thus becomes an all-inclusive concept, embracing both the inner and outer activity of the soul. In this capacity feeling is rightly, in Herder's words, "the true origin of the true, the good, and the beautiful". Without feeling, the soul would never come to a realization of any of these great concepts, for it is only after the soul has developed with the aid of feeling that it is able to perceive that which is true, good, or beautiful.

Herder makes it quite clear at the very beginning of his final version of *Vom Erkennen und Empfinden* that he sees no dichotomy between the "outer" and the "inner" when he writes: "Der empfindende Mensch fühlt sich in Alles, fühlt Alles aus sich heraus, und druckt darauf sein Bild, sein Gepräge" (VIII, 170). Haller had made the first beginnings of an effort to close the gap between the living organism and "outer" reality with the introduction of what he termed *Reiz* – Herder called it his strange phenomenon. But since Haller's term referred to a purely physiological nerve process, involving only outer sensations, the gap still remained open. Although Herder profited greatly from Haller's ideas, and although he accepted the importance of Hal-

[16]   *Ibid.*, p. 86.

ler's *Reiz* for sensation, i.e. the outer, he could hardly be content until he had tied sensation together with perception. Four years before this he had written: "Alle Empfindungen sind nur Mittel, Materialien, Symbols, woraus sich etwas entwickeln soll, was bleibt! ... Durch Empfinden lernts nehmlich erkennen" (VIII, 225). And again: "Nehmlich das *Erkennen der Seele* kann als ein *deutliches Resultat* all' ihrer *Empfindungszustände* betrachtet werden; die Empfindung kann nichts anders seyn als gleichsam der *Körper, das Phänomenon* des Erkennens, die *anschaubare Formel*, worin die Seele den Gedanken siehet" (VIII, 239). Herder's choice of words here is perfect to illustrate the relationship, as he sees it, between sensation and perception. Sensation is to perception as the body is to the soul. But just as was the case with the body and soul, this is not a dualistic relationship.

Despite the fact that Herder cannot accept Haller's results as the final word on the relationship between perception and sensation, he nevertheless found in Haller's explanation of the phenomenon of stimulus the basis for his final solution of the problem. The stimulated nerve fiber first contracts, then expands. This same principle can be observed in every physiological phenomenon, in man, animals, and plants. As a muscle strains to lift a load, it tightens, and then relaxes. As the heart palpitates, it contracts and expands. As man breathes, the intake of air causes tension in the body: as he exhales, the tension is relaxed. Herder sums up this principle in these words: "Zum Empfangen und Geben ist der Mensch geschaffen, zur Würksamkeit und Freude, zum Thun und Leiden .... In dieser Anziehung und Ausbreitung, Thätigkeit und Ruhe liegt Gesundheit und Glück des Lebens" (VIII, 173f). The usual explanation for these physiological phenomena was that the reactions of the muscles to stimuli, or the functioning of some organ of the body, were purely mechanical. Rejecting the mechanical explanation, Herder says that the processes and functions illustrated by these physiological occurrences are "supermechanical" (*übermechanisch,* VIII, 174), held together by a "spiritual bond" (*geistiges Band*) created especially by the Creator for this purpose. This spiritual bond is Herder's solution to the problem of the gap between perception and sensation. This bond, which is the essential factor of psychical unity, also becomes the integrating factor of both the physical and mental functions.

The existence of this bond must be accepted as a matter of belief. There is no proof for it beyond the fact that it manifests itself in thousands of phenomena. The name which Herder gives to this bond is *Kraft,* and he conceives of this *Kraft* as an inexplicable absolute. Herder makes no attempt to explain *Kraft.* He only wants to point out its existence. "Ich sage nicht, dass ich hiermit was *erkläre*: ich habe noch keine Philosophie gekannt, die, was *Kraft* sei, erkläre, es rege sich Kraft in Einem oder zween Wesen. Was Philosophie thut, ist *bemerken,* unter einander *ordnen, erläutern,* nachdem sie Kraft, Reiz, Würkung schon immer *voraussetzt*" (VIII, 177). In spite of his penetrating analysis of the psychic process, Haller had made the same error as Riedel. Instead of *one* force (*Kraft*), Haller defines *three* forces (*Kräfte*). Herder's reply to this is: "Der innere Mensch mit alle seinen dunklen Kräften, Regen und Trieben ist nur *Einer*" (VIII, 178).

At the same time Herder corrects Haller's false division of one force into three forces, he also cleanses his psychology of the last vestiges of Leibniz' influence. In the versions of 1774 and 1775 Herder was still under Leibniz' influence. Statements such as the following occur in the 1774 version: "Die Menschliche Seele als ein eingeschränktes Wesen hat auch keine unendliche Kraft zu erkennen und umfasset nicht das Weltbild in seinem Ersten Grunde" (VIII, 245). Ideas such as these reflect Leibniz' concept of the monad. According to Leibniz each individual unit of force is a monad. He retained the Carthesian concepts of "clear" and "distinct" and said that each monad must be primary, indivisible, and absolutely distinct from every other unit. Although each unit, i.e. monad, possessed some degree of individual spontaneity, each had absolute individuality, which Leibniz expressed with the metaphor that "monads have no windows". Therefore, no monad can communicate or be influenced by another. There is no organic relationship with nature. Herder rejects Leibniz' concept of organic exclusiveness from nature and replaces it with a concept of organic oneness with nature. "Ueberhaupt ist in der Natur nichts geschieden, alles fliesst durch unmerkliche Uebergänge auf- und ineinander; und gewiss, was Leben in der Schöpfung ist, ist in allen Gestalten, Formen und Kanälen nur Ein Geist, Eine Flamme" (VIII, 178). It is therefore difficult to understand how Haym can say of this final version: "Es bleibt doch dabei, dass der Grundstock der Herderschen Ideen in der Lehre Leibnizens zu suchen ist".[17] The fundamental concept of Leibniz' doctrine is the exclusiveness of the soul monad, that it is completely self-contained, and that only through a pre-established harmony does it fit into the general plan which regulates all of creation. On the other hand, Herder's whole psychology rests upon the assumption that the soul is in contact with nature, and that only through the growth and development which results from this contact does it assume its rightful place in God's creation.

Herder's formulation of the spiritual bond, which not only united all the functions of the individual organism, but also allowed each organism to communicate with every other living being, opened up entirely new psychological vistas. It must be remembered, of course, that Herder considered the soul and this bond one and the same. "Sie [die Seele], die ja von der Natur jener und selbst innigste, würkendste Kraft ist, . . ." (VIII, 178). First and foremost, of course, was the conclusion that sensation and perception are integral parts of one vital process. There can be no perception without sensation, neither can there be sensation without a resulting perception. To the one vitalistic process Herder likewise adds volition, which had also been treated as a separate faculty. "Auch *Erkennen* ohne *Wollen* ist nichts" (VIII, 198). In fact, there is one passage where Herder seems to collect every conceivable term applied to man's faculties just so he can emphasize their unity. "Ihre [der Seele] innere Kraft aber ist gewiss nur Eine: *Apperception* ists, innere sich selbst erblickende Thätigkeit, Göttliches *Bewusstseyn,* mit der so denn selbst *Freiheit, Gewissen, Verstand, Wille* (Modificationen

[17]   Haym, I, 709.

von aussen) im Grunde Eins sind. Nur so viel hat ein Mensch *Freiheit, Wille, Gewissen,* als er innere tiefe *Apperception, Thätigkeit, Bewustseyn* hat: gerade so viel hat er auch *Verstand"* (VIII, 290). Just as the individual senses possess media, so too the soul has one which expresses its vitalism. "Und dies Medium unsres Selbstgefühls und geistigen Bewusstseyns ist – *Sprache"* (VIII, 196f). Language is especially suited for this function as it reflects the same unity that has been the main theme of this essay. "Auch in den tiefsten Sprachen ist *Vernunft* und *Wort* nur *Ein* Begriff, *Eine* Sache, *logos"* (VIII, 197). In the essay on language Herder had already written: "Der Mensch empfindet mit dem Verstande und spricht, indem er denkt" (V, 100).

Man's capacity to sense, to perceive, and to will all reflect a freedom of action. This freedom is not absolute, however, but is organically conditioned, because man's functions are coordinated and integrated with all of organic nature through the spiritual bond. Since volition and perception are one, there is no problem. Man simply recognizes that freedom of will actually is the recognition of the fact that he is *not* free. "Da ist wahrlich der erste Keim zur Freiheit, fühlen, dass man *nicht* frei sei, und an welchen Banden man hafte? Die stärksten freisten Menschen fühlen dies am tiefsten, und streben weiter; wahnsinnige, zum Kerker gebohrne Sklaven, höhnen sie, und bleiben voll hohen Traums im Schlamme liegen" (VIII, 202). For Herder true freedom exists in love, which he defines as movement in the great sensorium of God's creation, in the flame of all thinking and feeling. This is why he writes: "Wo Geist des Herrn ist, da ist Freiheit" (VIII, 202).[18] Freedom in perception and volition, says Herder, is the very depth and divine treasure of our soul (VIII, 294).

Although the preceding discussion may seem to be a digression from the main theme of this section, namely the development of the soul, in reality the matters presented here touch upon one of its most vital aspects. Sensation, perception, and volition are all inextricably tied together with development,

[18]   See 2nd Corn. 3 : 17.

because without them there would be no development. A dead organism does not grow or develop, it remains static. Only when there is life is there development. Or to use Herder's words: "Erkenntniss und Empfindung leben nur in *That,* in *Wahrheit*" (VIII, 217). Love, which Herder considered the most pure and most divine volition, is likewise designated man's most fervent activity. "Die tiefste innigste Thätigkeit des Organischen Geschöpfs ist also die Liebe" (VIII, 276). "Ihre [der Seele] Ausbreitung, ihr Durst zu erkennen, und zu lieben, ist *Thätigkeit*" (VIII, 290). Activity is not only the natural state in which the soul exists, it is also "höchster Genuss der Seele" (VIII, 293). The soul considers activity its greatest pleasure because simultaneous with the activity is perception, and simultaneous with perception is the soul's realization that with every act of sensation and perception it is growing and developing. There can be no development, however, unless that perceived by the soul is truth. "Die Seele muss fühlen dass, indem sie erkennet, sie Wahrheit sehe, mithin sich geniesse, ihre Kräfte des Erkennens wohl angewandt, sich also fortstrebend, sich volkommner wisse" (VIII, 236). The very fact that there is activity indicates that the active organism must be undergoing some sort of change. Either the activity must result in the building up of the organism, i.e. development, or the activity must contribute to a breakdown of the organism. Only when this activity is positive, i.e. only when truth is sensed and perceived, does the organism develop. Now it is possible, of course, for the soul to be deceived, but this is not the fault of the soul. It is the fault of the senses that convey the sensations to the soul. Since the soul rejoices and seeks to strive only in truth, it is imperative that it be convinced of the truth of its perceptions, even though they be false in reality. A simple example will suffice to illustrate this. When we view a tree our soul is, in effect, deceived. The image which is transported to the soul has only one dimension. Yet the soul is not led astray by this incongruity because it knows from previous experience that the tree is not the one dimensional object it would seem to be at first glance. Herder is referring to just such occurrences when he writes:

So bald man sich einmal denkt, dass die geistige, wahre Kräftenwelt eine andre ist, als die körperliche, die wir mit dunkeln Sinnen und ungeheuren Massen und Verwirrungen sehen:
   so bald man sich denkt, dass die ganze Natur in jedem Punkt und Zielpunkt nichts als der allwürkende Gott sei, der nichts unordentlich, nichts im Sprunge thun kann: so bald verschwinden uns dergleichen Zweifel aus den Halbbegriffen der Sinnlichkeit geschöpft, aus den Augen. (VIII, 253f)

Empirical knowledge is not the only criterion man has to arrive at the truth. Faith, metaphysical knowledge – call it what you will – also plays a role of the greatest importance. Man's faith, however, is frequently supported by his experience. Since his experience tells him, for example, that the sun rises and sets daily, he had faith in the continuance of this phenomenon, even though he may not understand how or why it takes place. We have previously observed that the soul never operates in an arbitrary manner and that it always seeks the essentials in the objects with which it is concerned. In other words, the soul is primarily concerned with the spirit of any object with which it comes into contact. Since the soul reacts directly to this spirit, its powers of perception are more intense than those of reason alone. Thus the activity of the soul does man's faith an important service by linking the soul together with the spirit of the rest of creation, thus supplying it with the experiences and sensations needed to sustain and support faith.

   We have already seen that Herder's *geistiges Band* is not only the means whereby all the various functions of the psychic process are coordinated and integrated, but also the link between the individual soul and the rest of organic nature. The importance which Herder attaches to this principle is most clearly illustrated in the *Ideen*. Here Herder discussed the anthropological development of man and stressed the role which the world in which he lives plays in this development. Since even before the composition of the *Ideen* Herder had already established the unity of the body and soul, it is logical to assume that spiritual growth accompanies any other kind of growth, in this case especially physical growth. In the *Ideen* Herder develops his important concept of man as "ein Mittelgeschöpf unter den Thieren der Erde" (XIII, 68). As Herder elaborates on this concept in the *Ideen* it becomes clear that he is speaking anthropologically. That is, that man is physically a composite of the features of other animals: "... *d.i., die ausgearbeitete Form sei, in der sich die Züge aller Gattungen um ihn her im feinsten Inbegriff sammeln"* (XIII, 68). Yet that this is not the only meaning that can be ascribed to the concept of a *Mittelgeschöpf* can be seen clearly in two other places in the *Ideen.*[19] Here Herder is looking for the cosmic significance of his concept. The physical world is conceived of having many spheres and systems. The earth is the middle of the solar system and man, as the *Mittelgeschöpf,* is the connecting link between the living organisms of this system and the others. But lines from a later essay on this subject allow still another, and for our purposes even more important interpretation of this concept. Herder wrote in the *Seelenwanderung:* "Und vielleicht sind wir ... Mittelgeschöpfe, zwischen der dunklen Saturnusart und dem leichten Sinnenlichte, dem Quell aller Wahrheit und Schönheit" (XV, 277). Metempsychosis can be understood to mean the transpiration of the soul from one world to the next. The more immediate application, however, is to be found in the soul's existence here and now. Man's so-called middle position also means that in every phase of his existence he can and must supercede his previous state. That is, there must be growth and development. Thus the statement of the *Ideen:* "Alles ist auf der Erde Veränderung" (XIII, 26).

Herder is primarily interested in the growth and development of the spirit, because this is the part of man that is divine and immortal. "In allen Gestalten und Ständen der Menschlichkeit, dünkt mich, kommt es freilich weniger auf Ausbildung unsers Witzes, oder Scharfsinnes, oder andere Sprossen menschlicher Seelenkräfte, als auf *Erziehung des Herzens* an; und dies ist bei allen Menschen ein *Menschenherz.* Es kann auch in allen Formen und Situationen der Menschheit bis auf einen gewissen Grad gebildet werden. ... *Reinigung des Herzens, Veredlung der Seele mit ihren Trieben und Begierden,* das dünkt mich, ist

[19]   Book IV, I, 4, *SWS,* XIII, 25f; Book V, 6, XIII, 194f.

die wahre *Palingenesie dieses Lebens,* nach der uns gewiss eine
fröliche, höhere, aber uns unbekannte Metempsychose hervor-
steht" (XV, 303). When speaking of growth and development
Herder never understands a progression from one species to
another. Statements of his such as, "Je mehr . . . sich die
Menschlichen *Geistes*kräfte sich entwickeln, desto mehr ersterben die Fähigkeiten der sinnlichen Thierseele" (XXXII, 69),
have sometimes led investigators to the conclusion that Herder's
idea of growth is a forerunner of Darwin's theory of evolution.
There are innummerable passages where Herder has conclusive-
ly denied any such thoughts. Speaking of man's capacity for
language as opposed to the lack of such in animals, he writes:
*"Der Unterschied ist nicht in Stuffen, oder Zugabe von Kräf-
ten, sondern in einer ganz verschiedenartigen Richtung und
Auswickelung aller Kräfte"* (V, 29). And elsewhere: "Der edle
Mensch hat die Himmelsleiter in sich, die er hinauf seyn muss"
(VIII, 299). Consequently, Herder sees in the effect of a stimulus
the beginnings of all sensations, passions, and actions; he sees
in the *tönende Verba* man's first step on the way to the development of language; and he sees in the vast mass of mythology,
legends, folklore, and traditions – he terms them "rohen, kleinen,
veracteten Samenkörnern" (IX, 53) – the origins of the magnificent forest of English literature. The stimuli, verbs, and folk
traditions are only the seeds from which the more fully developed product grows up, but at all times the potential for the full
growth is present.

There are two places where Herder has set down his own
systematic ideas on how the soul can best be developed. The
first of these is the *Reisejournal* of 1769, the second the numerous *Schulreden,* extracts, studies, proposals, etc. which he
composed in his official capacity as teacher or director in the
various school systems which he served. To do justice to the
ideas of Herder recorded here would require a separate study
for this specific purpose. Nevertheless, it does seem possible to
find a basic concept which undergirds all of Herder's ideas on
education. This concept is, that all thought, every idea, no matter how abstract, must have lived. "Auch die abstrakteste Wis-

senschaft hat ihre Anschauung, und meistens ward der glück-
lichste Blick auch in ihr nur in Geschäft, That, Handlung gebohren" (VIII, 216). To be effective ideas must have their basis
in man's experience and feeling. Dry, metaphysical, *a priori*
ideas do not help the soul grow. They deaden it. Life is the basic
factor of any organism, and all ideas originating from an organism must reflect this life. The seed that is never planted can
bear no fruit. The knowledge which the soul gains from experience and living is that which causes it to grow. "Von Sinnen
und der Erfahrung gehet unser Erkänntniss aus und auf sie
kommt alles zurück" (XV, 527). In this growth, in man as a
composite of living forces who is always striving forward, Herder sees the main spring of human history. "Die ganze Men-
schengeschichte ist eine reine Naturgeschichte menschlicher
Kräfte, Handlungen und Triebe nach Ort und Zeit" (XIV, 145).
"*Lebendige Menschenkräfte sind die Triebfeder der Menschen-
geschichte* und da der Mensch seinen Ursprung von und in
einem Geschlecht nimmt: so wird hiemit schon seine Bildung,
Erziehung und Denkart genetisch" (XIV, 84).

The *Reisejournal* is Herder's own personal statement of the
necessity he felt to live. The sea voyage which he embarked upon
in 1769 undoubtedly marked the turning point in his life. The
time spent in Königsberg, and then more recently in Riga, had
offered many valuable experiences. But looking back upon these
years from the vantage point of the open sea Herder regards
them as so many lost years. "Ich beklage mich, ich habe gewisse Jahre von meinem *Menschlichen* Leben verlohren" (IV,
346). Those years had been a time when many seeds had been
sown, but instead of growing and bearing fruit they had lain
dormant. Addressing God in a fervent outburst, Herder asks
Him to instruct him how he can cast off this stupor and escape
from a life that has been more death than life. Finally Herder
finds the answer to his prayer in the reflections and analogies
which life aboard the ship on the open sea suggests to him.
The ship becomes a symbol of freedom, of life as it should be
lived without restrictions, of a life which is free to reach out and
drink in new sensations and experiences. Just as the ship sails

on toward new horizons, so are new vistas opened up to the soul as it continues on its upward climb. Herder has left us a record of the two feelings which were raging within him, of the old feeling of stagnation and stupor on the one hand, and of the new found freedom of the soul on the other. "Wo ist das veste Land, auf dem ich so veste stand? und die kleine Kanzel und der Lehnstul und das Katheder, worauf ich mich brüstete? wo sind die, für, denen ich mich fürchtete, und die ich liebte! – o Seele, wie wird dir seyn, wenn du aus dieser Welt hinaustrittst? Der enge, veste, eingeschränkte Mittelpunkt ist verschwunden, du flatterst in den Lüften, oder schwimmst auf einem Meer – . . . Welch neue Denkart!" (IV, 349).

We can conclude, then, that according to Herder's psychology the soul is in a continual state of development and growth which in part is the result of its own organic unity, in part the result of organic unity with every other living organism. The growth and development is in the direction of the Godhead from which the soul originated, and to which it shall ultimately return. Herder sums this up as follows: "Sein [des Geschöpfes] Gang ist immer fortschreitend: das Weltall muss ihm immer mehr und tiefere und hellere Phänomene des Wahren und Guten liefern: mit jeder Enthüllung derselben zum Erkennen und zum vollständigen Erkennen, der That, muss seine innere Kraft wachsen. Er strebt hinauf zur Gottheit und wird höherer Glückseligkeit fähig" (VIII, 262).

C. COMPLETION OF THE SOUL

Man's striving forward toward the godhead is indicative that a purpose and a goal have been set, which is the ultimate reason for his growth and development. If man at best is a harmonious being living in harmony with a harmonious creation, then his growth and development must also reflect this harmony.[20] As

---

[20]   See the most recent contribution to this general theme which appeared after this was written. Wilhelm Dobbek, "Die Kategorie der Mitte in der Kunstphilosophie J. G. Herders", in *Worte und Werte,* ed. Gustav Erdmann and Alfons Eichstaedt (Berlin, 1961), pp. 70-78.

man's soul unfolds, it must do so in an orderly manner. There can be no aimless, purposeless growth branching out into all directions without regard to an ultimate goal or purpose in man. Herder was not the first, of course, to recognize that man is constantly progressing from one state of development to another. But he was the first to explain this development according to genetic principles and to advance his own unique interpretations concerning these principles which have since firmly established him as one of the most important, if not the most important thinker on these questions in eighteenth century Germany. The prevailing idea of growth and development, and progress in general, was the Rationalistic interpretation that growth is a linear progression from one state or stage to another. Any illusions that Herder's thoughts may be identified with those of the Rationalists are dispelled as early as 1774 in *Auch eine Philosophie*. In this work, which served him as a sort of proving ground for many of the ideas of the *Ideen*, Herder aimed his barbs at the shallow Rationalistic concept of history and the belief in a unilateral progress that resulted from it.

Gemeiniglich ist der Philosoph alsdann am meisten *Thier*, wenn er am zuverlässigsten Gott seyn wollte: so such bei der zuversichtlichen Rechnung von Vervollkommung der Welt. Dass doch ja alles hübsch *in gerader* Linie ginge, und jeder *folgende Mensch* und jedes *folgende Geschlecht* in *schöner Progression*, zu der er allein den Exponenten von Tugend und Glückseligkeit zu geben wusste, nach *seinem* Ideal vervollkommet würde! Da trafs nun immer auf ihn *zuhinterst*: 'Sehet, zu solcher Aufklärung, Tugend, Glückseligkeit ist die Welt gestiegen! ich, hoch auf dem Schwengel! das *goldene Zünglein* der Weltwaage: *sehet* mich!' (V, 557f).

The idea of unilateral progress is destroyed in order to make way for the true idea of the development and growth of man. Herder does not see this growth and development taking place in a linear manner, but rather spirally, i.e. both horizontally and vertically. Man must strive for perfection, his activity must lead him to a goal and purpose. These, however, are not necessarily found on the highest point, but rather in the soul of man, in his universal truth and goodness by virtue of the divine semblance within him, and in his reflection of the divinity of the Creator. "Vom mindesten aber bis zum höchsten herrscht nur Ein Gesetz, das All zu repräsentieren, von Dunkelheit zur Klarheit, vom Empfinden zum Erkennen zu steigen, die beide auch Eins sind, und wo sich in Allem Eine Gottheit spiegelt" (VIII, 247).

Just as the soul has within it, from the very moment of its creation on, the full potential of its powers, so too is the potential for perfection one of its inherent characteristics. "Der Zweck einer Sache, die nicht blos ein todtes Mittel ist, muss in ihr selbst liegen" (XIV, 207). "Vollkommenheit einer Sache kann nichts seyn, als das Ding sei, was es seyn soll und kann" (XVII, 115). "Jede nicht ganz misbildete und verworrene Gestalt trägt eine Idee mit sich, die ihr Wesen ausdrückt, *was sie seyn soll*" (XXII, 296). Although *Zweck* and *Vollkommenheit* are often used synonymously by Herder, there is one important distinction which must not be lost sight of. Any object can have a purpose, but only the organism can attain perfection. For though the potential for this perfection is present in all organic beings, this potential is realized only through growth and development. A lifeless form neither grows nor develops. It remains static. Whereas the true being of man, or any other organism, lies in its growth and development (*Werden*),[21] the purpose of the inorganic being is in its mere existence (*Dasein*). Now it is obvious that even inorganic substances are subject to change and that such a change is sometimes necessary before its immediate purpose can be realized. But this is only an external change brought about by external factors. There is no growth and development from within, no emulation of the creative process such as takes place within the soul of man. The lack of ability to act (*wirken*), and therefore to develop and grow from within, also signifies an inability to communicate with the rest of organic nature. We have already seen that the *geistige Band* within man both unites all of his diversified physiological and psychological functions into a harmonious whole and places

---

[21]　Berger, p. 37.

him into a direct line of contact with every other organic being. This contact with other beings is essential to the growth and development of the organic being and is therefore one of the factors which helps it along the way toward perfection.

In his efforts to achieve perfection man constantly has before him a model which embodies within it the highest possible degree of perfection. This model is none other than man's creator, God. "In Gott ist die höchste Wahrheit, Lebhaftigkeit und Klarheit" (XV, 527). Although God is a spirit and as such remains invisible to man, man's soul, that part of him which is most like its creator and that part of him which constantly strives to attain the perfection of its creator, enjoys a spiritual relationship with God. It must be apparent, however, that it is primarily during its earthly existence that the soul concerns itself with the attainment of perfection. Although the soul originates in the heavenly realm, it passes almost immediately over into its second state, that of earthly existence. While never losing sight completely of its heavenly origins, the soul's drive toward perfection takes place within an earthly sphere while it dwells within a mortal, earthly form, the body, for in man's experience there is no such thing as a disembodied spirit. During its earthly existence two major tasks face the soul: the ordering of the mutiplicity of matter and thereby the bringing about of unity to this mutiplicity. The greater the soul's success in performing these tasks the closer it comes to attaining the perfection it seeks. The final stage in the existence of the soul, which may be viewed as a sort of circular process, is the disembodiment of the soul, i.e. death, and its return to its heavenly origins. That the soul is conscious of the perfection within the Creator and strives to attain this perfection within itself is indicated by the fact that it has prescribed for itself the same standards in the production of images that it envisages the Creator to have. "So sind doch allen diesen Kräften *dieselben Gesetze der Vollkommenheit eines Bildes* vorgezeichnet; *Wahrheit* nämlich, *Lebhaftigkeit* und *Klarheit*" (XV, 527). The whole creative process of image production which we have already considered in some detail is of immense importance to the soul in its drive for perfection. For as the soul creates and translates images, these act upon it and present it with the possibility of growth and development. This is what Herder is saying when he writes: "Woran die Seele sich übe und durch welche Sinne sie würke, was sie daher erbeutet ist Wahrheit: mit welchen Leidenschaften sie strebe, was sie sucht, ist Glückseligkeit, Vollkommenheit, Gutes. Alle Menschen arbeiten an Einem Produkt nur aus verschiedenen Aufgaben und Zahlen und jeder auf seine Weise" (VIII, 255). This one product toward which all of mankind is working is perfection, and this can be achieved only if the soul can act, can grow and develop. But lest this concept of growth and development be misunderstood it must be again called to mind that this is a process whereby the soul develops its innate potential, and not one whereby it adds to this potential.

That man is striving and developing is evidence of his desire to attain perfection. Just as the functioning of the soul becomes increasingly harmonious with habit, so too does its degree of perfection. The closer man is able to approach the Divine, and this can be done only within the soul, the more perfect he becomes. "Wo Geist des Herrn ist, da ist Freiheit. Je mehr uns Gottes Erkenntniss, das allgemeinste und kräftigste Licht überall anblitzt und Gottes Triebe, die reinsten, kräftigsten und allgemeinsten anziehen und beleben, desto edler vergeistigen wir Körper und alle Körper, alle sichtbaren Wesen um uns her. Aus allem ziehen wir nur *die* reine Flamme, die Gott ist, und so sind wir, wie Gott, frei und allmächtig. Allerdings hier nur im Streben und nicht im Genusse: nicht im Seyn, sondern im Werden" (VIII, 295). The emphasis in these lines is on *Streben* and *Werden,* without which man neither knows freedom nor can he attain perfection. And to apply the words of Faust, man's freedom must be earned daily. To attain perfection, which is his goal and purpose, man can permit himself no indolence. He must constantly be striving onward and upward.

If the human soul, and for that matter all of creation, reflects the order and harmony of the Divine Soul, then both must have within them the same qualities. For Herder one of the basic characteristics of the human soul, which also reflects its harmony, is its innate goodness and truth. By analogy this characteristic is likewise reflected in the cosmic soul, the universe. "Die Menschliche Seele und das Universum für sie ist voll Anlagen zur Weisheit, Güte und Tugend in jeder Leidenschaft, in jeder Erscheinung" (VIII, 244). "Ihre Natur ist Wahrheit und Güte" (VIII, 245). "Die allweise Natur . . . hats also so gefüget, dass ihr nichts zuströmen kann, was ihr nicht Symbol der Wahrheit, Güte und Vollkommenheit sei" (VIII, 245). In these lines Herder has made several points which are not only basic to his psychology as a whole, but also to his insistence that man has a purpose and a goal toward which he must constantly strive. The innate goodness of the soul, like all the rest of its characteristics, is an undeveloped resource. But to be effective this resource must be developed. Secondly, Herder does not speak of human "souls", but of *the* human soul. He is not concerned here with individualities, but with generalities. The predisposition for goodness and truth is present in every soul, not just one. The more the soul grows and develops the closer it will come to realizing this predisposition and the nearer it will approach oneness with all other souls. "Wie steigen und erhöhen sich die Organizationen aus allen Punkten, auf allen Seiten! Und wie sind sie sich einander wiederum so ähnlich! Gerade, als ob auf unsrer ganzen Erde die Formenreiche Mutter nur *Einen* Typus, *Ein* Protoplasma vor sich gehabt hätte, nach dem und zu dem sie alles bildete. – Wissen Sie, was dies für eine Form ist? Die Nämliche, die auch der Mensch an sich trägt" (XV, 287). Development for Herder means that the organism moves from the individual toward the universal, for it is only in universality that perfection can be realized. Herder sees this same leveling tendency of history everywhere about him. "Durch hundert Ursachen hat sich im Verfolg der Jahrhunderte die alte Stammesbildung mehrerer Nationen gemildert und verändert; ohne welche Verschmelzung der Allgemeingeist Europas schwerlich hätte erweckt werden mögen" (XIV, 287).

Despite the fact that Herder frequently talks about the worth of the individual, stresses the value of the individual personality, admonishes critics to consider each work and each artist individually, and never tires recounting how time, place, climate, and a host of other factors influence the development of each organism, Herder's primary interest lies in universals. Recognition of this important premise is the key to an understanding of the Shakespeare essay. Herder's statement that Sophocles' drama and Shakespeare's drama are two things which hardly have even a name in common is an indication of the individuality of the artistic creations of these two dramatists. Yet elsewhere in the same essay Herder can point to Shakespeare as the sole heir to the tragic traditions exemplified in the drama of Sophocles. Why, because although each of the dramatists has created a drama which is uniquely his own, each has incorporated into his own individual creation a sense of the tragic which is common to all of mankind. Although this point has already been stressed several times, we dwell upon it at length here because it is critical to the results of this discussion and at variance with the majority of voices of Herder scholarship. Careful examination of Herder's own statements can, however, leave little doubt about what he is saying. "Dass jede Nation zu ihrer Zeit, auf ihrer Stelle nur das war, was sie seyn konnte; das wissen wir alle, damit aber wissen wir noch wenig. Was jede in Vergleich der andern war, wie sie auf einander wirkten und fehlwirkten, einander nutzten oder schadeten, aus welchen Zügen nach und nach das Bild zusammengeflossen sei, das wir als die Tendenz unsres gesammten Geschlechts, als die höchste Blüthe der Schönheit, Wahrheit und Güte unsrer Nation verehren, das ist die Frage" (XVIII, 149). The individual and particular are not important as ends in themselves, but rather to the extent which they reflect the tendencies of all of mankind. Herder strives for that one human state in which he sees the divine reflected. In lines already cited above he calls it a form which man usually bears with him. More often he terms it *Humanität*.

For Herder man passes through two distinct, yet closely related stages on his way to ultimate perfection. The first of these he designates *Humanität,* which is the goal and purpose of man's earthly existence and as such may be distinguished from the goal and purpose of man's existence in the hereafter. *Humanität* is, so to speak, a preparatory state through which man must first pass before he can attain ultimate perfection. This term ultimate perfection is, however, somewhat ambiguous, and must be used with care. Strictly speaking man can never realize ultimate perfection, at least not during his earthly existence. Perfection, in this case *Humanität,* is a goal and purpose which must be constantly strived for, but which is never completely attained. Any admission that *Humanität* is completely attainable would be contrary to the whole purpose of man's existence. *Humanität* itself defies any concise conceptual formulation because it is the infinite sum of the good in all human beings and is in a state of unending change. As a composite of living, active powers man is destined to grow and strive onward continually, not aimlessly, but with a goal and purpose – *Humanität* – ever in mind. But should this goal ever be reached, then the reason for man's striving would be removed. Instead of a dynamic being, he would be reduced to a static being, which in itself is contradictory, since no organism can exist permanently in a static state. Man can attain a degree of *Humanität,* but never fully acquire the finished product.

Perfection, it must be remembered, whether in this world or the hereafter, is a spiritual matter. Only man's soul, that part of him which is immortal and divine by virtue of its creation in the likeness of the Great Creator, strives for perfection. The very fact that during its earthly existence the soul is housed in the body, which is mortal and earthly, and is bound by considerations of space and time, precludes the soul from actually attaining perfection. Although the body itself does not actively participate in the drive for perfection on its own initiative, it is nevertheless Herder's firm belief that the degree of perfection of the soul is reflected in the body. But whether or not the transition of man's soul from its earthly, mortal existence to existence in an immortal, spiritual realm constitutes the ultimate attainment of perfection is not a question to which Herder has given us an unequivocal answer. On the one hand it can

be argued that the spiritual state after death when man's soul
returns to its creator is the highest possible state man will ever
attain, and hence can rightly be considered his ultimate perfection. This assumption gains in credibility when one remembers
that according to Herder's psychology the soul is endowed by
the Creator with the same rights and characteristics that are
His own. Man's soul is a miniature reproduction of the Divine
Soul. But herein lies the bone of contention when one attempts
a final solution to the problem. If man's soul is only a miniature
of the Divine Soul, then the question follows if it can ever
realize perfection to the same extent as has the Divine Soul,
which is the very essence of perfection. Although Herder remains silent on this point, we can attempt an answer to this
question in keeping with his psychological principles which have
already been noted. Perfection means ultimate development of
an innate potential. As long as this potential has reached ultimate development, i.e. perfection, within its sphere, questions
of magnitude are of little consequence. For perfection is ultimately a matter of degree, not extent. Perfection is, as Leibniz
had earlier remarked in his essay *Von der Weisheit*, dependent
upon the ability of the soul to act on its own initiative. This
perfection remains hidden from view within the soul until it is
revealed through some creative activity, for only after the activity is it possible to ascertain the perfection of the soul. Consequently, the drive for self-development and growth is always
of primary concern to the soul. Since man is incapable of judging
pure activity, the best indication of the degree of perfection
within the soul comes from the product which results from this
activity. Thus in his discussion of the genius in the *Kalligone*
Herder reminds us that during its creative activity it is the
nature of the genius to portray itself. The result of this activity
and drive for self-portrayal is a work of art which exists as a
visible image of the degree of perfection which the soul of the
genius has reached. Since no work of art ever exhibits complete perfection, it must follow that no soul ever fully develops
its potential or attains ultimate perfection while in this world.
We can conclude then, that Herder did consider it possible for

the soul to attain ultimate perfection, but only in the spiritual realm of the hereafter.

Humanität is an all inclusive concept which touches upon every possible characteristic of the human soul. Herder wrote in the *Ideen:*

> Ich wünschte, dass ich in das Wort *Humanität* alles fassen könnte, was ich bisher über des Menschen edle Bildung zur Vernunft und Freiheit, zu feinern Sinnen und Trieben, zur zartesten und stärksten Gesundheit, zur Erfüllung und Beherrschung der Erde gesagt habe: denn der Mensch hat kein edleres Wort für seine Bestimmung als Er selbst ist, in dem das Bild des Schöpfers unsrer Erde, wie es hier sichbar werden konnte, abgedruckt lebet. Um seine edelsten Pflichten zu entwickeln, dörfen wir nur seine Gestalt zeichnen (XIII, 154f).

Herder reiterates here many of the characteristics of *Humanität* which have previously been enumerated. As the very word itself suggests, *Humanität* is a trait restricted to man and is inextricably linked together with his existence here on earth. *Humanität* does not exist as a finished product, but is the result of man's gradual growth and development. As Clark has observed, *Humanität* "is an abstract term referring to the ideal state capable of attainment by mankind" and "the latent possibility which mankind has for the attainment of that ideal".[22] "Das ganze Gebilde der Humanität in ihm hängt durch eine geistige Genesis, die Erziehung, mit seinen Eltern, Lehrern, Freunden, mit allen Umständen im Lauf seines Lebens, also mit seinem Volk und den Vätern desselben, ja mit der ganzen Kette des Geschlechts zusammen, das irgend in einem Gliede Eine seiner Seelenkräfte berührte" (XIII, 346). Man's effort to pull himself up to *Humanität* is not solely an internal process dependent upon the inherent creative and organic powers of the soul. An important aspect of this climb toward *Humanität* is the oneness among organic beings resulting from the organic and spiritual band which connects all organic beings and enables them to communicate with one another. Since every indi-

---

[22] Clark, *Herder*, p. 315.

vidual is a link in the chain of mankind, *Humanität* must be applicable to the whole chain, and not just one individual link. *Humanität* is, as we have already noted, a universal quality. Fricke is correct when he says that Herder believed he could bring all differences together under the common denominator *Humanität*.[23]

In a rather lengthy passage from one of the *Humanitätsbriefe* Herder has admirably summarized his concept of *Humanität*. Although he calls *Humanität* the character of our species, here again he emphasizes that it is no mere gift to man. Rather, it is a quality which must be sought and earned daily if it is to be attained. Elsewhere Herder has termed it man's goal in life, his great future toward which he must work with courageous and joyous heart.

Humanität ist der Charakter unsres Geschlechts; er ist uns aber nur in Anlagen angebohren, und muss uns eigentlich angebildet werden. Wir bringen ihn nicht fertig auf die Welt mit; auf der Welt aber soll er das Ziel unsres Bestrebens, die Summe unsrer Uebungen, unser Werth seyn: denn eine Angelität in Menschen kennen wir nicht, und wenn der Dämon, der uns regiert, kein humaner Dämon ist, werden wir Plagegeister der Menschen. Das Göttliche in unserem Geschlecht ist also Bildung zur Humanität; alle grossen und gute Menschen, Gesetzgeber, Erfinder, Philosophen, Dichter, Künstler, jeder edle Mensch in seinem Stande, bei der Erziehung seiner Kinder, bei der Beobachtung seiner Pflichten, durch Beispiel, Werk, Institut und Lehre hat dazu mitgeholfen. Humanität ist der Schatz und Ausbeute aller menschlichen Bemühungen, gleichsam die Kunst unsres Geschlechts. Die Bildung zu ihr ist ein Werk, das unablässig fortgesetzt werden muss; oder wir sinken, höhere und niedere Stände, zur rohen Thierheit, zur Brutalität zurück (XVII, 138).[24]

Thus in the *Humanitätsbriefe* such diversified individuals as Benjamin Franklin, Friedrich II of Prussia, and Joseph II of Austria are singled out because of their significant contributions to the humanitarian ideal. The further addition to this

---

[23] Gehard Fricke, "Das Humanitätsideal der klassischen deutschen Dichtung und die Gegenwart", (II. Herder), *Zeitschrift für Deutschkunde*, XLVIII (1934), p. 681.
[24] Cf. also *SWS*, XIV, 209; XVII, 153.

list of such names as Homer, Milton, Shakespeare, Luther, Klopstock, and Ossian would also most certainly be entirely in keeping with Herder's intent when he speaks of the contribution made by all great men to the furtherance of *Humanität*.

The theoretical attainment of *Humanität* is not a prize limited to a chosen few. It is available to every individual man, regardless of the link he occupies in the chain of mankind. "Was also jeder Mensch ist und seyn kann, das muss Zweck des Menschengeschlechts seyn; und was ist dies? Humanität und Glückseligkeit auf der Stelle, in diesem Grad, als dies und kein andres Glied der Kette von Bildung, die durchs ganze Geschlecht reichet. Wo und wer du gebohren bist, o Mensch, da bist du, der du seyn solltest: verlass die Kette nicht, noch setze dich über sie hinaus" (XIII, 350). The degree of *Humanität* attainable by the individual may be determined and conditioned by his own particular circumstances and conditions, but whatever these are, they are a part of that incalculable whole of God's creation, just as each individual is a link in the vast chain of humanity. Herder's emphasis is not on individual *Humanität*, but rather on the *Humanität* of the individual as a symbol and reflection of a universal *Humanität*. "Alle Werke Gottes haben dieses eigen, dass ob sie gleich alle zu Einem unübersehlichen Ganzen gehören, jedes dennoch auch für sich ein Ganzes ist und den göttlichen Charakter seiner Bestimmung an sich träget" (XIII, 350).

Herder never doubts for a moment that every positive activity of man furthers the cause of *Humanität*, while everything negative he does is detrimental to it. "Also haben wir auch nicht zu zweifeln, dass jede gute Thätigkeit des menschlichen Verstandes nothwendig einmal die Humanität befördern müsse und befördern werde" (XIV, 242). "Was also in der Geschichte je Gutes gethan ward, ist für die Humanität gethan worden: was in ihr Thörichtes, Lasterhaftes und Abscheuliches in Schwang kam, ward gegen die Humanität verübt" (XIV, 209). Man's goodness and the goodness which he does are only possible because of the divine semblance within him. The closer he comes to complete development of body and soul, the nearer he approaches the divine semblance, i.e. *Humanität*, perfection, call it what you will. Rudolf Stadelmann has written concerning Herder's *Humanität*: "Humanität ist weder eine Foderung, noch eine Erkenntnis, sondern ein allgemeinstes Ziel der Sehnsucht, ein höchstes Gut, von dem ein Strom von Beseeligung ausgeht".[25] Stadelmann's characterization of *Humanität* as "ein höchstes Ziel" penetrates to the very crux of the matter and echoes Herder's own words: "Betrachten wir die Menschheit, wie wir sie kennen, nach den Gesetzen, die in ihr liegen: so kennen wir nichts höheres, als Humanität in Menschen: denn selbst wenn wir uns Engel oder Götter denken, denken wir sie uns als idealische, höhere Menschen" (XIV, 208). Since man is the highest being known to man through empirical knowledge – "Eine höhere Gestalt als die unsre kennen wir nicht" (XIII, 163f) – he consequently conceives of any supreme being or beings anthropomorphically. *Humanität* signifies complete development of the mind and body according to its innate potentials, is the highest good known to man, and the measure which universally applies. The function of the soul in man's quest for *Humanität* does not have to be sought far afield, for without the power derived from the innate energy of the soul man would be a lifeless organism, incapable of striving toward any goal. Then too the soul is the seat of that part of man most closely linked to the divinity of the Creator. As such it reminds him of his orgins and gives him the will to strive for the perfection – *Humanität* – inherent in them.

Religion is an important factor in all of Herder's considerations. But with *Humanität* religion is more than a factor, for here what might seem to be two separate philosophies of life come together until one is hardly distinguishable from the other. Zeller has characterized the relationship between religion and *Humanität* for Herder as follows: "Mit der Humanität fällt für Herder die Religion ihrem Wesen nach zusammen. Die Religion ist die höchste Humanität des Menschen, sie ist es aber auch, die den Völkern die erste Kultur und Wissenschaft brachte; das religiöse Gefühl unsichtbarer Kräfte ist die Bedingung jedes

[25] Rudolf Stadelmann, *Der Historische Sinn Bei Herder* (Halle/Saale, 1928), p. 30. Cf. also p. 75.

höheren Vernunftgebrauchs".[26] Thus we see that the essence of religion is basically identical with that of *Humanität*. In the fourth book of the *Ideen* Herder says: *"Zur Humanität und Religion ist der Mensch gebildet"* (XIII, 154). In addition he declares: "Endlich ist die *Religion* die höchste Humanität des Menschen und man verwundere sich nicht, dass ich sie hieher rechne" (XIII, 161). As the highest *Humanität* religion gains a special significance because it is the human institution with the highest degree of perfection possible to man during his earthly existence and therefore the closest man can come to the perfection which awaits him in the hereafter. Religion is the loftiest expression of man's relationship with the Divine Being, the supreme development of the soul, and the nearest man approaches a realization of oneness with his Creator. "Religion ist also, auch schon als Verstandesübung betrachtet, die höchste Humanität, die erhabendste Blüthe der menschlichen Seele" (XIII, 163). This "gottähnliche Humanität", as Herder calls it, is the only acquisition made by man while in this life that he can take with him into the next. Herder tells us that man's need of religion is ultimately based on the category of causality. Man is not only organized for *Humanität* and religion, but also for understanding and reason. The business of man's understanding is to seek out and establish the connection between cause and effect. In nature, however, man's understanding is frequently confronted with the task of finding the hidden cause of a visible effect. The end result of this "Gang der Philosophie" (XIII, 162) is always religion, i.e. man inevitably comes upon the idea of God. Where he can see no visible cause, man supplies one. Herder concludes that whether true or false, religion is the proof of God and man's hope for immortality. In true religion, however, the emphasis is on the relationship between God and man. "Wahre Religion also ist ein kindlicher Gottesdienst, eine Nachahmung des Höchsten und Schönsten im menschlichen Bilde, mithin die innigste Zufriedenheit, die wirksamste Güte und Menschenliebe" (XIII, 163). Since Herder con-

---

[26] Eduard Zeller, *Geschichte der deutschen Philosophie seit Leibniz* (München, 1873), p. 540.

siders the attainment of *Humanität* the primary task of the soul, and since he equates *Humanität* with religion, which leads to man's discovery of God, it can be said that recognition of the existence of God is the most important one perception of the human soul. Until the soul has perceived His existence, there can be no *Humanität*, there can be no perfection. "Vom Anfange des Lebens an scheint unsre Seele nur Ein Werk zu haben, *inwendige Gestalt, Form der Humanität* zu gewinnen und sich in ihr, wie der Körper in der Seinigen gesund und froh zu fühlen" (XIII, 187). This work of the soul finds expression in several ways. For the genius it means the creation of artistic works which reflect the *Humanität* of his soul. For the non-genius, i.e mankind as a whole to whom it has not been given to express itself through creative acts, it means a projection into, an empathizing with the creation of the genius and thereby benefiting from it. But whether it be through the creative act, or an attempt to partake of the product of the creative act of another, man's soul is never at rest. It is constantly active, growing and developing.

In spite of his tolerance and the liberalism of his views, there was for Herder, however, only one true religion. And this was Christianity. This is the theme of the seventeenth book of the *Ideen*. In the fourth book Herder had talked about religion in general, in the seventeenth he deals only with Christianity. All other religions are the product of a people, place, climate, or time, but Christianity Herder sees as "die lauterste Philosophie der Sittenlehre, die reinste Theorie der Wahrheiten und Pflichten, den menschliebensten Deismus".[27] Herder wrote in the *Humanitätsbriefe*: "Das Principium des Christenthums ist nicht Gesetz, sondern *Evangelium*" (XVIII, 338). And for Herder there was only one gospel. This is the gospel of Jesus Christ. For him the Incarnation is the highest manifestation of *Humanität* known and the most potent proof of its existence. In the person of Christ the two elements humanity and Divinity are united in perfect harmony. In everything Christ did, *Humanität* is reflected. Moreover, Herder strongly hints that without Christ

---

[27]   Fricke, p. 686.

there could be no *Humanität*. "Die *ächteste Humanität* ist in den wenigen Reden enthalten, die wir von ihm haben; Humanität ist, was er im Leben bewies, und durch seinen Tod bekräftigte: wie er sich denn selbst mit einem Lieblingsnamen, den *Menschensohn*, nannte" (XIV, 290). Herder goes on to say that Christ's mission on earth "was the foundation of a kingdom of truth and goodness in which men should co-operate together for the common good of all, adding that such a goal as this for the human race must be the aim and intention of providence".[28] Both in its purpose and its execution Christianity is *Humanität* itself. "Dass der Zweck der Religion Christi ... reine Humanität sei, ist... Sonnenklar" (XVIII, 338). "Die *Religion Christe*, die Er selbst hatte, lehrte und übte, war die Humanität selbst" (XVII, 121). Herder saw in Christianity the one institution of man universally capable of uniting all of mankind, which, by the way, is one of the fundamental tenets of Christianity even today. At the same time he saw man's attainment of a relationship with God through this institution as his supreme achievement. "Die Religion Christi ... ist die Humanität selbst, und auf den fortstrebenden Bau der geistigen verbundenen Menschheit ist Alles in der Geschichte angelegt. In Liebe und Wahrheit, kraft des Geistes der Freiheit, sollen wir Alle Eins werden." [29]

The earthly state of man has imposed upon his soul the limitations of time and place. The soul is anchored to the body in which it dwells, and not until death is the soul set free from its mortal form. Such questions as what happens to the soul after death, where does the soul go, what is it state, does it assume a recognizable form, etc., have long challenged the ingenuity and knowledge of man. Although numerous answers have been offered, none can be accepted as absolutely conclusive, for ultimate answers to these questions lie in a realm beyond human experience and comprehension. The immortality of the soul is generally conceded, but here too empirical proof is

---

[28]   Frank McEachran, *The Life and Philosophy of Johann Gottfried Herder* (Oxford, 1939), p. 72.
[29]   Haym, II, 575.

lacking and the concepts of how immortality is attained are many. A vital part of man's religion is his hope for immortality. He believes in immortality, but as Herder has observed, he can produce no metaphysical proofs. "Dass mit der Religion als auch Hofnung und Glaube der Unsterblichkeit verbunden war und durch sie unter den Menschen gegründet wurde, ist abermals Natur der Sache, vom Begriff Gottes und der Menschheit beinah unzertrennlich" (XIII, 164). In addition to its function as the expression of the highest *Humanität*, of man's relationship with the Supreme Being, religion has the added task of bringing man to an awareness of the immortality of the human soul. Herder's ideas on the immortality of the human soul, like his thoughts on language, religion, or any other of his major areas of concern, are never codified.[30] It is important, therefore, to resist jumping to conclusions or making any final formulations about Herder's actual position until a number of his utterances have been examined. For example, Herder sometimes gives the impression that he, like the Barock poets, believes that the only immortality for man is that attained through the legacy he leaves to posterity. Nevertheless, Herder did believe in immortality in the orthodox, Christian sense, and on the basis of his psychology he did see the possibility of a definite proof of this immortality. The soul is a force (*Kraft*), and in Herder's words: "Keine Kraft kann untergehen" (XIII, 170). Herder also refers to the soul as a spirit or pneuma, which symbolizes the connection between man's soul and God, for this breath is none other than that of the Creator. For Herder it would be a crass contradiction to assume that anything in which the spirit of God is present could perish. "*Geist Gottes* heisst ihnen [Geschöpfen] in menschlichen Seelen *jede edelste Kraft*, wenn sie sich in vollem Genuss ihres Daseyns auf die verzüglichste Weise äussert. *Geist Gottes* heisst ihnen endlich jene fortwährende *Tendenz* des Menschen, immer vollkommener zu werden, heller im Verstande, reiner im Herzen, kräftiger im

---

[30]   Haym, II, 239-246 has surveyed the range of Herder's ideas on immortality.

Willen, von innerm Vorwurf frei, der Gottheit nahe, ihr verwandt, nach ihr gebildet" (XXX, 229).

Having established Herder's belief in the immortality of the human soul, we can now turn our attention to the significance of this belief for his psychology and his concept of the perfection of the human soul. Herder often uses the chain as a metaphor and compares man's various stages of existence to the links of a chain. One of the difficulties which face Charikles and Theages in *Ueber die Seelenwandrung* is how to resolve the problem of the initial and final links in the chain, i.e. where was man's soul before birth and where does it go after death. Both concede the difficulty of imagining man outside of "der Kreis der Menschheit" and its "veste Grenzen". Finally however, Charikles is forced to admit that Theages' idea of the soul released from its earthly bonds opens up to it entirely new vistas and possibilities. "Die Schranken, die Sie eröfnen, sind allerdings grösser: das Feld zu dem Sie einladen, ist unendlich – die Schaar aller Welten, die auf meinem ewigen Wege zur Gottheit liegen" (XV, 274). But there is still a problem for Charikles: 'Wer giebt mir dahin Flügel?" Theages answer: "Wollen Sie sie nicht aus *heiliger* Hand nehmen, . . ." (XV, 274). In other words, palingenesis for Herder is only another link in the chain of man's existence and development and is just as much a part of God's plan for the soul as the period spent as life on earth. "Moral ist nur eine höhere Physik des Geistes, so wie unsere künftige Bestimmung ein neues Glied der Kette unsers Daseyns, das sich aufs genaueste, in der subtilsten Progression, an das jetzige Glied unsres Daseyns anschliesst, wie etwas die Erde an die Sonne, wie der Mond an unsre Erde" (XV, 275).

The *Reisejournal* is Herder's own personal statement of the importance of new situations for the soul. When the soul finds itself in a new situation, it comes into contact with new sensations, makes new perceptions, and thus grows and develops. And so it is when the soul passes into its new existence after death. "– haben Sie nie, mein Fr. erfahren, was eine neue Situation der Seele für neue Schwungkraft giebt, die sie oft in ihrem alten Winkel, im erstickenden Dampf ihrer Gegenstände und Geschöpfe, sie nie zugetraut, sie nie derselben fähig gehalten hätte – " (XV, 273). During life the soul is incarcerated in the body. After death it is set free, and, simultaneous with palingenesis, finds itself in its rightful habitat. "Entkörpert ist er [der Geist] sogleich an *seinem* Ort, in *seinem* Kreise, in dem neuen Staat, dazu er gehöret" (XV, 272). The soul has no concept of this new location. It might be roundabout it, it might be far away from it. But the soul is assured that wherever this location is, that it will always be in '*Gottes unendlichem Schoosse*".

There can be no doubt that the rebirth of the soul after death constitutes its ultimate perfection for Herder. Created to grow and develop and destined to strive always to reach perfection, the soul attains this state only when it returns to its original spiritual state of oneness with God. Life on earth is only a sojourn, an intermediate state, a middle link in the chain of man's existence. Only in "that world", as Herder refers to it, does the soul find the absolutes necessary for ultimate perfection. "Nehmen Sie die reinsten Verhältnisse auf dieser Welt, ... mit welchen Sorgen sind sie vermischt, ... *In jener Welt,*' ... Da ist *Liebe* befreit von gröbern Trieben, reinere Freundschaft ohne die Abtrennungen und Bänden dieser Erde, wirksamere Thätigkeit mit glücklicher schöner Eintracht, und einem wahren und ewigen Endzweck, kurz überall mehr *Wahrheit, Güte, Schönheit*, als uns diese Erde auch bei hundertmaligem Wiederkommen geben könnte" (XV, 279). Only in "that world' does the soul become one with God, Who is perfection itself. "Wenn endlich der Geist sich zum höchsten Ideal der Schöpfung, zu Gott, erhebt: ein Meer, in dem alle Vollkommenheiten zusammen fliessen: ein Mittelpunkt, aus welchen alle Radien strömen: ... Von Dir, durch Dich, in Dir bin ich; zu Dir gehe ich wieder. Du bist alles, Du hast alles, Du gabst mir alles; gib mir das Edelste, Dir ähnlich zu seyn; hilf mir!" (XVI, 257).

Our examination has shown that Herder sees the soul passing through three definite stages. First of all there is the inherent state of unity within the soul which remains constant. Since the soul is created by an act of God, it exists in His likeness and reflects His attributes, above all His universality. Second, the soul is endowed with a potential, which must be developed and expanded by the energy and life within the soul. This development not only takes place from within, but is also dependent upon outside factors which find entry into the soul through the *geistiges Band* which links it with all of creation. The creative energy within the soul manifests itself in several ways, in its embodiment, in its creation of images, and in the genius in its creation of artistic products in emulation of the creative act of the Great Creator. And third, there is the drive toward ultimate achievement of the highest possible development – perfection. During man's earthly existence attainment of perfection is synonymous with reaching a state of *Humanität*, which, in turn, is closely identified with Herder's philosophy of religion.

It may well be asked what this excursion into psychology has to do with Herder's aesthetics, which is the main subject at hand. Interestingly enough, the *Viertes Wäldchen*, which even Herder's critics have praised, not only contains the germs of Herder's psychology, but also is a work of greatest importance for his aesthetics. The mere fact that Herder's treatment of psychology and aesthetics in the *Viertes Wäldchen* is so entwined that one is dependent upon the other should give some indication as to why we have begun our investigation of his aesthetics by first trying to obtain a clear concept of his psychology. Although the final answer to the question posed above must await our detailed treatment of the aesthetic writings and theories themselves, a partial answer is already possible at this time. Again and again it has been emphasized that the entirely new and revolutionary concept in Herder's psychology, that which in a marked way distinguished it from the psychology of the Enlightenment, was his premise that the soul not only grows and develops from within, and in so doing influences the world round about it, but that the influence of the outside world upon the soul is also of great importance to its growth and development. This give and take process has been characterized by Berger as follows: *"Im Ausdrucksbild und in der Verstandeserkenntnis wirkt die Welt auf unsre empfängliche Seele: im Trieb- und Willensakt wirkt die Seele auf die Aussenwelt: Wirkung und Gegenwirkung, Eindruck und Ausdruck charakterisieren auch hier den Lebensvollzug.*" [31] Just as language may be said to be "die sinnliche Erscheinung der Seele",[32] so too can every other one of man's creations lay claim to this designation. Thus after completion the products of the creative energy of any one soul become a part of the outside world, which in turn may aid in the growth and development of some other soul. The greater the degree of perfection evidenced by this creation, i.e. the more beautiful, the truer, the better it is, the more capable it will be of stimulating growth and development in another soul. The two functions of the soul, growth and development and creation, thus become inextricably entwined, with each to a large degree dependent upon the other. The same can be said for psychology and aesthetics. Aesthetics is primarily concerned with the creative aspects of the soul, whereas psychology deals with the effects of what is created upon the soul. Yet it is impossible to draw any strict line of demarcation and to isolate completely the area of concern of the one from that of the other. Korff has characterized this relationship as follows: "Denn der Gipfel der Humanität, der Zustand, in dem der Mensch am vollkommensten Mensch sein kann, das sollte jener ästhetische Zustand sein, der uns zuteil wird in Anschaun und Genusse der Kunst." [33] It remains the task of the main body of this study to point out more fully this relationship through a detailed examination of several of Herder's individual writings.

---

[31]   Berger, p. 137.
[32]   Max Kommerell, *Der Dichter als Führer in der deutschen Klassik* (Berlin, 1928), p. 68.
[33]   H. A. Korff, *Geist der Goethezeit* (Leipzig, 1957f), I, 8.

II

THE ROLE OF THE CRITIC AND THE POSSIBILITIES
OF AESTHETIC EVALUATION: *DIE FRAGMENTE*

A. LANGUAGE

In 1766 the first important work of Herder, *Über die neuere deutsche Litteratur, Fragmente,* was offered for sale at the Leipzig book fair. This work, like Herder's writing from beginning to end, consists of unfinished fragments, "fragments", however, which are frequently of considerable size and proportion. In spite of this fragmentary character the importance of the *Fragmente* for the future course of German literature can hardly be over-emphasized.[1] But what is perhaps of greater importance for any discussion of Herder's aesthetic is, that the germs of many of the ideas which Herder developed later in life are to be found here in the *Fragmente.*[2]

The primary purpose of the *Fragmente*, which was also that of the *Litteraturbriefe* which Herder singled out as his model, is a critical one. As Herder himself makes clear in the forward to the *Fragmente*, he envisages his work as a continuation of the *Litteraturbriefe*, and as a step forward in the same direction already taken by the earlier publication. Although Herder intends to subject German literature to a critique, it is significant that his purpose is not solely a polemic one. Foremost among his hopes is that his critique will bear fruit in a positive manner, i.e. that literary standards and tastes in Germany will be improved by his

---

[1]   See Suphan's introduction in SWS, I, xxiv.
[2]   Alexander Gillies, *Herder* (Oxford, 1945), p. 3, Wolfdietrich Rasch, *Herder, Sein Leben und sein Werk im Umriss* (Halle, 1938), p. 25.

efforts.[3] But Herder does not only use the *Litteraturbriefe* as a
model, he also approaches them as a critic, and in so doing he
had to come to terms with the problems of criticism in general.

In his *Versuch einer kritischen Dichtkunst* (1730), in a statement representative of his age, Gottsched had termed poetry the
vehicle of scientific, i.e. philosophical thought. Unwittingly perhaps, but none the less accurately, Gottsched's statement points
a finger at many of the problems besetting the literary and critical
scene in the Germany of his day. The preeminence of the demands of the theoretical elements upon the production of literary
works, the indiscriminant imitation of foreign models, and the
preoccupation with reducing every area of inquiry to some sort of
a philosophical system along with a language suited to the system were, to mention only a few, some of these. The one-sided
emphasis of the philosophical to the apparent exclusion of the
work of art itself was the very point where Herder disagreed with
Baumgarten,[4] for whom he otherwise had the highest regard.
This is by no means to say that philosophy was foreign to Herder.
One must remember, however, that while philosophical considerations are present in nearly everything that Herder did or said,
he did not allow them to take the upper hand and thereby to obscure other, equally important considerations. Herder not only
wanted to judge, but to understand, not to reason, but to feel, not
to theorize, but to realize. "Wir kritisieren ... aus unsrem Gefühl" (IV, 311). Indeed, Herder's ability to "feel himself into a
work" (*sich einfühlen*) has been universally recognized as one
of his foremost gifts.[5] As has already been noted in Chapter I,
but which must never be lost sight of because of its critical role in
both Herder's psychology and aesthetics, Herder's concept of

---

[3]   Cf. Dilthey's statement about Lessing in *Das Erlebnis und die Dichtung,*
3. Auflage (Leipzig, 1910), p. 36: "... die aufstrebende deutsche Literatur durch Kritik zu födern".
[4]   *SWS*, XXXII, 61 & 83: Cf. Rene Wellek, *A History of Modern Criticism* (New Haven, 1955), I, 145.
[5]   Rudolf Haym, *Herder*, ed. Wolfgang Harich (Berlin, 1954), II, 751;
Frank McEachran, *The Life and Philosophy of J. G. Herder* (Oxford,
1939), pp. 27, 28; Bruno Markwardt, *Herders Kritische Wälder* (Leipzig,
1925), p. 91f; Gillies, p.3; cf. SWS IV, 346.

feeling goes far beyond the usual meaning associated with this word. Feeling for Herder signified a process in which all the senses and the combined, harmoniously operating faculties of the soul take part. Feeling (*Gefühl*) alone, but even more so empathy (*sich einfühlen*), indicates that the soul of man has penetrated directly to the essence, the spirit or soul if you will, of the object with which it has come into contact, and has not been content with any superficial sentimentality or sensitivity. Herder's ideas were diametrically opposed by those of the rationalists, who were concerned with rules and discussion of *what* the poet *should* aim at, and *how* he *should* work, instead of *how* he *does* and *has* worked. In Herder's opinion, rationalistic perceptions had to be replaced by empirical perceptions from the realm of natural sciences, history, and psychology.[6] The critic had to have an understanding of the sources in the author's mind, and above all these sources and the work itself had to be viewed as a product of their day, time, and environment. "Jede gesunde Kritik in der ganzen Welt sagts, dass um ein Stück der Literatur zu verstehen, und auszulegen, man sich ja in den Geist dieses seines Stücks setzen müsse" (VI, 34). Thus the prevailing ideas of literary criticism are all pointedly rejected by Herder.[7] Criticizing the tenor of the judgments in the *Litteraturbriefe*, he writes: "Ein wahrer Kunstrichter in solchem Journal muss nicht Bücher, sondern den Geist beurtheilen, sie mit ihren Schwächen und Grössen gegeneinander abwägen und nicht System, sondern ihr Urbild verbessern" (I, 142).

In a short preliminary discourse which precedes the second collection of the *Fragmente* Herder traces the origin of the critic and the various points of view he represents. The opening sentence of the discourse, "Der erste Kunstrichter war nichts mehr als ein Leser von Empfindung und Geschmack", (I, 245) introduces at the very outset two important factors in Herder's criticism: feeling and taste. With his emphasis on feeling rather than reason Herder opposed the critical currents of his day, while with his interests in questions of taste he shared a concern common to

---

[6]   This is, of course, the crux of the argument with Kant in the *Kalligone*.
[7]   Wellek, I, 183.

most of his literary contemporaries. Continuing in a rather fanciful metaphor, he compares the first critic to a bee, who only drains the nectar from a flower and does not leave behind the skeleton of the plant as does the caterpillar or grasshopper. This was the age of literature when wisdom was not yet science, when experiences were not experiments. This was the age when man thought, instead of learning what others have thought. This, suggests Herder, was perhaps the Golden Age of Literature.[8] The Golden Age of Literature for Herder is always a time when literature springs directly from the soul and feeling of man without any artificial encumbrances such as rules, or the necessity of applying a philosophical system. But what or who is meant by the caterpillar and grasshopper? Undoubtedly Herder refers here to Gottsched and his school of criticism, who with their emphasis on philosophy, rules, and imitations were anathema to Herder. The Golden Age was no more, for philosophy and reason had replaced feeling, rules the right of free artistic expression, and imitations of objective nature the imitation of the creative act. But as soon as this reader of taste and feeling began to seek the reason for the higher quality of one work as opposed to another, the modern critic was born. ". . . er prüfte, lehrte und besserte" (I, 246). This was the true critic, the critic with a threefold responsibility: to the reader, to develop his taste and insight; to the writer, a friend and servant; to literature in general, a fellow citizen. This critic must

---

[8] Cf. Robert T. Clark, Jr., *Herder: His Life and His Thought* (Berkeley-Los Angeles, 1955), p. 67: "This is the same Rousseauism as that of the fragment on the "Ages of Language." Nowhere else have I seen this metaphor discussed. It is interesting to note that it was a favorite with Herder and that in one other place (*SWS*, IX, 498) the metaphor appears again, but this time Herder is not so vague. "Philosophie nährt sich von Abstraktionen, Schwärmerei auch. Jene zerfrisst das Blatt als Raupe, diese entsaugts als Schmetterling: durch beide wird das Blatt dürre. Der Schmetterling erzeugt Raupen, aus der Raupe wird wieder Schmetterling werden; das ist die ganze Geschichte jener beiden Extreme des menschlichen Geistes." Cf. also Hamann's statement in *Werke*, ed. J. Nadler (Wien, 1949f.), II, 341 in *Leser und Kunstrichter* (1762): "Die heutige Fruchtbarkeit der Schriftsteller giebt mir Anlass ein Bild von den Insecten zu entlehnen, und die schöne Natur einiger Leser mit den grünen Larven, welche kriechen und Blätter fressen, die schöne Natur anderer Leser hingegen mit den fliegenden, honigsaugenden bunten Schmetterlingen zu vergleichen."

always be able to put himself in the place of the author whose work he is concerned with. ". . . Im Geist eines Autors zu *wohnen*, seine *Sprachweise* sich eigen gemacht zu haben, von Plan und Zweck seines Werks aus dessen eigner Seele gleichsam unterrichtet zu sein" (XXIV, 182). An at this, Herder had few peers! Indeed, for Herder the critic himself had to be recognized as a writer if his pronouncements were to carry any weight and be worth any consideration. Thus he writes in tribute to Lessing: "Wo Lessing in seinem Laokoon am vortrefflichsten schreibt, spricht – der Critikus, der Kunstrichter des Poetischen Geschmacks: der Dichter" (III, 9).

In their diverse approaches to the question of imitation and its place in artistic production can be seen one of the fundamental differences between the critical methods of Herder and the majority of critics of his day. The doctrine of imitation was an old one and, as the long history of criticism makes clear, one which could be given many different interpretations.[9] Aristotle was probably the first to make a concrete formulation of the doctrine of imitation, and most of the critics of the late seventeenth and early eighteenth centuries still held to some extent to his idea of *mimesis*. Nearly all of them regarded poetry in some way as an imitation of nature, though most agreed that this did not mean copying in any literal sense. Neo-Platonism was able to meet some of the objections to Aristotle's *mimesis* by the theory that art is not an imitation of the phenomena, but of the noumena, i.e. the world of ideas. Among the British critics and philosophers who were read and highly esteemed in eighteenth century Germany all, with the exception of Shaftesbury, thought of nature as a mechanism and of nature's processes as mechanistic. It is true that Shaftesbury followed most of his contemporaries in regarding poetry as some kind of imitation, but his understanding of imitation departs radically from the usual interpretation. For Shaftesbury nature is not a mechanical, but a creative process. Thus if

---

[9]   For an interesting discussion of this question see R. L. Brett, *The Third Earl of Shaftesbury* (London, 1951), pp. 100ff. My information on Shaftesbury follows this account closely.

poetry, i.e. any artistic invention, imitates nature, it too becomes a creative process. Shaftesbury, and after him Herder, agreed that poetry was an imitation not of objective nature, but of the creative process. In remarkably similar passages both of them draw an analogy between the human creative act and the divine creative act.[10] Just as the divine creative act not only produces the visible form, but also the spirit, so too must the human creative act seek to produce more than mere outward form. Concerning the task of art, Herder writes: "Seele im Körper darzustellen . . . das bilde die Kunst und das hat sie gebildet" (VIII, 17).[11]

The endless futile attempts of the critics of the eighteenth century to resolve such questions as hexameter versus free verse, or strict adherence to the unities of Aristotle versus the less rigid style of Shakespeare, illustrate vividly how concern with problems of literary form and structure had obscured the more important questions relating to content. In the quotation above (I, 142), Herder speaks up for a criticism which takes cognizance of the inner form, of the spirit. As we have seen earlier, Herder does not intend to say by this that form is of no consequence. This spirit refers to those transtemporal, universal, infinite, and human ideas which can serve definite purposes toward the shaping of mankind. With this in mind it will be easier to understand the following, little noticed lines from the first version of the *Humanitätsbrief* 76: "Es giebt nur Eine Poesie, nur Einen guten Geschmack auf der Erde; haben wir diesen nicht, so haben wir gar keinen oder einen falschen. . . . Poesie macht die ganze Natur zur Kunst, die Natur in und ausser uns; die Regel ihrer Kunst tragt sie in sich. Trotz aller Abweichungen des Geschmacks ist dieser vest und bleibend: denn die Philosophie des

---

[10]   Shaftesbury, *Advice to an Author:* "Such a poet is a second Maker; a just Prometheus under Jove." Herder, *SWS,* XII, 7: "Indem er alles nennt, und mit seiner Empfindung auf sich ordnet, wird er Nachahmer der Gottheit, der zweite Schöpfer, also auch *poietes,* Dichter."

[11]   This should be compared with the approach of Erich Auerbach as outlined in his *Mimesis,* 2. Auflage (Bern, 1959). Auerbach writes: "Der Gegenstand der Schrift, die Interpretation der Wirklichen durch literarische Darstellung oder 'Nachahmung,' . . ." p. 515. See especially p. 515ff and pp. 509/510 for an explanation of Auerbach's method.

Wahren, Schönen und Guten ist nur Eine" (XVIII, 516). It is hardly necessary to point out that Herder is not saying that poetry has remained static throughout the ages. Even the most naïve reader is quick to perceive the many differences between the dramas of the ancient Greeks and those of Shakespeare. Yet in the dramas of both there is a quality which has made them eternal and which has enabled them to transcend their own temporal and special limitations. Herder has justifiably distinguished all those works of art which possess this quality as "one poetry", and all others, for him at least, are not worthy of consideration. Thus for Herder one of the primary functions of criticism is to seek out and examine this spirit, or as he has criticism say for herself: "Ich die Richterinn des Wahren, Guten und Schönen" (XXIV, 189). Criticism for Herder therefore, like aesthetics, history, literature, and all the other worthwhile pursuits of man is consciously active in the service of one definite effort aimed at the further cultivation of man – in the furtherance of *Humanität*.[12]

Herder's demand that the critic must never lose sight of the poetic work as a whole in its entire historical setting, which is one of the dominant thoughts in his critique of the *Litteraturbriefe*, further strengthens his premise that it is the function of criticism to concern itself with matters pertaining to the soul and the spirit of the author and his work, as well as those of mere form or technical skills. Since for Herder criticism must express the soul of the author and his work, he wants a history of literature which would answer such questions as: What was the status of the nation that produced the author and his work? What was the current taste? What were the general and scientific interests of the time which produced the author and his work? [13] The importance which Herder assigns to this basic principle can easily be seen in his argument against Klotz in the *Zweites Wäldchen*. In the manner typical of the time Klotz attempts to impose standards of the eighteenth century on Homer and then to ascertain

---

[12]   Places in Herder's writings that will back this up are legion. I mention just a few: *SWS*, XVIII, 121; XVIII, 82; XIII, 343ff.
[13]   *SWS*, I, 140.

his merit or lack thereof according to these standards. In so doing Klotz completely ignores the necessity of capturing the spirit of the author's work and time. Herder calls Homer *"Ein Barde voriger Zeiten für seine Zeit"* (III, 200), which is precisely the point wherein his value for the present lies. But no more than it would be possible to return to Homer's day and time to view them at first hand can one expect Homer to meet the requirements of a more modern age. Herder says of Homer: "Er sang" (III, 197), i.e. he found his own original manner of expression which succeeded in accurately portraying the spirit of his day and time, and this spirit he has passed on to the present day through his works. For Herder this is the standard which must be employed when judging Homer, and not a standard based on meanings of words as Klotz apparently does it. Since in the course of three thousand years the meaning of words has undergone numerous changes, this can hardly be an acceptable criterion of judgement. Consequently, Herder's concern is not with mere word meaning, but with feeling and the value of the feeling produced by words and the spirit reflected by them, i.e. *der innwohnende Geist* of the word, or what Herder refers to as "Gefühl seiner epischen Würde in der Sprache" (II, 198). Herder is ever mindful that any judgments of feelings or critiques of the human soul must be undertaken with extreme caution, and to have any claims to validity these must be based on a conscious effort to understand the spirit of the writer, his work, and his times. If the writer has succeeded in capturing this spirit, if his work reflects the customs and events of the time, and Homer's did, then the work can be judged to possess that universal quality which transcends time or place, and that is the mark of all great works of literature. For Herder there could be no absolute measure in the same sense as was understood by most of his contemporaries. But there is a belief in an absolute development and in hard and fast forms within this development which is characteristic of Herder's attitude toward aesthetics. In everything about him he sees a historical uniqueness. His denial of the rationalistic concept of indefinite progress is further strengthened by his strong affirmation of its direct opposites – the development of definite self-contained linguistic and literary areas which can best be understood by an evaluation of their spiritual and cultural content.[14]

In order to carry out his announced program Herder chooses for the *Fragmente* what Clark calls a topical treatment.[15] Thus the problems to be considered are divided into four areas. "Sprache, Geschmackswissenschaften, Geschichte und Weltweisheit sind die vier Ländereien der Litteratur, die gemeinschaftlich sich zur Stärke dienen und beinahe unzertrennlich sind" (I, 142). The order in which Herder lists the four topics is indicative of the importance which he assigns to each one. Language is the first mentioned and language is the first to demand the writer's attention. "Die Sprache ist ein Werkzeug der Wissenschaften und ein Teil derselben; wer über die Litteratur eines Landes schreibt, muss ihre Sprache nicht aus der Acht lassen" (I, 147). This problem of language has been termed one of the two major themes of the *Fragmente*.[16] But in order to understand fully the impact of Herder's ideas one must have some knowledge of what had previously been done in this area. The seventeenth century witnessed a number of language societies, all modeled on French and Italian counterparts, and all dedicated to the purification and furtherance of the mother tongue. Nor were poetics anything new to the German scene, Opitz' having appeared in 1624, G.P. Harsdörffer's in 1641ff. Leibniz – he himself wrote mostly French or Latin – recognized the need of improving German. In his *Unvorgreiffliche Gedanken* (1697) he advanced a number of interesting ideas on the origins and developments of German and even had some practical suggestions that would have been worthy of Herder himself. But although Leibniz considers German an excellent vehicle for the expression of concrete ideas, he questions its use for philosophical subjects. And thus we come to the point where Herder parts ways with Leibniz. Leibniz is primarily interested in the purposiveness of language.[17] For him

---

[14] Cf. Hermann Nohl, *Herder* (Berlin, n.d.), p. xxvi.
[15] Clark, p. 62.
[16] Gillies, p. 30ff; Haym, I, 155.
[17] Cf. Gustav Konrad, *Herders Sprachproblem im Zusammenhang der Geistesgeschichte* (Berlin, 1937), p. 9ff.

it is the means of rational understanding. He is not concerned with a poetic language or a history of language representative of a developing spirit.

Another writer who belonged to the same philosophical school as Leibniz was Johann Georg Sulzer. He had spoken out in the *Litteraturbriefe* in favor of philosophical correctness, even at the expense of beauty.[18] As is to be expected, Herder not only completely rejects this idea of Sulzer's, but also his proposal that one should subject language to a "general philosophical grammar", according to the rules of which the beauty and perfection of language would have to be judged. Herder's friend and mentor J. G. Hamann had also busied himself with the problem of language, and had to a great extent paved the way for many of the ideas expounded by Herder himself in his essay on the origin of language. Hamann's world view was essentially pantheistic. The "Word" for him is an expression of the divine voice.[19] "Er ist, wo sein Wort ist, wo sein Sohn ist. Ist sein Wort in uns, so ist sein Sohn in uns, ist sein Wort in uns, so ist der Geist dieses Worts in uns." [20] His God was a personal God and for him the God was "The Word".[21] As one critic has recently observed, "there was nothing new in interpreting the logos as a statement about the incarnation; what was new was to interpret the logos as a statement about language in terms of the incarnation".[22] This Hamann does at the very beginning of his *Ueber die Auslegung der Heiligen Schrift*. "Gott ein Schriftsteller!" [23] Exactly what Hamann means by this is best explained in two lines from *Biblische Betrachtungen*. "Gott offenbaret sich – der Schöpfer der Welt ein Schriftsteller." [24] But not only did Hamann believe in the revelation of God through His divine word, the Bible, he also saw

[18] Cf. *SWS*, I, 159f.
[19] Konrad, p. 13ff.
[20] Hamann, *Werke*, I, 64.
[21] See John 1 : 1; see also the interesting discussion in Ronald G. Smith, *J. G. Hamann* (New York, 1960), pp. 64-87; Cf. Wellek, I, 179; cf. Herder in *SWS*, VII, 356 (*Erläuterungen zum Neuen Testament*).
[22] Eric A. Blackall, *The Emergence of German as a Literary Language* (Cambridge, 1959), p. 428.
[23] Hamann, *Werke*, I, 5.
[24] *Ibid.*, I, 9.

God revealed in nature. "Gott hat sich geoffenbart den Menschen in der Natur und seinem Wort." [25] Hamann's assertion that poetry is the mother tongue of the human race is cited by Herder again and again.[26] But perhaps his greatest service was the denial of the rationalistic view of language. Language for him was an expression of the individual's feelings and not a matter of reason. What is perhaps even more pertinent to our discussion is Hamann's demand: "Rede, dass ich Dich sehe!" [27] Thus according to Hamann the expressive power of mankind is reflected in language and through the medium of language the whole figure of man, the unity of the outer and inner, is grasped and revealed.[28] Of importance too in this whole matter of language were the various attempts to explain the origin of language by Rousseau, Süssmilch, and Condillac. But Herder did not actively concern himself with this problem until some years later in his prize essay *Über den Ursprung der Sprache.*

It is not difficult to understand why Herder was so concerned with this problem of language. In comparison with the English and French, German literary achievements had been conspicuously meager. Herder himself realized that language and literature are inseparable, but on the whole this fact seems to have been ignored in Germany. In the *Fragmente* he writes: "Der Genius der Sprache ist also auch der Genius von der Litteratur einer Nation" (I, 148). Within Germany itself comparatively little had been done to put German into its proper place as the vehicle of a literature. An extreme example is the Prussia of Friedrich the Great, where everything pertaining to language and

[25]   *Ibid.*, I, 8.
[26]   *Ibid.*, II, 197. "Poesie ist die Muttersprache des Menschengeschlechts".
[27]   *Ibid.*, II, 198.
[28]   Cf. Katherine E. Gilbert and Helmut Kuhn, *A History of Esthetics* (New York, 1939), p. 313. "According to him [Hamann] the whole creation is Word, communication of a meaning by images. It is the creature's answer to the creator's 'Speak that I may see you!' " Hamann himself wrote, *Werke*, II, 197: "Sinne und Leidenschaften reden und verstehen nichts als Bilder." See also the perceptive remarks by Smith, p. 64ff. Contrary to the view represented by Unger, who sees in the Logos a mythological significance for Hamann, Smith sees an eschatological significance. Wellek's discussion also supports the standpoint represented by Smith. See also Blackall, p. 428ff.

literature had been gallicized. In the essay *Preussische Krone* Herder takes Friedrich to task for writing French and ignoring his native German. At the other extreme were the poets of the Anacreontic, whose works were just as stilized and foreign to the general masses as if they had been written in a foreign language. As a result, German literature was virtually unknown outside of Germany and the German speaking world, and even here it was regarded by many more as an object of curiosity, the expression of the hearts of a few simple souls, than as a literature with any lasting aesthetic value.

But even more important than a language's function as a tool, as a vehicle of literature, is its importance as the vehicle of our thoughts. "Durch die Sprache lernen wir bestimmt denken, und bey bestimmten und lebhaften Gedanken suchen wir deutliche und lebendige Worte" (I, 147).[29] The entire psychological process of thinking is thus made dependent upon language.[30] Now whenever Herder speaks of language, it must be kept in mind that he nearly always means native language. In 1770 he wrote:

Unsere Muttersprache war ja zugleich die erste Welt, die wir sahen, die ersten Empfindungen, die wir fühlten, die erste Würksamkeit und Freude, die wir genossen (V, 118).

In one of his earliest writings, *Über den Fleiss in mehreren gelehrten Sprachen*, 1764, he calls special attention to the importance of the mother tongue.

Hat nun eine jede Sprache ihren bestimmten Nationalcharakter, so scheint mir die Natur blos zu meiner Muttersprache eine Verbindlichkeit aufzulegen, weil diese meinem Charakter angemessener ist, und meine Denkungsart ausfüllet. Fremden Nationen werde ich vielleicht ihre Sprache nachlallen können, ohne bis auf den Kern ihrer Eigenheit und Schönheit zu dringen (XXX, 8).

In language, in history, in aesthetics, and in the aesthetic experience Herder is always concerned with the nucleus, the uniqueness of the individual object. In this same work he repeatedly supports his convictions about the necessity of a cultivated mother

[29] Cf. *SWS*, XVIII, 384.
[30] Cf. Benno von Wiese, *Herder, Grundzüge seines Weltbildes* (Leipzig, 1939), p. 38.

tongue, as in the following: "Insonderheit ist die Muttersprache zur Dichtkunst und Beredsamkeit unentbehrlich" (XXX, 12).

Throughout his lifetime Herder continued to attempt to impress upon his countrymen the necessity of knowing and appreciating their German mother tongue. As has been alluded to above, there is a very good reason for Herder's concern. By emphasizing the monistic character of the relationship between thought and word Herder is simultaneously stressing the necessity for a language sufficiently developed and cultivated to serve as a vehicle for thought. A direct point of contact between Herder's linguistic views, his psychology, and his art philosophy can thus be drawn. For as no more than word or thought, or the body and the soul, can exist in a dualistic relationship, can the two elements of art, the form and the content, exist in such a state. The work of art must be a harmonious whole if it is to fulfill adequately its purpose. The harmony and perfection within the word and its artistic products, poetry, are expressed by an intangible that Herder calls power. According to the theories developed by Herder in the *Viertes Wäldchen* this harmony is revealed to man through the senses, specifically feeling, that term which Herder uses to designate the complete involvement of a harmoniously functioning soul in the process of revelation. Herder's linguistic philosophy and his philosophy of art have so many points in common that to understand the one without the benefit of the other is hardly possible.

But there is an additional dimension to Herder's concept of language which we have hardly touched upon. Herder emphasizes in the *Fragmente* that "language is more than a tool." It is also, however, something more than Leibniz' or the rationalists' notion of a medium for philosophical concepts, a so-called language of understanding. As we have already noted above, Hamann saw God revealing Himself to man through both nature and His word. According to him these two revelations had to be constant with one another, i.e. nature and the word had to be organized in a similar manner. "Die ganze Natur ist voller Zeichen, und siehe, so wie die Schrift ist."[31] "Alle Werke Gottes sind

[31] Hamann, *Werke*, I, 68.

Zeichen und Ausdrücke seiner Eigenschaften; und so, scheint es, ist die ganze körperliche Natur ein Ausdruck, ein Gleichnis, der Geisterwelt." [32] Now if corporeal nature is an expression of a spiritual universe, and nature is comparable to scripture, i.e. God's word, then the word must likewise be an expression of its spiritual counterpart, i.e. the soul of man. And this is precisely how Hamann and Herder thought of it, for in their sight the invisible nature of the soul is revealed by words. Indeed, language is not only the measure of our perceptions and understanding, but also a representation of the soul in all its forms and states.[33] Herder's letters to his future wife, Caroline Flachsland, are full of references to the function of language as the revealer of the soul. Shortly after Herder passed through Darmstadt and had seen his friend for the second time, he wrote her on 20 April 1771 from Bückeburg: "Unsre Briefe sollen die Geschichte unsres Herzens, unsrer Gedanken und unsres Bestimmungskreises enthalten." [34] Since he and Caroline could not be together, Herder sees their letters as taking the place of what would normally be accomplished in a conversational interchange. Each one's letters were to record for the other the writer's innermost thoughts and feelings, and as we have them preserved today, they are truly this. They are literary outpourings of the soul, which, by the way, Herder several times labels his letters. On 25 August 1770 Herder wrote to Caroline: "Edle, rechschaffene Seele, glauben Sie es mir, der ich jetzt vor Ihnen stehe und meine ganze Seele sprechen lasse." [35] Herder was not interested in communicating concepts to Caroline. He wanted to convey the feelings and passions directly from his soul. In a letter from Caroline to Herder we find the same idea about language applied to the writing of poetry. "O, vernachlässigen Sie dies Talent nicht, aus der Seele zu dichten." [36] (The poems referred to here are those sent by Herder to Caroline which she entered into the so-called *Silbernes Buch*.) As we have

---

[32] *Ibid.*, I, 112.
[33] Cf. Konrad, p. 18.
[34] *Herders Briefwechsel mit Caroline Flachsland,* ed. Hans Schauer (Weimar, 1926-28), I, 169.
[35] *Ibid.*, I, 4.
[36] *Ibid.*, I, 257.

already seen, Herder refers both to the form and the content of language. The form is that part which can be printed on paper, or scientifically described and discussed. The content is the spirit or genius of the word, and this is the part that Herder is most concerned with, for it is through the inner meaning of the word that the inner being of man, the soul, is revealed. But language is even more than an expression or revelation of the soul. As Herder develops it in the essay on the origin of language, language is also a product of the soul. "Dies *Erste Merkmal der Besinnung war Wert der Seele! Mit ihm ist die Menschliche Sprache erfunden"* (V, 35). This concept will be developed more fully in our discussion of this essay.

Having once formulated his basic ideas on language and noted the various functions which he expected a language to fulfill, Herder's next problem was to ascertain what form of language could best meet these needs and where exactly his own native German fitted into the overall language picture. In his essay *Von den Lebensaltern einer Sprache* Herder projects the three roughly defined groupings of Thomas Abbt, who had been his predecessor in Bückeburg and who had made the beginning of a historical approach to language in the *XIII. Litteraturbrief*, into four criteria analogous with human growth. In this essay Herder decides in favor of the third or prose age of language, which he says is our only natural language, because it alone of all the forms of language can retain its philosophical clarity without sacrificing poetic beauty. In his desire to improve German so that it could better meet its obligations and take its place as the basic element of a national German literature Herder was not alone. The *Litteraturbriefe* had been full of the suggestions of these *Sprachverbesser*. One of their favorite proposals, entirely in keeping with rationalistic thinking, was to "improve" German by translations of the classics. Although in general Herder rejected such proposals, on occasion he was prepared to admit that some benefit could be derived from the use of other literature as a model. What he then expected from the model in such cases can quite clearly be seen from his preference of Greek over Latin. First and foremost is the fact that Greek had developed into a prose and poetry "des guten Ver̦standes", while Latin had not. This element of reasonableness is precisely that which leads Herder to a differentiation between Latin and Greek. Herder does not tell us here what he means by *Verstand*, but a look at the *Metakritik* and the *Ideen* should help to clarify his concept of *Verstand* and *Vernunft*, since he often seems to use these terms interchangeably. In the *Metakritik* the functions of *Verstand* and *Vernunft* are considered similar. *"Aus einer dunkeln Wolke von Allgemeinen uns das hellere Bild eines Besonderen zu schaffen,* ist das Bestreben unsrer Sinne, unsrer Vernunft, unsres Verstandes" (XXI, 208). Earlier in the *Metakritik* he had tried to distinguish between *Vernunft* and *Verstand,* but as he himself readily admits, the distinction remains blurred. "Offenbar ergiebt sich heraus, dass die Vernunft ein *anwendendhöherer Verstand* sey, die Grundsätze beider stehen einander nicht entgegen. Auch der Verstand *erkennet,* d.i. er unterscheidet das Wahre vom Falschen durch ein Merkmal; mittelst dieses spricht er den Namen der Sache bezeichend aus. Die Vernunft *erkennet* auch; nur schliessend, d.i. beschliessend aus vorgelegtem Grunde" (XXI, 201). One of the most important factors in keeping *Vernunft* and *Verstand* pure (not Kant's purity) so that they can properly perform their function is language.[37] In the *Ideen* Herder goes even further and maintains that without language there can be no *Vernunft.* "Alle kommen wir zur Vernunft nur durch Sprache" (XII, 362). ". . . kurz Sprache ist der Charakter unsrer Vernunft, durch welchen sie allein Gestalt gewinnet und auch fortpflanzet" (XIII, 358). Thus Herder's concepts of language, reason, and understanding become inextricably intertwined, with each owing something to the other. Furthermore, the very number of the quotations listed here dealing with reason should make it clear that Herder by no means fails to recognize the important role played by reason in man's whole psychological make-up. Herder never opposes reason, which indeed he considered one of man's unique and distinguishing traits, but he never tires of campaigning against the evils of pure reason, i.e. reason based on other than empirical concepts, or against a supremacy of reason which excluded other

37 Cf. *SWS,* XXI, 221.

equally important factors. When Herder writes that Greek developed into a poetry and prose "des guten Verstandes", he is indirectly commenting on the whole Greek way of life. In effect, he is saying that all elements of Greek life – religion, art, language, literature, even environment – were compatable, and as such sprang directly from an understanding of a way of life as it should be. It was a way of life which was national and original. On the other hand, he found the Romans too much occupied with abstractions and with borrowings from others and too much a hodgepodge of elements from the far reaches of the empire. Accordingly, their language reflected this way of life and was less suitable as a model than Greek.

As did Latin among the ancient languages, so did French among the more modern bear the brunt of Herder's campaign against the evils of using foreign models. Herder's campaign against French leads him to a consideration of the nature and value of inversions, which because of the completely original approach is considered by Haym to be one of the most important sections of the *Fragmente*.[38] Since the whole idea surrounding Herder's discussion of inversions is of considerable importance to his concept of language and the place it occupies in his psychology, we must concur with Haym's evaluation. Here, as always, Herder is concerned with the dynamics of language. As Haym puts it: "Immer steht vor seinem Geist die *werdende* Sprache." [39] To meet this requirement a language must grow, and to grow it must be free. One sign of this freedom is inversion. "Je mehr eine [Sprache] derselben von Grammatikern und Philosophen gebildet werden, desto härtere Fesseln trägt sie; je mehr sie ihrem ursprünglichen Zustande nahe ist, desto freier wird sie seyn. Je mehr sie lebt, desto mehr Inversionen; je mehr sie zur todten Büchersprache zurückgesetzt ist, desto mindere" (I, 194). Herder agrees that if a language were conceived by a philosopher solely for philosophers and philosophical purposes, then it would obviously have to reflect this purpose in its sentence structure. It would require no inversions. But as long as we do not have a language that is solely philo-

---

[38] Haym, I, 163.
[39] *Ibid.*

sophical, and German is not, then a certain flexibility is desirable. Herder's understanding of a *werdende Sprache* is undoubtedly not restricted to historical or temporal considerations alone. To decide what he actually means here one must also decide what is meant by philosopher and philosophical. Throughout the eighteenth century the term "philosophic" in reference to language usually meant "scientific".[40] The philosophic, i.e. scientific approach was used almost exclusively by rationalists. It was a factual method dominated by reason, from which feeling and sensuousness were excluded. At least this seems to be the type of philosopher Herder has in mind at the beginning of *Auch eine Philosophie* where he compares the idyllic heroic features of the patriarchal age with his own cold, philosophical age,[41] an age which cannot be content to corrupt itself with philosophical excesses, but also attempts to judge all time by its own distorted standards. He warns against the misleading words of the *Fachphilosophen* (Voltaire, Boulanger, Helvetius),[42] and an age when man tries to learn by cold, dry reason. To his readers he exclaims: "Gehe hin . . . und fühle noch jetzt hinter Jahrtausenden die so lang erhaltene *reine Morgenländische Natur*, belebe sie die aus der *Geschichte der ältesten Zeiten*" (V, 486). In condemning his age for being cold and philosophic Herder is not being fatalistic. He does not think or mean that it has to be this way.[43] He is merely expressing his opinion of how things stand. Herder's use of the words philosophy and philosophic is both inclusive and exclusive. The exclusive aspect is what concerns us here, for it designates a failure to come to terms with the sensuous aspects of life. A language which is designated philosophical has this same deficiency and can never reach perfection, i.e. it cannot fulfill all of its functions. It cannot "feel" or "enliven", as Herder admonishes his readers to do. Such a language is the opposite of what Herder favors in the *Fragmente* when he discusses a *werdende Sprache* and inversions. He wants a German

40   Clark, p. 19.
41   *SWS*, V, 484.
42   *SWS*, V, 482.
43   See *SWS*, V, 482.

language like the Greek language, which he designates "die vollkommenste ihrer Art" (XIV, 98). Why does this distinction belong to Greek but not to German? Because Greek fulfilled all its purposes, it developed its full potential; it was suitable as a tool and vehicle for philosophy, for poetry, for history, and it met the everyday demands of the people who spoke it. But above all it was a language which could serve as the vehicle for the outpourings of the soul of the people who spoke it. It was a language which grew and developed along with the soul of the people, and thus became, so to speak, a phenomenon of the soul. With this in mind it is easy to see that Herder is by no means saying that German is thus removed from any philosophical considerations, nor is he advocating that philosophy be done away with altogether. Quite the contrary, for to his way of thinking a flexible, dynamic German would be even more suited to the needs of philosophy than one stilted and static. In fact, Herder is in complete agreement with the statement from the *Litteraturbriefe* which today would undoubtedly cause eyebrows to rise. "Zur Weltweisheit scheint die deutsche Sprache mehr als irgendeine von den lebendigen ausgebildet zu seyn" (I, 196). Herder wants his native German to be a language with sufficient flexibility to be a ready tool for the poet, the prose writer, and the philosopher.

All these questions about inversions, hexameter, meter in general, etc. which Herder takes up in the *Fragmente* are essentially centered around concern for one aspect of language to the complete neglect of another, even more important aspect. Insofar as these problems are symptomatic of Herder's age, his reaction against them is likewise characteristic of the point of view consistently maintained by his philosophy of language and philosophy of art. The points discussed so far deal primarily with the outer form of language. They fail to take into consideration the even more important factor of content. Language for Herder was analogous to a living organism and for any living organism to develop properly all of its various members must grow simultaneously. There must be unity within this growth so that the harmony within the organism can be maintained. Herder was perceptive enough to realize that external improvements alone, or external improvements contrary to the inherent being of German, are more of a hindrance than an aid.

Throughout this first collection of fragments, in every admonition he directs to German writers, in every polemic uttered against the restrictive ideals of the *Aufklärung*, one idea more than any other seems to dominate Herder's concept of literature and literary production. "Genies, ihr müsst die Regeln durch euer Beispiel gültig machen!" (I, 211). Although a detailed treatment of this whole matter of genius is beyond the scope of this study, some brief comments on Herder's remarks in this context are nevertheless in order. Klopstock, along with Hamann, Hagedorn, Moser, and Abbt are all mentioned favorably in the concluding section of the first collection. If it is possible to reduce the sum total of their desirable qualities to one statement, then this would probably be it: All these writers write like Germans, and not like Frenchmen or Englishmen. Thus they have a clain to the title genius. It must be remembered that Herder did not subscribe to the general accepted notion that the poet was an imitator of nature. Through his imitation of God in a creative process man, i.e. the poet himself, becomes a creator. "In dem er alles nennt, und mit seiner Empfindung auf sich ordnet, wird er Nachahmer der Gottheit, der zweite Schöpfer, also auch *poietes*, Dichter" (XII, 7). At this point Herder rejects one of the main tenents of neoclassicism and thus hastens a process of dissolution which had already set in.[44] When Herder holds up the works of certain authors as a model and maintains that rules come from the language and the literature, he is never forgetting for a moment that a creative genius like the Great Creator himself stands behind each work. Only through the individual shaping power and will of the genius does the work itself come into its own. In designating any author genius, Herder is giving him the highest possible praise.

The influence of Hamann's ideas on Herder's concept of genius has long been recognized. For Hamann it was genius that replaced Homer's lack of knowledge of literary rules and it was genius that compensated for Shakespeare's uncertainty and trans-

[44]   Wellek, I, 200.

gression of literary laws.[45] It was also this same genius, that as creator in his own right, could imitate the creative act. The very name Shakespeare was synonymous with genius for Hamann, as indeed it also later became for Herder in the Shakespeare essay. In this essay the drama of Shakespeare is seen as a microcosm, as an artistic reflection of a universe which was just as much the product of the creative power of the genius as the objective world is an active reflection of the creative power of a divinity. Shakespeare is a genius, and as such he creates his own world, which for Herder is born out of the spirit of the Germanic North. In the same essay in which Hamann calls Homer and Shakespeare genius, he takes to task the *Aufklärung* view of truth and maintains that knowledge is not solely a matter of the mind, but rather is dependent on the whole of human activity, on feeling as well as thinking. The quality of genius is equated with what Hamann rather obscurely terms "Socratic ignorance." This Socratic ignorance is further described as *Empfindung*,[46] which in this context is perhaps best translated "sensibility",[47] i.e. "experiencing by means of the senses." Smith has quite rightly called attention to a certain affinity between the thinking of Socrates and Hamann. Present in both is a sense of the insufficiency of reason and the sense of being guided by a higher power variously referred to as a genius or demon.[48] Scattered in among the often

---

[45] Hamann, *Werke*, II, 75.

[46] *Ibid.*, p. 73. "Die Unwissenheit des Socrates war *Empfindung.*"

[47] Smith, p. 55. As the *OED* points out, this is the original meaning of the word, although its usage with this meaning is rare today. The German *Empfindung* also has the original meaning of to feel or to perceive through the senses. *Empfindung* has a more subjective, innerspiritual connotation than *Gefühl*. (S. Grimms *Deutsches Wörterbuch* sub *Empfindung*.) But as Markwardt has observed (*Geschichte der deutschen Poetik*, Berlin, 1956, II, 231), the meaning of the word *Empfindung* was extremely fluid in the 18th century, and depended upon individual usage almost entirely. See also his discussion in II, 517f and Blackall, p. 390. For an indication of how Herder used the word see Schauer, I, 231, 234, 268, 269 and many others.

[48] Cf. Hamann, *Werke*, II, 75: "Ob dieser Dämon Socrates . . ." Hamann's use of *Dämon* must not be confused with the modern day interpretation of the word or the meaning attached to it in connection with Goethe. Hamann undoubtedly thought of *Dämon* in terms of its original Greek meaning. *Daimon* is synonymous with genius and denotes a positive, creative power

vague and incomprehensible utterances of the *Socratische Denk-würdigkeiten* there seems to be sufficient hints to justify seeing a definite connection between Hamann's genius and Socratic ignorance, and the Platonic doctrine of the soul. For Plato the soul was not human, but divine, immutable, and indivisible. Insofar as a genius imitates the creative act, he assumes for himself a certain divine quality. In any creation resulting from the divine act, but particularly in the case of man, the worth of the creation does not lie primarily in its outward form, i.e. in the mortal body, but in the immortal soul, i.e. the inner content. This soul is an absolute, for it is divine, immutable, and indivisible. The body, the means by which the soul is seen, is human, mutable, and divisible. Hamann alludes to this function of the body at the beginning of the essay when he refers to the body as the figure or image of the soul.[49] As has previously been observed, Herder is never interested in mere form alone. It is doubtless true that he recognizes a certain uniqueness in every creation, be it the result of the divine or the artistic creative act. But what is even more important than the mere expression of a unique individuality is the creation of an organism in which something absolute is embodied – the soul in the case of the divine creation, an inner content of humanity in the case of the artistic creation. Thus the observation that Herder's whole concept of genius and individuality results from the direct influence of Hamann seems warranted,[50] while more indirectly the thoughts of Leibniz,[51] Shaftes-

---

within the soul, and not a demon or evil spirit. For a discussion of this term in the Goethean sense see Franz Schultz, *Klassik und Romantik der Deutschen* (Stuttgart, 1952), I. Teil, pp. 42-44, and Benno von Wiese, "Das Dämonische in Goethes Weltbild und Dichtung," in his *Der Mensch in der Dichtung* (Düsseldorf, 1958), pp. 72-91.

[49] Hamann, *Werke*, II, 66: "... so scheint *der Leib eine Figur oder Bild der Seele zu seyn.*"

[50] Cf. Hermann Wolf, "Die Genielehre des jungen Herder", *DVJS*, III (1925), p. 429ff.

[51] Cf. Schultz, p. 164. "Auch in der Herderschen Humanitätslehre wirkt die mit Leibniz in Verbindung zu bringende Anschauung von dem System individueller Kräfte und Einheiten, deren jede der lebendige Spiegel des Universums, eine in der anderen wirkend und lebend, alles zum Ganzen webt."

bury, and Plato, all of whom Herder had known and read, also doubtless play a role in the final formulation of his concept of the genius.

In his conclusions to the first collection, in which he again relies heavily on the *Litteraturbriefe,* Herder reaches some decisions about the ideal of language which are neatly summed up in the following lines: "Aus alle diesem folgt, dass unsre Sprache unstreitig von vielen andern was lernen kann, in denen sich dies und jenes besser ausdrücken lässt ... dass sie von der Griechischen die Einfalt und Würde des Ausdrucks, von der Lateinischen die Nettigkeit des mittleren Stils, von der Englischen die kurze Fülle, von der Französischen die muntere Lebhaftigkeit und der Italienischen ein sanftes Malerische lernen könne. Allein man sieht auch, dass in jeder Gattung der Schreibart kein Genie seiner Muttersprache schämen soll oder sich über sie beklagen darf ..." (I, 240). These lines must not be interpreted to mean that Herder is reversing himself in the position he has constantly advocated, for essentially, what Herder protests against, is extremes. He is reiterating his basic standpoint that language is not something hard and fast, but that it is a growing organism. To deny it influences that would aid this development and growth would be just as much an extreme as the position of the neoclassicists. Furthermore, Herder's insistence on the cultivation of the *Muttersprache* is by no means a chance thought or passing whim. "... eine jede Sprache [hat] ihren bestimmten Nationalcharakter ..." (XXX, 8). Not only does the language itself have a national character, it, more than any other single factor, is responsible for the national character of all the people who speak it,[52] much in the same manner that it serves as the formative element of the soul. According to Herder the genius of the people lies in its language. Language is therefore never something arbitrary or by chance, but with inner necessity is a national language, the mother tongue.[53] This relationship has been aptly described by Benno von Wiese as follows: "Nationalsprache ist daher zunächst nicht das literarisch gestaltete, sondern das ur-

[52]   Konrad, p. 51.
[53]   v. Wiese, *Grundzüge,* p. 24.

sprünglich gesprochene, sinnlich anschauliche Wort, das aus der Eigentümlichkeit des eigenen Volkstums hervorgeht." [54]

B. THE PROBLEM OF IMITATION AND EMULATION

Beginning with the second collection of fragments, Herder takes up the second of the two great themes which determine the contents of the *Fragmente*: the relation of German literature to the foreign literature which serve it as a model, above all to the classical and oriental literatures. "Ich will also die Deutschen Nachahmungen mit ihren Originalen vergleichen, ihren Werth gegen einander abwägen . . ." (I, 257). Again Herder is assuming for himself the role of a critic, a part which he played with such uniqueness and originality that the entire course of modern literary criticism stands in his debt.[55] The basic question which Herder raises is: "Können wir die Morgenländer nachahmen?" (I, 258). Then he "leads the reader over paths" to supply the answer. "Die schöne Natur des Orients ist nicht völlig die unsrige" (I, 258). "Auch die Vaterlandsgeschichte der Morgenländer ist nicht unsere" (I, 261). "Der Geist der Religion hat sich verändert" (I, 267). Without considering individually every point made by Herder, there is nevertheless a lesson to be learned here which is basic to Herder's critical method. Nature, the source of the poet's images, history, the source of his associations, allusions, and events, religion, man's loftiest pursuit on earth which is symbolic of his relationship to the Supreme Being, and as developed by Herder in his later works the highest good in life, have all changed. Mankind develops in history and must be of a different nature during each stage of history.[56] (Herder had already developed this idea in his treatment of the ages of language.) This difference in the nature of man at any given stage in history is characterized by both a gain and a loss.[57] A gain, because in the

[54]   *Ibid.*, p. 25.
[55]   Wellek, I, 182, 183, 200.
[56]   Eduard Spranger, "Johann Gottfried Herder: Ahnung und Erfüllung," in *Vom Geist der Dichtung*, ed., Fritz Martini (Hamburg, 1949), p. 42.
[57]   Benno von Wiese, "Der Philosoph auf dem Schiffe", in his *Der Mensch in der Dichtung* (Düsseldorf, 1958), p. 68.

course of the development certain new thoughts, characteristics, and beliefs are acquired; a loss, because certain others, the heritage of another people and time, are irrevocably lost. At no one time is the development static nor does it operate in one direction only. Like language, mankind reaches out its branches to the new, while at the same time it sinks its roots after the old. The sum total of all these factors in the soul of a people at any one time Herder designates *Nationalgeist*. Closely related to this *Nationalgeist* are the *Nationalvorurteile*. In Herder's own words: "... Meinungen des Volks über gewisse ihnen unerklärliche Dinge ..." (I, 263). Or as Haym interprets them: "... d.h. ihre poetischmythologischen Anschauungen und Vorstellungen ..." [58] This is the very reason why it is not possible for a German to sing a psalm with the same fervor as a Hebrew – there exists no common national spirit. In a later work, *Vom Geist der Ebräischen Poesie*, Herder offers some advice to those who would understand the Psalms. (1) "Man vergesse alle neuere Nachbildungen und Commentatoren; auch wenn es die gepriesensten, die besten für ihre Zeit wären. Sie lasen ihrem Zweck gemäss für ihre Zeit, mit Anwendung des Psalms in Sprache, Trost und Lehre auf ihre Zeiten; hier aber wollen wir die Urzeit sehen und in ihr das Herz, den Verstand Davids und seiner Dichter. (2) Sonach suche man zurerst die Gegenstände und Situationen, auf welche gedichtet ward" (XII, 208). The conclusion which Herder finally reaches here is: "Ueberhaupt hat sich die ganze Poetische Sphäre bei den beiden Nationen geändert" (I, 270). And for Herder history is synonymous with "the whole poetic sphere". Just as the origin of language is seen as a history of poetry as well as language, so it is not chance that the concept of the poet and poetry are seen in terms of a history of poetry in which the origins of poetry describe its very nature.[59] Herder's solution to the original question is, that German can learn from Oriental literature, but there is a prerequisite. That is, that the Orient, its history, and its literature must first be understood and explained. Then and only then can it be of value for German language and literature as a model and

[58]   Haym, I, 167.
[59]   Wellek, I, 188.

a source. Furthermore, insofar as the value of translations is concerned, translators are required who are explicators, philosophers, poets, and philologists. Unfortunately, few if any can meet this high calling.

The point which Herder is intent on making here and which may not be too apparent is one of tremendous importance for his aesthetic, and is essentially the same as the theme which he develops in such other works as the Shakespeare essay. For Herder it is not only a question of can we imitate, or do we imitate, but what, if anything, should be imitated. Herder's advice to his reader is to forget the imitations and commentaries on the Psalms if one wishes to understand them. Now at first glance this may seem like a strange bit of advice, for there are few readers who can read and understand the full meaning of the Psalms without some outside help. There are, however, in Herder's opinion, some very good reasons for this advice. The commentators, whoever they are, have evidently restricted their attention to the external characteristics of the Psalms, to the form, and have never attempted to deal with their internal aspects, the content. As Herder says, we want to understand the origins of the Psalms and their spirit and the spirit of their poet, all of which are concerned with the content. The translator or commentator is not the translator or commentator of form or of words alone. He must also grasp and translate the spirit, the national spirit if you will. This, of course, is the quality which Herder misses in so many of the works of his day. The Shakespeare essay unequivocally establishes Herder's position in regard to this point. Herder is not opposed to imitation *per se*, but he is opposed to imitations, criticism, or commentaries which limit themselves to questions of form and ignore the content. It is entirely possible and worthy to imitate content, for as Herder sees it, there is only one true content anyway, and this of course is *Humanität*.

Woven in among Herder's attempts to reach some conclusions on the question of imitations we find an alternative solution, an alternative, however, which in time was to become the preferred solution. We have already noted how Herder pleaded for an understanding of the *Nationalgeist* and the *Nationalvorurtheile* of the Hebrews, and we have attempted to define these terms as Herder understood them. In parts of his discussion Herder seems to consider the term *Nationalvorurtheile* synonymous with the fables, fairy tales, and other forms of literary expression of a primitive people. He talks about collecting them, citing them, listing them, etc. He expresses a wish which he himself was to fulfill later. "Es wäre ein angenehmer und nützlicher Versuch, diese *Nationalvorurtheile* vieler Völker zu sammeln, zu vergleichen und zu erklären" (I, 265). In short, Herder wants his readers to consider the heritage that has influenced their own national literature. Any doubts about this are dispelled when he writes:

Wer es also beklagen möchte, dass keine solche Morgenländische Invasion nicht auch bei uns den Samen Poetischer Fabeln gestreut; dem rathe ich, diese Dichterische Schweisstropfen der Cultur seines Bodens zu widmen. Er durchreise als ein Prophet in Ziegenfellen die Mythologien der alten Skalder und Barden sowohl, als seiner eigenen ehrlichen Landsleute. Unter Scythen und Slaven, Wenden und Böhmen, Russen, Schweden und Polen gibt es noch Spuren von diesen Fusstapfen der Vorfahren. Würde man, jeder nach seinen Kräften, sorgsam seyn, sich nach *alten Nationalliedern* [emphasis supplied] zu erkundigen: so würde man nicht blos tief in die Poetische Denkart der Vorfahren dringen, sondern auch Stücke bekommen, die, wie die beide Lettische Dainos, die die Litteraturbriefe anführten, den oft so vortreflichen Ballads der Britten, den Chansons der Troubadoren, den Romanzen der Spanier, oder gar den feierlichen Sagoluids der alten Skalder beikämen; es möchte nun diese Nationalgesänge Lettische Dainos, oder Cosakische Dummi, oder Peruanische, oder Amerikanische Lieder seyn (I, 266).

For the first time Herder speaks out pointedly and forcefully and calls for a consideration of that segment of the national literary heritage which embodies the feelings of each individual of the linguistic and ethnic community and is therefore considered common to all — the national or folk song.[60] He quite rightly forsees that these songs can become the basis of a literature which will reflect the development of the history, language, culture, and society of any people — a national literature. By his own example

---

[60]   Cf. what Herder has to say in the preface to *Nordische Lieder*, *SWS*, XXV, 81ff. See also Elizabeth Blockmann, "Die Volksdichtungsbewegung in Sturm und Drang und Romantik", *DVJS*, I (1923), p. 427ff.

several years later he kindled a fire which has continued to burn brightly to our own time.

From the German-Oriental poets Herder turns his attention to the German-Greek poets. The main idea here, as in the preceding section, is from the imitation of others to the imitation of ourselves. As Herder puts it: ". . . ihr Deutsche, müsst ihr schon nachahmen, so ahmt lieber eure Landsleute nach als fremde Nationen, um lächerlich oder verächtlich zu werden!" (I, 337) Much of what is said here is similar to what has already been expressed in the first section, the only difference being in the point of reference. A brief résumé will therefore suffice to show how Herder strengthens and develops his basic ideas.

Without a doubt, concedes Herder, the Greeks are worthy of imitation. Their poetic sense is matchless, indeed, the entire thirteenth book of the *Ideen* is given over to a hymn of praise of the Greeks. But before the Greeks can possibly be imitated, they must first be understood. To help the Germans do this and to catch up with the French and others in the field of literature Herder has three suggestions: (1) Someone must reveal the secret of the beautiful sciences *(schöne Wissenschaften)* to the Germans; (2) Translators must be found who not only study the author they are translating, but also his particular time and character, tone, style, etc.; (3) Even the best translations must be equipped with notes and explanations of high quality. In a prize essay submitted to the Bavarian Academy in 1779 Herder makes it clear what he understands by *schöne Wissenschaften*. "Die schönen Wissenschaften heissen humaniora: sie dienen der *Menschheit* und sollen in *allen Ständen und Formen* dienen" (IX, 304). "Schöne Wissenschaften sind die, welche die sogenannten *untern Seelenkräfte*, das *sinnliche Erkenntniss*, den *Witz*, die *Einbildungskraft*, die *sinnlichen Triebe*, den *Genuss*, die *Leidenschaften und Neigungen ausbilden*" (IX, 295).

These lines here are an excellent statement of the purpose of art as Herder sees it, and of the reason why with him psychology and aesthetics are so inseparable. The three expressions critical to an understanding of these lines are "dienen der Menschheit," "die sogenannten *untern Seelenkräfte*", and "ausbilden". The basic thought expressed here is that the purpose of the beautiful sciences, i.e. humanities and arts, is to transform, to recast, and to cultivate the "so-called" lesser faculties of the soul. As the word *sogenannt* hints, and as Herder makes clear in the *Viertes Wäldchen* (IV, 48ff), the term *untern Seelenkräfte* does not constitute a qualitative evaluation. Although the expression was widely used pejoratively in Herder's time to designate faculties which for some reason or the other were thought to be less potent, Herder uses the term with exactly the opposite meaning. *Untern* would better be translated "deeper" rather than the usual "lesser" to convey the meaning Herder had in mind, for in comparison with these powers the faculties of understanding and reason seem impotent and superficial. Herder's term here refers to those human faculties which are better able to feel, to sense, and to experience as Herder would have them do. The idea that a final state of perfection is brought about within these faculties through training and instruction is implicit in the use of *ausbilden*.[61] In this way, in Herder's words, mankind is served, for the growth and development of the individual's soul is furthered. But entirely in keeping with his psychology Herder never attributed to these senses the ability to raise these lesser faculties to a higher potency. Rather, the whole process of *ausbilden* is restricted to the development of the innate potential of these lesser faculties. In this respect Herder's use of the terms *bilden* and *erziehen* departs from that of Lessing's. Whereas Herder uses the terms to signify an immanent development, Lessing nearly always uses them to mean a transcendent development.[62] The whole problem as Herder sees it is to refine and sharpen the faculties of the soul until they are receptive to the arts and humanities. Furthermore, part of the process of refinement is the task of the very arts and humanities for which Herder wants to prepare the soul. But as Herder views his own age he finds that the very forces which have the power to do this have been suppressed by the rationalistic

[61] Cf. *Trübners Deutsches Wörterbuch* sub *ausbilden*: "Im Anschluss an *bilden* hat *ausbilden* seine Bedeutung verinnerlicht zu durch Erziehung und Unterricht vollkommen machen."

[62] Schultz, p. 166.

culture of the age. One of the solution's which he therefore proposes is, that in Germany someone do for literature what Winckelmann had already done for art.

In the highly complex and even contradictory personality of this man were two qualities for which Herder had special affinity: his sensualism and his historicism. As one writer has aptly put it: "Winckelmann taught his age to see things with the eye and to feel them with the hand." [63] So strong was this sensualism within Winckelmann that it has even been suggested that his experience of Greek statues was sexual.[64] The manner in which he described statues is an emotional experience which, when transferred to literary criticism by Herder, heralded the dawn of a new style in this discipline. His historical sense gave him a feeling for and an insight into the ancient world which surpassed any previous achievements. His *Geschichte der Kunst des Altertums*, though based on scant first hand knowledge, is the first internal history of any art. The methods used in this work profoundly influenced Herder and the future course of literary history. In his monument to him Herder writes: "Er schrieb statt Geschichte, die nicht geschrieben werden kann, ein historisches *Lehrgebäude*: d.i., er setzte aus den Nachrichten oder Denkmählern, die ihm bekannt waren, nur zuerst *Unterscheidungszeichen* zwischen Völkern, hernach in ihnen zwischen Zeiten und Classen, oder Arten des Styls fest und so fing er an zu ordnen und zu schreiben" (VIII, 469). In Winckelmann Herder saw one of the first Germans who had spread the fame of Germany abroad, a fame which was based on Winckelmann's uniquely personal, spiritual experience of the Greek art which he glorified in his writings. There can be no doubt that conceptual abstractions, philosophical reasoning, and metaphysical speculations were completely foreign to his methods of art appreciation. The hand which

[63]   McEachran, p. 25.
[64]   Wellek, I, 150. Also Gilbert and Kuhn, p. 312, here in reference to Heinse: "When we turn from Baumgarten and his followers to Heinse, we leave a lectureroom to attend a Bacchanalia. The cautious admission of a sensuous perfection of idea had given way to the proclamation of sensuality as extreme esthetic value ... Thus, according to Heinse, esthetic enjoyment is largely due to sexuality."

Winckelmann taught his age to feel with, and the eye to see with, were not philosophically, but rather spiritually and psychologically oriented. In one point, however, Herder could hardly agree with Winckelmann. This was his exaltation of Greek art and culture to the exclusion of all others. In *Auch eine Philosophie der Geschichte* (1774) Herder rejects Winckelmann's judging of Egyptian art by a Greek standard, while at the same time he recognizes Winckelmann's indisputable claim to greatness. "Der beste Geschichteschreiber der Kunst des Altertums, Winckelmann, hat über die Kunstwerke der Ägypter offenbar nur nach Griechischem Masstabe geurtheilt, sie also *verneinend* sehr gut, aber *nach eigner Natur und Art* so wenig geschildert, dass fast bei jedem seiner Sätze in diesem Hauptstück das offenbar Einseitige und Schielende verleuchtet" (V, 491). So when Herder appeals for a Winckelmann of literature, he is looking for someone who can point out and explain the true ideals of the Greeks in each of the literary genre, just as Winckelmann had done this for art. For both Winckelmann and Herder these were ideals which reflected a universal human soul not limited by special or temporal considerations. In passing it might be noted that Herder hoped to fulfill this high calling himself. The immediate application of this discussion was to encourage the Germans to imitate themselves, i.e. life as they lived it and as it had been lived by their Germanic ancestors. For as Herder points out over and over again, the literary and artistic ideals of the Greeks, indeed, of any people, are inextricably interwoven with life as it was or is lived at a given place and time.

One of the most important contributions made by Herder in this discussion of the German-Greek poets is his concise definition of literary history, which is both characteristic of his thoughts on literary history and, for the time, highly original. "He is also, in many ways, the first modern historian of literature who has clearly conceived of the ideal of universal literary history, sketched out its methods, and written outlines of its development which are not merely an accumulation of antiquarian research, as the works of Warton and Tiraboschi or the *Histoire littéraire de*

la France tended to be." [65] Seeking to characterize the essence
of Herder's theory of literary history, Gisela Ulrich has written:
"Das Wesen von Herders Literaturgeschichte, die sich immer
wieder als reine Geistesgeschichte erweist, ist die Synthese, hier
den Zusammenschluss zur geistigen Gestalt der Sprache. ... Im
Bereich nationaler Literaturgeschichte dient die Synthese der
Herausbildung der nationalen Geistesform. Literaturgeschichte
wird zur Physiologie des ganzen Nationalkörpers." [66] Because of
its importance for the future of literary history, this passage
deserves close attention. "Die Geschichte der Griechischen
Dichtkunst und Weisheit, zwei Schwestern, die nie bei ihnen
getrennt gewesen, soll den Ursprung, das Wachstum, der Veränderungen und den Fall derselben nebst den übriggebliebenen
Werken des Altertums durch Proben und Zeugnisse beweisen.
Sie sei keine blosse Erzählung der Zeitfolge und der Veränderungen in derselben, sondern das Wort *Geschichte* behalte
seine weitere Griechische Bedeutung, um einen Versuch eines
Lehrgebäudes liefern zu wollen" (I, 294). Several important
points are made here that deserve further comment. First of all,
Herder emphasizes the relationship of poetry to knowledge in
general. This relationship here is an intimate one which permits
no separation. As Cassirer remarks: "Thus, understanding through
linguistic communication becomes for Herder, as it had been for
Heraclitus, the genuine and typical expression of our understanding of the world. *Logos* creates the bond between the individual
and the whole." [67] Furthermore, this understanding is a denial of
the narrow basis imposed on the judgement of literature by a
purely theoretical aesthetic, for literature is the expression of a
total human attitude – of the sensuous as well as the intellectual. Literature for Herder is undeniably linked together with the
past and tradition, with the time and place. It cannot exist as a
free being in space. Secondly, growth and change both take place

[65] Wellek, I, 195.
[66] Gisela Ulrich, *Herders Beitrag zur Deutschkunde* (Würzburg, 1943),
p. 85. Cf. also p. 81ff. See also Friedrich Berger, *Menschenbild und
Menschenbildung* (Stuttgart, 1933), p. 100.
[67] Ernst Cassirer, *The Logic of the Humanities*, trans. Clarence Smith
Howe (New Haven, 1961), p. 58.

within the bounds of poetry and knowledge, and an understanding of this change and growth is an important prerequisite to an understanding of literature. Throughout the fragments this has been emphasized again and again. Thirdly, and most important in that it is something entirely new, is Herder's definition of literary history. Such a history is not a mere listing of facts, or of events, or of dates, but interpreting, explaining, choosing, and bringing together all the potential facts and moulding them into what Herder calls a "complete painting" of literature in the first collection.[68] Today, we take all this for granted, but not until over a century later did these ideas come into their own in the writings of the historical school of literary history in the latter part of the nineteenth century. Gervinus, Scherer, and Haym are only a few of the many who followed in the path originally blazed by Herder.

It is doubtless true that the historicists of the nineteenth century owe their very existence to the ground work laid by Herder.[69] But whether or not the critical methods of Herder and Haym and Gervinus are one and the same is a moot question, the answer to which is by no means as simple as has been generally believed. Among literary historians and scholars it has become an established custom to relate Herder's ideas to those of the historicists and to label him their most important forerunner.[70] If one examines what at first seems to be the basic premises of Herder's method and the method of the historicists, it is not difficult to see how the establishment of this relationship has so easily come about and been accepted. One of the most influential and widely read of present-day works which deals with theories of literature characterizes the methods of the historicists as follows: "It is not denied that acts of judgment are necessary, but it is agreed that literary history has its own peculiar standards and criteria, i.e., those of the other ages. We must, these literary reconstruc-

---

[68] Cf. this with what he has to say about history in general. *SWS, XX,* 178; XX, 224; XIX, 148; XX, 304 and many others.
[69] For a good, solid discussion of historicism in literary criticism see William K. Wimsatt, Jr., and Cleanth Brooks, *Literary Criticism, A Short History* (New York, 1957), Chapter 24, p. 522ff.
[70] See Otto Mann, "Wandlungen des Herderbildes", *Deutschunterricht* X (1958), pp. 27-48.

tionists argue, enter into the minds and attitudes of past periods and accept their standards, deliberately excluding the intrusion of our own preconceptions." [71] This statement, which is echoed by Herder himself in countless passages, can quite clearly be used to describe one of the points most basic to Herder's critical method. So far there would be little justification to deny the historicists' debt to Herder. There are, however, several other facets of this problem which must be considered before any final judgement can be pronounced. Contrary to most of the historicists, Herder never denies the necessity of acts of judgement. His critical methods are not restricted to question of *what* and *when*, but also extend to those of *how* and *why*. The attack against the influence of French literature was not prompted by a lack of understanding or appreciation of them in their historical context on Herder's part, for to mention only the most obvious case, Herder was profoundly influenced by the ideas of Rousseau.[72] But at the same time he was preceptive enough to realize that the thoughtless imitation of French models was not what German literature needed to get it on its feet. The rejection of French literature and preference of English literature as a model in its stead involves a value judgement, a judgement which was based on a historical knowledge of temporal and spacial considerations and conditions, but which also took into account the basic incompatibility of the German and French cultural and physiological make-up. Secondly, others of the historicists saw in the individual personality the bearer and representative of the spirit and ideas of an age. It was accordingly possible for them to single out one figure and point to him as the embodiment of all that was representative of his age. Up to a certain point this view is likewise representative of Herder. For example, Herder most certainly saw in Sophocles and Shakespeare the most illustrious representatives of their age. But he also saw in each a quality that transcends his own age, and it

[71]   René Wellek and Austin Warren, *Theory of Literature* (New York, 1956), p. 29.
[72]   Karl S. Gutke's "A Note on Herder and Rousseau", *MLQ*, XVIII (1958), pp. 303-06 has a succinctly summarized account of the prevalent views concerning Rousseau's influence on Herder. For a more detailed treatment see H. A. Korff, *Geist der Goethezeit* (Leipzig, 1957f), I, 76ff.

is at this point that Herder takes a step which differentiates his method of criticism from that of the historicists. According to the Shakespeare essay the Greeks had succeeded in revealing in their tragedies a basic state of the human being. The primary purpose of the tragedy is to shock, which in turn leads to a purgation of human emotions. In the centuries that followed the flowering of Greek drama many had attempted to emulate its basic qualities, but few had succeeded in penetrating to the core of the matter. Corneille was one of these, but his dramas were similar to those of Sophocles in outer form only. Shakespeare's however, were like Sophocles' dramas in inner form, in content. Only in the dramas of Shakespeare did Herder find fulfilled the demands of the Greek drama (V, 225f). Of primary importance to him in the Shakespeare essay is the fact that in the works of both Shakespeare and Sophocles there is an absolute which is not limited by special and temporal considerations, and not that there are historical differences between Sophocles and Shakespeare as has been stated by Haym, Kühnemann, Hettner, and a host of others.[73] Thus if one accepts the fact that Herder is emphasizing the similarities rather than the differences between Shakespeare and Sophocles, then such a statement as "Es giebt nur eine Poesie, nur Einen guten Geschmack auf der Erde". (XVIII, 516) immediately becomes pregnant with meaning and opens up new vistas which Herder scholarship has hardly considered. Commenting on this concept of universality, Ernst Cassirer writes: "Every universal in the sphere of culture, whether discovered in language, art, religion, or philosophy, is as individual as it is universal. For in this sphere we perceive the universal only within the actuality of the particular; only in it can the cultural universal find its actualization, its realization as a cultural universal." [74]

A third area of historicism with which Herder seems to have affinity at first glance is romantic primitivism, which has been defined as "the notion that the poetry of uncivilized times, or poetry written about uncivilized times, is the most natural, the most directly human, the most powerfully emotional – pathetic

[73] See Mann, p. 38f.
[74] Cassirer, *Logic,* p. 25.

and sublime – and is hence the best." [75] Here again one must
readily admit that this is an adequate statement of one of Herder's
most characteristic critical views. What such an assertion fails to
take into account however, is Herder's belief in hard and fast
forms of development. The essay on the ages of language is a
good example of this belief. Herder recognizes in this essay that
language has undergone a process of development much like a
human organism. Although development is not necessarily synonymous with betterment, it does imply that certain stages have
been passed which can never again be reclaimed. In order to
critically justify collecting and reading poetry of uncivilized
times, one is thus compelled to seek reasons which extend beyond
any mere antiquarian value as examples of the products of a by-
gone golden age of poetry. In the *Fragmente* Herder has given
us an answer to this problem. He is under no illusions that the
golden age of poetry can be brought back or even that this would
be advisable were it at all possible. His main purpose is to hold up
the simple works of art as examples to his own age of what can
be done. His own age had the potential, but to be effective the
potential had to be developed. As we shall see, Herder was even
prepared to admit the possibility of a time when poetry and philosophy could exist side by side. Martin Schütze has correctly observed: "It is important to note that Herder makes no essential
distinction between ancient folk poetry and purely intellectual
poetry, provided they have the characters of spontaneity and
individuality in common." [76] In this point, as was also the case
with the two previously discussed, Herder's main concern is that
the literary form, be it drama, poetry or prose, serve as a vehicle
for an absolute content. The folksong, the Bible, and the poems
of Ossian were all ideally suited for this purpose.

As was so often the case with Herder's works, the *Fragmente*,
which according to the original plan had forseen four collections,
realized only three of these and so, in fact as well as name, remained a fragmentary product. From the main theme of the third

[75]   Wimsatt and Brooks, p. 528.
[76]   Martin Schütze, *The Fundamental Ideas in Herder's Thought,* serially
in *MP*, Part IV, XIX (1921-22), p. 365.

collection, the idea that Latin language and literature had influenced German literature and thought more negatively than positively, and that nothing is to be more desired than a complete cleansing of German from this influence, Herder makes an excursion into the realm of psychology, which is by far the most arresting part of the collection. We have already seen that it was Herder's contribution to show clearly the importance of the union between thought and expression. In the *Fragmente* he compares this union to the relationship between the soul and body, "... wie die Seele zum Körper, den sie bewohnet" (I, 394), and in so doing goes beyond the more usual imagery of his day which described the relationship "wie der Körper zur Haut" (I, 286 & 394). The prime purpose of this image is not to emphasize the union, although it admittedly is important, but rather to direct special attention to the spirit or soul, which in the final analysis is Herder's main concern. The spirit here is representative of all the connotations and denotations of a word, of the very *logos* itself. It is of greater importance than the mere outer form of the word itself, i.e. how the word is spelled or how it looks in print, which is of significance only insofar as it is the medium whereby the more important content can be apprehended. Since form and content mutually complement one another, one cannot be separated from the other without diminishing the effectiveness of both. Thought cannot be divorced from expression, nor the meaning of the word from the word itself.

Herder's psychological excursion is closely linked with his idea of language as the phenomenon of the soul, and as such touches upon several problems basic to his aesthetic. If language is the phenomenon of the soul, then the language with which the soul is accustomed to working must be the language which will most accurately reveal the condition of that soul. Accordingly, it is important for a writer to express himself, i.e. the workings of his soul, in a living language, without taking recourse to a dead tongue, such as Latin, or without attempting to express himself in a foreign tongue where his powers of expression will be limited by his command of that foreign tongue. Herder's watchword to the poet was: Be original! This not only meant that the poet must use his mother tongue as his vehicle of expression, but also that the Aristotelean theory of imitation already overthrown by Shaftesbury is also denied by Herder.[77] The true poet is never an imitator, but a creator in his own right. Only insofar as he imitates the creative process can he be considered an imitator.

From the relation of thought and expression in literature attention is focused on this same relationship in philosophy. A sharp distinction is made between the two phases of language. "In der Sprache der sinnlichen Welt, über all, wo ich blos *klar* denken muss, ohne doch immer des Unterschiedes mir bewusst zu dörfen; vorzüglich in der Dichtkunst, wo der sinnlich lebhafte Ausdruck alles ist: klebt also der Gedanke sehr am Wort – aber jetzt treten wir auf ein ganz ander Feld, wo sich alles verändert zeigt. Die Weltweisheit: wiefern kann und muss in ihr Gedanke am Ausdruck haften" (I, 414-15). By his use of the words *klar,*[78] *sinnlich,* and *lebhaft* Herder emphasizes the nearness of poetic language to sense images. But as he remarks, when the field is shifted to philosophy, these criteria no longer apply. In his discussion of philosophical language three points are sketched: the sensuous, i.e. through the senses, the technical, and the grammatical. In the end Herder finds that in these three respects philosophy differs from literature. Instead of dealing with the concrete, philosophy deals with the abstract, a claim also made by Kant for philosophy in the introduction of his first *Kritik.* "Was noch weit mehr sagen will, *als alles vorige,* ist dieses, dass gewisse Erkenntnisse sogar das Feld aller möglichen Erfahrungen verlassen, und durch Begriffe, denen überall kein entsprechender Gegenstand in der Erfahrung gegeben werden kann, den Ursprung unserer Urteile über aller Grenzen derselben zu erweitern den Anschein haben." [79] In denying philosophy an empirical aspect Kant, in so many words, assign qualities to it which are the exact opposites of those in Herder's poetic language. For once Herder and Kant seem to be in agreement! Herder makes a further claim

---

[77]   Wolf, p. 401ff.

[78]   Baumgarten spoke of "extensive clarity". "Extensive clarity is quantitative richness of imagery". Gilbert and Kuhn, p. 293.

[79]   Immanuel Kant, *Werke,* ed. Wilhelm Weischedel (Wiesbaden, 1956), II, 49.

for philosophy for which we find support in Kant – it is an analytical discipline. It seeks to explain the whys and wherefores. Writes Kant concerning this analytical aspect: "Diese Analytik ist die Zergliederung unseres gesamten Erkentnisses a priori in die Elemente der reinen Verstandeserkenntnis. Es kommt hierbei auf folgende Stücke an. (1.) Dass die Begriffe rein und nicht empirische Begriffe sein. (2.) Dass sie nicht zur Anschauung und zur Sinnlichkeit, sondern zum Denken und Verstande gehören." [80] One sees from this that philosophy would be killed if thought were thought *implicite* with the expression. The main purpose of philosophy is to develop concepts from words and to make these concepts clear. Thus expression cannot be chosen in place of thought, nor can expression be allowed to swallow up thought.

With these remarks Herder has broached a subject which is still current today in literary circles. In their beginnings language and poetry were one and the same. This was the position which had been formulated by Hamann and adopted by Herder. This primitive language was essentially figurative, imaginative, synthesizing, and mythological. It was ideally suited to the needs and purposes of the poet. But with the advance of civilization another kind of language gradually evolved. The imaginative, mythological, and poetic turns of speech have progressed toward the logical, precise, and nonfigurative. Emphasis is placed on logical, analytical clarity, rather than synthetical (Herder's "one from many") imagination. Since images are replaced by theoretical abstractions, the language of the soul and heart has become a language of reason and intellect. From the standpoint of philosophy this development in language was certainly to be welcomed. The need for a vernacular adequate to the demands of philosophy had long been present in Germany, and was not met until the beginning of the eighteenth century by Christian Wolff, "who introduced into Germany both the reasoned presentation of philosophy and a stable philosophical terminology".[81] But Herder was not interested in a reasoned aesthetic, and consequently this reasoned language of philosophy was not acceptable

[80] *Ibid.*, II, 107.
[81] Blackall, p. 26.

to the requirements of poetic expression as he saw them. Herder wanted an aesthetic based on personal experience with the work of art, and whenever this work of art is a work of literature, then language is of a prime consequence. The emphasis with Herder is therefore on the psychological, rather than the philosophical. Because he thought Baumgarten leaned too far toward the philosophical, Herder rejected his definition of aesthetics (XXXII, 62 & 83). Herder was ready to admit that philosophy and poetry each present language with a different set of demands which must not be confused. Thus his concept of philosophical language did not differ greatly from that of Kant. But despite this momentary agreement, Kant and Herder followed paths which were soon to separate, never to meet again. Kant's attempt to apply his philosophical system, which for Herder was detached from life, to all aspects of life, is viewed as a serious mistake by Herder, and as the *Kalligone* makes clear, on this point there could be no compromise with Kant. Herder emphasizes here that his goal is a language commensurate with a psychological aesthetic, i.e. a language of the soul where the main interest is in conveying feeling, rather than rational concepts.[82]

Remarks in Klotz' *Epistolae Homericae* occasion a continuation of the general theme of imitation, this time however with limitation to a particular aspect, the use of mythology in recent literature. A renewed interest in this topic had been stimulated by the publication of the Ossianic poems of Macpherson and by Klopstock's use of Norse mythology in his poems. Clark has maintained that Herder's position, like Hamann's, was neutral, and that in the third collection he merely proves that mythological allusions should be functional to the poem.[83] Now mythology in its primary meaning is generally defined as the body of myths of a people. Comparatively recently it has taken on a new meaning, this the systematic, scientific, investigation of this body of myths in an effort to further our insights into the cultures of the past. Each mythology is composed of individual myths –

---

[82]   Ernst Cassirer, *The Philosophy of Symbolic Forms*, I: *Language*, trans. Ralph Manheim (New Haven, 1955), pp. 147-55.
[83]   Clark, p. 72.

stories of gods, demons, heroes – often times highly symbolically and allegorical in meaning. All true myths nevertheless have certain qualities in common – they are the spontaneous product of a primitive unreflecting and uncritical consciousness. In Hamann's complex personality the myth was regarded as the origin of poetry. Although Herder did not agree with Hamann, he did recognize in mythology a source of poetry and culture which could hardly be ignored. In the essay *Iduna, oder der Apfel der Verjüngung* (1796) the whole problem of mythology is reviewed and summed up as follows: "Ich will mir nichts zugestanden wissen, als was jedem Dichter und Märchenerzähler aus einem fremden, fernen oder verlebten Volk zusteht, nämlich *dass er den Reichtum, den ihm dies Volk und dessen Zeitalter gewahrt, brauchen* dörfe" (XVIII, 502). This is clearly a plea for the functional aspect and thus supports Clark's assertion.

But exactly what was mythology to Herder? The mythology of the ancients was part history, part allegory, part religion, and part poetic structure. They took all of these elements, wrapped them creatively in poetic bodies and breathed into them a poetic spirit. This was the mythology of the ancients.[84] As the course of history has shown time and time again, mythology is a creation of and for the soul. For the intellect and reason mythology is without substance, and whenever these have attained dominance over the soul, mythology has lost its vitality. Only the soul possesses the power to bring together and to comprehend the various component parts of mythology, even as mythology itself is a synthesis of the most varied elements. But Herder is quick to see that this is nothing restricted to the ancients alone. "Himmel!", he exclaims, "das habe ich alles in meinem Land, in meiner Geschichte; rings um mich liegt der Stoff zu diesem Poetischen *Gebäude*" (I, 442). With all the elements necessary for mythology present in Herder's own cultural history, he sees only one reason for studying the mythology of the ancients, a reason which Clark has overlooked. "Kurz! Als Poetische Heuristik wollen wir die Mythologie der Alten studieren, um selbst Erfinder zu werden" (I, 444). This is the same answer which he gives to

[84] *SWS,* I, 441, 42.

every question on imitation. Imitate to learn to use one's own history and culture to produce a literature which can stand up in its own right as a representative of the people and time who produce it, in short, a national literature.

More closely examined, however, Herder's concept of mythology reveals other characteristics which equal in importance the suggestion that mythology be used as a poetic heuristic. This suggestion, with slight variations, is essentially the same solution which Herder proposes for all of the questions centered about imitation in the *Fragmente*, and as such is no startling innovation. What is entirely new and different and what establishes Herder's claim to the distinction as the most original thinker on mythology in eighteenth century Germany is the reasoning which lies behind his more practical suggestion. Ernst Cassirer calls Giambattista Vico the real discoverer of the myth and Herder, followed by Schelling, his most important successor. Only these two, he states, recognized and grasped clearly the distinction between the mythical and rational.[85] With Herder this distinction manifested itself in several ways, all of which are characterized by the exclusion of rational elements, but with a marked emphasis on the spiritual, original, and sensuous. Originality and return to origins are omnipresent themes in Herder's writings which constitute one of the most important facets of his critical method. For the young Herder mythology is one of the forms and manners of experience in which the primitive and original is expressed. Moreover, while Herder maintains the distinction between the national and mythical within this merger, the same cannot be said for the mythological *per se* and the poetic. These two fuse together and become one so that myth is regarded and interpreted as something purely aesthetic. Insofar as Herder is concerned, this merger of the primitive-original with the mythological produces two distinct aesthetic avenues of inquiry. The first of these is the functional approach which we have already considered above. In the short essay *Iduna* Herder extolls the advantages of Germanic mythology over Greek mythology for much the same

---

[85] Ernst Cassirer, *The Problem of Knowledge,* trans. William H. Woglom and Charles W. Hendel (New Haven, 1950), p. 296.

reason he states in the Shakespeare essay that he is closer to Shakespeare than the Greeks. This mythology is the product of a Nordic people, it grew up in a Nordic environment, and it is recorded in Nordic languages. Not only the closely related linguistic, ethnic, and environmental features of this mythology caused it to be preferred by Herder, but also the fact that this mythology represented an independent, original effort on the part of Germanic peoples who conceived it to explain their origins.

It was no accident that the primitive Germanic thinkers turned to mythology for a solution to their questions on origins, for since the beginnings of time man had resorted to myths to explain phenomenological occurrences beyond his powers of comprehension.[86] Herder's recognition of the fact that the earliest cosmologies and theogenies were the results of a poetic-mythological approach and treatment of the problem of origins is graphically illustrated by the following statement from the short treatise *Ueber Bild, Dichtung und Fabel*: "Die älteste Mythologie und Poetik also ist *eine Philosophie über die Naturgesetz*; ein Versuch, sich die Veränderungen des Weltalls in seinem Werden, Bestehen und Untergehen zu erklären" (XV, 535). Herder himself makes use of this very technique in his *Aelteste Urkunde*, thereby illustrating the second of the aesthetic avenues of inquiry resulting from the fusion of the primitive-original with the mythological. In the *Aelteste Urkunde* Herder mythologizes himself, i.e. thinks himself into an existing myth and uses it as an instrument of his own thought.[87] Cassirer praises the *Aelteste Urkunde* as a fine example of how far the aesthetic interpretation of a myth can go and how fruitful it can be,[88] while Clark flatly pronounces it Herder's poorest work.[89] Despite Clark's reservations, there can be no doubt that Herder's interpretation of Genesis by this method, which was based on his own unique, personal experience of the

[86] I have found Ernst Cassirer's introduction to *The Problem of Symbolic Forms*, II: *Mythical Thought*, trans. Ralph Manheim (New Haven, 1955), pp. 1-26 especially helpful for the following.
[87] Elizabeth Sewell, *The Orphic Voice* (New Haven, 1960), p. 82.
[88] Cassirer, *The Problem of Knowledge*, p. 296.
[89] Clark, p. 164.

Bible, injected an entirely new and fructifying influence into theology and Bibical criticism. The opposing views of Cassirer and Clark further lead to the conclusion that mythological interest is comprehensible and explicable only with regard to Herder's doctrine of the soul or some like key which opens up to full view the entire realm of the mythological.

A recent study has suggested that the poet can do three different things with myth. "He can study its nature and its origins, in its traditional forms; interpret myths according to his own theories; or mythologize himself, either by thinking himself into existing myths and using them as instruments of his own thought, or by inventing new myths and using them in the same way." [90] The last of these, as we have previously noted, is the method pursued by Herder in the *Aelteste Urkunde*. It is an entirely poetic method. While the first activity need not be poetic, it usually is, and if we accept Cassirer's view, with Herder it is always poetic. The second is nonpoetic, or even antipoetic, and so has no application for Herder. In his dealings with mythology Herder escaped involvement in the negative modern-day approach which regards all myths as fiction (as opposed to fact), and accordingly looks upon them disapprovingly. Herder recognized that myths are the products of a primitive imagination and hence cannot be considered objective, factual information. Myths are not history in the scientific sense, yet they are history in the sense that they provide a record of events before the dawn of recorded history and of primitive man's outlook on life. Cassirer claims, "the philosophical understanding of myth begins with the insight that it does not move in a purely invented or make-up world but has its own mode of *necessity* and therefore, in accordance with the idealist concept of the object, its own mode of *reality*".[91] Although application of the term philosophical to Herder might be questioned, this is essentially the manner in which Herder aesthetically, i.e. poetically, understood myths. With Herder it is not the question of material content that is significant, but rather the psychological intensity with which it is experienced and believed.

---

[90] Sewell, p. 82.
[91] Cassirer, *Mythical Thought*, p. 4.

As with Vico, myth became a problem for Herder as an expression of "an original direction of the human spirit, an independent configuration of man's *consciousness*".[92] Stated in the terms frequently used in this investigation, Herder is interested in the spiritual content of mythology, not in its form or material content.

Numerous places in Herder's writing could be cited to illustrate this,[93] but several from the digression on mythology in the *Fragmente* should suffice. Klotz had questioned the reasoning behind the names of the Greek gods. Herder agrees that this was completely arbitrary on the part of the Greeks. He is quick to add, however, that the gods are not important because of their names, but as poetic creations. Mythology is not used to provide images of truth, but for sensuous beauty and perception. "Aber wir nussen sie . . . der sinnlichen Schönheit wegen. . . . Der Wahrheit wegen brauche ich sie nicht; . . . der sinnlichen Anschauung wegen" (I, 427). The poet uses mythology to make abstracts perceptible and to speak to intuitive phantasy, not as religious and historical truths as did the Greeks and Romans, or as some holy antiquity as did the Reformation, or for countless similies as certain miserable babblers (Klotz is meant here) have done. Herder cares nothing for verse making. He wants to investigate the spirit of the ancients, and one of the ways to do this is through their mythology. "Ich sehe blos die Foderungen der Poesie an, so fern sie mit der Mythologie gränzen, oder nicht. So bald es in der Dichtkunst auf mehr ankömmt, als auf Verse machen, und fliessend reimen: so kann sie entweder für den Verstand reden, oder für die Einbildungskraft: für diese, um sie blos kalt zu vergnügen, oder zu rühren und gleichsam zu täuschen. Dies glaube ich, ist die Psychologische Eintheilung derselben" (I, 433). In much the same tone as the later Shakespeare essay Herder admonishes his reader that an imitation of Horace based on rhymes or meter with a dash of mythology added is not Horace, but only a bare skeleton. To be Horace the ode must fulfill the same purpose as Horace's odes, and to do this the content, as well as form,

---

[92] *Ibid.*
[93] Cf. e.g. *SWS*, XVIII, 490, 499; XV, 532, 539.

must be emulated. Herder's hope is to have shown that mythology can be used to enrich poetry and, as already noted, he finds all the elements for an indigenous mythology present in Germany. But one thing is lacking, and it is the most important aspect of all: poetic spirit. Without this spirit to breathe life into the dead material of mythology, mythology, whether as used by the Greeks or Germans, whether by ancient or modern poets, is meaningless and useless to literature.

The introduction of the concept of a national literature, which substitutes emphasis of the total literary achievements of a people for emphasis of the accomplishments of the individual, indicates a departure from the general eighteenth century concern for the individual, personal, and genial. Beginning with a few isolated voices in the seventeenth century and gradually gaining in prominence throughout the next two centuries until it attained wide acceptance in the eighteenth century, the idea that norms of beauty and art were closely linked together with the individual creative powers occupied in one form or the other most of the great minds of the age, including Herder's. Such a national literature as is suggested by Herder would by no means detract from the genius of the individual author. Instead, it would mean the widening of the literary perspective by considering the combined literary output of a people bound together by such factors as a common language and a common cultural and national heritage, the assumption being that although each individual product would maintain its peculiar identity, it would nevertheless have certain qualities in common with the literary output as a whole. This idea of a national literature is only another facet of Herder's belief that the universal is revealed in the particular, but that only in the universal can the particular find its realization. While Herder undoubtedly felt strongly the need of bringing it to the attention of his fellow countrymen that Germany had, or better could have, a national literature, and this need was present, it is hardly possible that he could foresee that the original significance of the term would frequently be distorted and lost by exaggeration of the original concept. Herder was nevertheless quite right in recognizing that there are distinct contributions of the individual nations to the general literary process. But as we have all recently had occasion to observe, the problems are all too often blurred by nationalistic sentiment and racial theories. Although Herder laid the groundwork for this invaluable aspect of literary evaluation over two centuries ago, the issue is by no means a dead one even today. With proper objectivity much could undoubtedly be brought to light which would add significantly to our understanding of individual national literatures and their own unique contributions to world literature.

On the whole, the third and final collection of the *Fragmente* is a weak echo of the forceful tones of the initial collections. The second fragment of this collection, which is dominated by Herder's plan for a *Lehrgedicht*, is another example of the universality he sees inherent in literature. Although this proposal for a *Lehrgedicht* may seem remarkably un-Herderean, it serves to illustrate one important aspect of Herder's aesthetic methodology that had all too often been overlooked. Herder is not a one-sided pedant. Instead, with his wide interests and knowledge Herder clearly demonstrates qualities approaching universality. One is tempted to attribute this plan for a *Lehrgedicht* to Herder's inability to shake off completely certain characteristics which identify him with his age.[94] But at least two observations we have already made demonstrate the inconclusiveness of any such explanation. In the essay on the ages of language Herder had placed German in the third or prose age. His reasons for doing this were twofold: so that German could benefit from the poetic age that preceded its present age, and so that it could also develop in the direction of the fourth or philosophical age. In another place, the passage where he defines literary history, Herder takes particular pains to point out the relationship of poetry to all knowledge. If poetry is the mother tongue of the human race, then it should be able to maintain its existence during all stages of human development. The *Lehrgedicht* not only shows that it is possible for poetry to exist side by side with or, as was the case in Herder's day, under philosophy, but can even utilize philosophical material and sources for its own purposes. But perhaps what is even more

[94] Cf. *SWS*, XXXII, 82, 83 and IX, 305.

significant is that the plan for a *Lehrgedicht* illustrates vividly that Herder's concept of art transcends any *l'art pour l'art* philosophy of art.[95] A lifetime activity as a teacher and minister, the numerous *Schulreden,* the detailed curricular outlines of the *Reisejournal,* and his omnipresent concern that the arts should develop *(ausbilden)* the powers of the soul all point to the emphasis which Herder places on the developmental value of art. Unrestricted in its powers, man's soul has distinct attributes of universality. It can just as easily apprehend and assimilate the *Lehrgedicht* as a pure lyric poem.

We can now clearly determine Herder's main intentions in the *Fragmente.* We have seen that questions of language, myth, imitation, and criticism are all vital to an understanding of his aesthetics in general, and his concept of literature in particular. Focusing his attention on language in the first part of his work, Herder shows that language, as the vehicle of man's thoughts, as the immediate expression of an individual's or people's soul, is the basis of all art, but particularly of all literature. Herder's philosophy of language and his philosophy of art thus become inseparable. Each mutually complements the other and an understanding of one is a necessary prerequisite for an understanding of the other. Herder has made it clear that language, like life itself, is constantly in a state of flux and metamorphosis, is never static nor subject to absolute fixed standards. Thus language does not serve as a vehicle for rational meaning alone. On the contrary, its most important individual function for Herder is to serve as a medium for what he terms *der innwohnende Geist,* a universal spirit which transcends all special and temporal considerations and restrictions. But whether in language or a work of art, the spirit is revealed only through a form, and for either to fulfill its destined purpose harmony must exist between the two. We thus come to the conclusion that a belief in certain absolutes and universals is fundamental to Herder's aesthetic methodology. Such a belief was also characteristic of the aesthetic outlook of many of

[95]   Cf. Wilhelm Dobbek, "Die Kategorie der Mitte in der Kunstphilosophie J. G. Herders", in *Worte und Werte,* ed. Gustav Erdmann and Alfons Eichstaedt (Berlin, 1961), p. 75.

his contemporaries, who, however, assigned their own meaning to the term absolute. For the rationalist this meant a theoretical aesthetic which demanded adherence to a hard and fast set of rules which had evolved from theory rather than practice. For Herder it meant certain universal absolutes which were revealed through various artistic creations, depending on the people, the time, and the place. In many of his writings Herder does point out the historical differences between individual writers or between the artistic products of different ages, but this must always be regarded as of secondary importance if Herder's aesthetic is to be understood fully. The historical differences are in form only. The inner content is universal and absolute. Herder's primary concern is to illustrate historical similarities, not differences, as the majority of Herder scholarship has maintained. We do find, however, that Herder is not alone in the eighteenth century with his concern for similarities. The difference here is that his contemporaries busied themselves with problems of form and never penetrated beneath the surface to more important questions of content. This superficiality led in turn to the whole host of evils which beset German literature during Herder's time, and there is hardly one of these that Herder did not hope to improve or remove by introducing his new principles and perspectives into the literary and aesthetic streams of his day and, what is even more important, by opening up new vistas to the human soul. Our discussion so far has attempted to show how Herder undertook to do this in his first significant work. We will further develop these points in discussions of Herder's other principal aesthetic works and individual literary genre.

III

THEORY AND ORIGIN OF THE INDIVIDUAL ARTS AND THEIR RELATIONSHIP WITH THE SOUL

A. *ERSTES WÄLDCHEN* — A DELIMITATION OF THE ARTS

The second of Herder's significant contributions to aesthetics, to which we now turn our attention, was the *Kritische Wälder*. The controversy centered about the person of the Halle academician Klotz, already begun in the *Fragmente*, is renewed here in the *Zweites* and *Drittes Wäldchen*, which are almost entirely a bitter polemic against Klotz, who by this time was regarded by Herder as a literary foe worthy only of complete annihilation. In fact, Herder becomes so engrossed trying to destroy his enemy that the fires of controversy consume much of the force which is otherwise characteristic of his writing and so render it ineffectual insofar as any contribution to his aesthetic is concerned. Since all of the important ideas of these two *Wäldchen* fortunately find expression in other works, our discussion can limit itself to the two really significant parts of the *Kritische Wälder*, the *Erstes* and *Viertes Wäldchen*.

Ostensibily a critique of Lessing's most important contribution to aesthetics, *Laokoon,* Herder's *Erstes Wäldchen* also plays, as Clark has recently observed, a subtle role in the whole Klotz controversy.[1] As the subtitle of the *Laokoon* suggests (*Über die Grenzen der Malerei und Poesie*), Lessing's main purpose is to attempt to establish some clear distinctions between these two arts. His point of departure was the blurring of these distinctions by Winckelmann, who in his *Gedanken über die Nachahmung*

[1]   Robert T. Clark, Jr., *Herder: His Life and Thought* (Berkeley-Los Angeles, 1955), p. 78.

der Griechischen Werke in der Malerei und Bildhauerkunst (1755) maintained that the face of Laokoon in the famous statue showed a great and composed soul despite all passion. This Laokoon, Winckelmann continues, does not intone a fearful shout as does Virgil's Laokoon. Instead, he suffers like the Philoctetes of Sophocles. Indeed, so great is his misery but likewise so composed the manner in which he bears this misery that we would wish to be able to bear suffering as he does. Thus Winckelmann's argument confirms his generalization of "edle Einfalt und stille Grösse" about Greek art. Apparently an attack against Winckelmann, the *Laokoon* is actually a step forward in the same direction already taken by him. Lessing makes it clear at the beginning that he is in partial agreement with him. In Chapter I of the *Laokoon* he writes: "Nur in dem Grunde, welchen Herr Winckelmann dieser Wahrheit gibt, in der Allgemeinheit der Regel, die er aus diesem Grunde herleitet, wage ich es, anderer Meinung zu sein." [2] Winckelmann had been overzealous to prove his generalization and in so doing had overstepped the bounds of sound critical procedure. It is clear that Lessing agreed with Winckelmann's description of the statue, but objects to the comparison with Philoctetes and the broad generalization. In this respect Herder's *Wäldchen,* which emphasizes agreement with Lessing's main conclusions, but objects to the manner in which he arrives at them, stands in a like relationship to the *Laokoon.*[3] Although the title page bears the dedication "Herrn Lessing gewidmet", at times the contents seem to have a decided polemic ring. In reality, Herder was using the same ironic technique used by Lessing in the *Laokoon* to blast Klotz and his pseudoclassic clique in Halle, for from the opening lines of the work it is evident that Herder held Lessing in high esteem, an observation that can be further substantiated by any number of remarks. Although the ideas of Lessing and Herder are indebted to those of their predecessors, Winckelmann and Lessing, respectively, at the same time each represents a new point of view. It is the unique and

[2] *Lessings Werke,* ed: Julius Petersen and Waldemar v. Olshausen (Leipzig, n.d.), IV, 294 (*Laokoon,* I)
[3] Bruno Markwardt, *Herders Kritische Wälder* (Leipzig, 1925), p. 49.

different in Herder's contribution that demands our attention
here.

That Herder recognized only too well the significant contribution of Lessing's *Laokoon* to aesthetics is evident from the
opening sentence of his work, where he labels the *Laokoon* the
most pleasant appearance in our present critical pestilence in
Germany. Although frequently in disagreement with Lessing,
Herder's work can nevertheless be said to stand as a monument
to the efforts of Lessing. Furthermore, it is clear that Herder fully
understood the intent of the *Laokoon* from the following lines
from the beginning of the *Erstes Wäldchen*: "Wo Lessing in
seinem Laokoon am vortreflichsten schreibt, spricht der Critikus,
der Kunstrichter des Poetischen Geschmacks: der Dichter ...
Dem falschen Poetischen Geschmack entgegenzureden, die Grenzen zwoer Künste zu bestimmen, damit die eine der andern nicht
vorgreifen, vorarbeiten, zu nahe treten wolle; das ist sein Zweck.
Was er auf diesem Wege von dem Innern der Kunst findet, freilich nimmt er's auf; – aber mir noch immer Lessing, der Poetische Kunstrichter, der sich selbst Dichter fühlt" (III, 9 & 10).
It is likewise just as clear that Lessing understood the purpose of
the *Wäldchen* and appreciated the efforts of its author, even
though at the time he was unaware of the author's identity. In a
letter to Nicolai dated 13 April 1769 Lessing wrote: "Der Ver-
fasser sey indes, wer er wolle: *so ist er doch der einzige, um den
es mit der Mühe lohnt, mit meinem Krame ganz an den Tag zu
kommen*." [4] In the broad sense Herder's purpose is the same as
Lessing's. He intends to compare the main differences between
Lessing and Winckelmann and in so doing to draw up distinctions between art and poetry as creative disciplines. And Herder,
not unlike Lessing, places the greater emphasis on the latter. Yet
the basic presuppositions of the two critics which determine their
aesthetics are largely dissimilar. Lessing's approach, despite all
his efforts to overcome the dominant rationalistic tendencies,
remains essentially under the spell of rationalism. Herder, however, although a product of the same literary and cultural traditions and heritages as Lessing, breaks with the rationalistic

[4] Quoted by Markwardt, p. 35.

view and argues from psychological-sensuous presuppositions.

Beginning his *Erstes Wäldchen* by first comparing the differences in style and approach between Lessing and Winckelmann, Herder then immediately takes issue with Lessing's statement that Laokoon suffers like Sophocles' Philoctetes (also the crux of the Lessing-Winckelmann disagreement), i.e. with a loud cry. Finding that he is in agreement with Winckelmann's claim that Laokoon's expression of suffering is more a sigh or stifled cry than an outburst, Herder proceeds to the second point of contention, introduced by Lessing's statement that Homer's warriors, when wounded, frequently *(nicht selten)* fall to earth with a cry. While Herder can agree with Lessing's observations, he cannot agree with the generalization which Lessing deduces from them. Lessing considered the loud cries, the falling to earth with creaking weapons and armour, the natural expression of bodily pain. Disputing this claim, Herder asserts that such a reaction is in keeping with the character of the individual, and not a universal which Homer constantly applies. "Es muss in dem Charakter eben dessen, den er schreien lässt, eine nähere Bestimmung dazu liegen, dass eben dieser schreiet und kein andrer" (III, 19). For as Herder observes, only the cowards and bullies among men and gods react with loud manifestations of their grief and pain. Now Herder was by no means the first to have emphasized the worth and importance of the individual. But in spite of the fact that Lessing's plays had presented to the theater characters who were individuals,[5] it was Herder who most clearly pointed out the importance of this dramaturgical matter. Just as each language has its own characteristic elements, so too does each human being have certain character traits which are solely his. In keeping with Herder's concept that the individual reflects the universal, the individual traits found in certain of Homer's figures do reflect certain universal character types, which is not to say, however, that these types are universally applicable. In the words of Martin Schütze: "Herder conceived of individuality not as an absolute finality but as the relative and variable product of a continuous

---

[5] Cf. Kurt May, *Lessings und Herders kunsttheoretische Gedanken in ihrem Zusammenhang* (Berlin, 1923), p. 104.

process of development." [6] Nevertheless, because of this reflection of the universal in the individual, and to some extent the reverse, it is essential that the poet, or indeed any artist, direct his attention to the personal and individual, for without a fashioning out of the individual for the individual, the effectiveness of his creative role in art will be diminished. As Ernst Cassirer has observed: "Every universal in the sphere of culture, whether discovered in language, art, religion, or philosophy, is as individual as it is universal. For in this sphere we perceive the universal only within the actuality of the particular; only in it can the cultural universal find its actualization, its realization as a cultural universal." [7] This is, according to Herder, the method used by the Great Creator, and must likewise be used by the artist who creates in a similar manner.

With his perspective analysis and fine feeling for art, in particular sculpture, Winckelmann revived an interest in things Greek in Germany, the effects of which are still apparent today in German arts and letters. In fact, Winckelmann's concept of Greece has been called the essential factor in the development of German poetry throughout the latter half of the eighteenth and the whole of the nineteenth century.[8] But in his zeal to right the wrongs of his age Winckelmann extolled Greek art to the exclusion of all others. Realizing fully the importance and validity of his observations, Herder venerated Winckelmann and considered him one of the truly greats of his age. But no more than could Herder's veneration of Winckelmann allow him to uphold those ideas of his which Herder considered against the best interests of German art and letters, could his esteem for and general agreement with Lessing permit silence whenever he considered Lessing in error. If Winckelmann had extolled the exclusiveness of the Greeks in art, then Lessing, following in his footsteps, with the one notable exception of Shakespeare, extolled the exclusiveness of the Greeks

[6] Martin Schütze, "Herder's Psychology", *The Monist*, XXXV (Oct. 1925), p. 510.
[7] Ernst Cassirer, *The Logic of the Humanities,* trans. Clarence Smith Howe (New Haven, 1961), p. 25.
[8] E. M. Butler, *The Tyranny of Greece Over Germany* (Cambridge, 1935), p. 6.

in literature.[9] Lessing wrote in the *Laokoon* that the civilized
Greeks were the only people who can weep and be brave at the
same time, thus reflecting the prevalent eighteenth century view
that the Greeks were the ideal in art, poetry, and beauty. Since
at all times his admiration for the Greeks is tempered by his enthusiasm for the poetry and way of life of other peoples, i.e. the
Orientals and Nordics, Herder never falls into the same trap to
which so many of his contemporaries had fallen prey. To be sure,
the Greeks had produced a poetry which was great and lasting,
because, as he tells us in the Shakespeare essay, Greek art, in
both form and content, is a natural outgrowth and reflection of
the Greek way of life. But for these very reasons that he so highly
esteemed Greek poetry Herder could never permit it to be applied
as a universal standard of excellence. Since the Greek way of life
can never be duplicated outside of Greece, the same must be true
of Greek forms in art. Consequently, Herder could point out that
even in Homer's works Lessing's statement is not always valid.
What about the Trojans? he asks. Searching for an example somewhat closer to his own interests, Herder turns to the Scandana-
vians. Here is a most heroic people, he reminds us, but their songs
are hardly elegies. In the Scots and their *Bardenlieder* Herder
finds the best refutation of Lessing's argument. Although Herder,
and many others as well, one might add, were fooled by the great
Ossian hoax, this in no way negates the fact that Herder knew
good folk poetry when he saw it, and he was convinced that the
songs of Ossian were exemplary of every quality of folk poetry.
These Scots, about whom the fictitious Ossian sang, could weep,
and at the same time be just as brave as any of Homer's heroes.

Throughout this entire discussion, which in the *Erstes Wäldchen* is centered about weeping figures, Herder's whole argument
rests upon his concept of individuality, which von Wiese has
called his *Urmotiv*,[10] and the necessity for objectivity in the matter of applying the Greek ideal as an absolute standard. Thus we

---

[9] Rudolf Haym, *Herder*, ed. Wolfgang Harich (Berlin, 1954), I, 255f.
Butler, p. 76.
[10] Benno v. Wiese, "Der Philosoph auf dem Schiffe", in his *Der Mensch
in der Dichtung* (Düsseldorf, 1958), p. 55.

can agree with both Markwardt [11] and Clark [12] that Herder's rejection of the supreme authority of Homer is one of the major points in which he opposes Lessing. Despite his rejection of the absolute authority of Homer, this in no way affected Herder's conviction that Homer's works, individual though they were in that they were a reflection of a particular way of life, were the very embodiment of certain universals which transcend time and place. Concerning this idea of individuality, Herder writes in the *Ideen:* "Was indess jeder Stein – und Erdart verliehen ist: ist gewiss ein allgemeines Gesetz aller Geschöpfe unsrer Erde; dieses ist *Bildung*, bestimmte *Gestalt*, eignes *Daseyn.* Keinem Wesen kann dies genommen werden: denn alle seine Eigenschaften und Wirkungen sind darauf gegründet. Die unermessliche Kette reicht vom Schöpfer hinab bis zum Keim eines Sandkörnchens, da auch dieses seine bestimmte Gestalt hat, in der es sich oft der schönsten Krystallisation nähert" (XIII, 47f). Even earlier, in a statement in his first historical work echoed by the lines above from the *Ideen,* Herder makes it clear that this individuality extends to the highest of creatures, man himself. "In gewissem Betracht ist also jede Menschliche Vollkommenheit *National, Säkular*, und am genauesten betrachtet, *Individuell*. Man bildet nichts aus, als *wozu Zeit, Klima, Bedürfniss, Welt, Schicksal,* Anlass gibt" (V, 505). By calling to mind some of the results of our excursion into Herder's psychology we can not only better grasp the intent of these two quotations, but can also come to a clearer understanding of what Herder means by individual and individuality. First of all, it must be evident that according to Herder's psychology von Wiese's designation of individuality as the *Urmotiv* is unacceptable. Only the spirit, the soul, can lay claim to this designation for Herder, since it is the basic unit of man's being, and it is that part of him which is most closely linked together with the creator. By virtue of its own innate power and energy this soul then emulates the creative act, and keeps on emulating this act, thus providing for itself a visible manifestation and the means whereby it may be stimulated to growth and

[11]   Markwardt, p. 132
[12]   Clark, p. 12.

development. This visible manifestation, i.e. the body, is not only the activity of the soul, but is further conditioned by external factors, which impose upon it a certain individual finiteness. Thus individuality, which Herder regards as the prerogative of every creation, lies in the very nature of the growth and development of any organism, and the factors which stimulate this growth and development are, in turn, those which determine its individuality.

At no time does Herder's concept of the individual suggest a closed unity, which neither gives nor receives from any other creation at some time, for Herder was only too aware that every individual is the recipient of a legacy determined in part by history, i.e. that which has already transpired. Having once ascertained that no two items in creation are identical, Herder can easily apply this to man-made creation. Regarding as he does the poet and artist as a creator in his own right, who imitates the creative process, Herder recognizes the same claim to individuality in their creations as in nature's own creations. Thus the style or form of one work can no more claim for itself universality than can any one of nature's creations make this claim. However, as has already been noted and as must constantly be borne in mind, this in no way prevents the individual creation from serving as a vehicle for a universal quality which transcends any temporal or spacial individuality. With this type of reasoning it was inevitable that the authority of Homer, based upon the universality of form and upheld by Lessing in the *Laokoon*, must crumble. In their different attitudes in regard to the relative importance of form and content lies one of the major differences in the critical methods of Herder and Lessing. In the words of Kurt May: "Lessing ist ein ganz unmittelbar auf das Gegenständliche gerichteter Geist." [13] Characterizing Herder, May writes: "Es ergibt sich am Ende ein einfacher Gegensatz: Herder hat somit das Schöne als notwendig gehalt-, lebend-, geisterfüllte Form erkannte, während Lessing, nach aussen jedenfalls, und mit seiner ganzen literarischen Wirkung, die Schönheit der reinen Form proklamiert." [14] Likewise for Markwardt, Lessing has remained on the surface

[13]   May, p. 10.
[14]   *Ibid.*, p. 29.

with definitions and defense of the Greeks in order to be able to produce a correct formula for poetic practice. "Herder, dem es mehr um das Wesen an sich als um praktische Kritik zu tun ist, geht tiefer: nicht bei den artikulierten Tönen, den Wörtern selbst bleibt er stehen. Vielmehr ist für ihn das, was hinter dem blossen Worte steht, das Lebendig-Geistige, der inhaltliche Kern in der formalen Fassung, das Seelische, der edle Rohstoff für die poetische Prägung." [15] These elements listed by Markwardt − "das Lebendig-Geistige", "das Seelische", "der inhaltliche Kern", − could properly be termed Herder's "Urmotiv", rather than the individuality so designated by Benno von Wiese. Commenting on the importance of the content of a work of art in relation to the human soul, Korff writes: "Die Kunst der Goethezeit dagegen − worunter hier zunächst die Dichtung verstanden sei − hatte ihren Ursprung in einer seelischen Not, und dementsprechend entstand auch ihre psychologische Kunstdeutung aus der Grundvorstellung, dass die Kunst in der Geschichte der menschlichen Kultur eine notwendige Stelle und eine sehr ernsthafte Funktion im Haushalte der menschlichen Seele hat, die durch nichts anders zu ersetzen ist." [16]

Finally, in passing it should be remembered that Herder's concept of individuality is closely related to his thoughts concerning perfection, already treated in detail in Chapter I. The often cited line "Jedes vollkommenste Werk nämlich, sofern man von Menschen Vollkommenheit fodern kann, ist ein Höchstes in seiner Art" (XIV, 148), leaves little room for doubt that individuality and perfection go hand in hand. That is, the degree of perfection, that state which reflects a harmonious functioning of all component parts of the organism, while at the same time it indicates the fullest possible development of the organism's innate potential, is of its very nature an individual state, since it is attained by one organism at one time only. Perfection is never something which man attains absolutely, but rather a state which he must continually strive to attain. "Jeder strebe also auf seinem Platz zu sein, was er in der Folge der Dinge sein kann, dies soll er auch sein

[15]   Markwardt, p. 146.
[16]   H. A. Korff, *Geist der Goethezeit* (Leipzig, 1957f), I, 24.

und ein andres ist für ihn nicht möglich" (XIV, 149). Since any organism, but of course most of all man himself, is in a continual state of growth and development, striving always for a goal which he partially but never absolutely attains, we can agree with Korff, who says: "In diesem Sinne muss man sagen: *Die Menschheit ist jeden Augenblick und – nie am Ziel.*" [17]

Returning to Herder's discussion of Lessing's *Laokoon*, we find that although Herder continues to center his argument about Lessing's claim that by giving vent to their feelings by loud cries, Homer's heroes remain true to human nature, Herder's main purpose is now shifted in an attempt to point out Lessing's lack of historical perspective, while at the same time he sees here an opportunity to expose the superficiality of his own age in matters of emotion and feeling. Choosing for his purposes what he terms "a philosophical history of the elegiac art of poetry concerning peoples and times", Herder finds three areas in which the Homeric heroes gave free expression to their emotions: in their relationship to the *Vaterland*, to the family, and to friends. Thus Agamemnon weeps over the losses of the Greeks, Priam over his slain son, and Achilles over the death of his friend Patroclus. But nowhere does Herder find the Greek heroes reacting to misfortune in such a way on the battle field. Although he disagrees with Lessing's assertion that the Homeric heroes remained true to human nature by weeping and crying out on the battle field, Herder finds no fault with the idea that feeling and emotion are essentials of human nature. Most of all he is at odds with Lessing when Lessing wants to restrict this basic human reaction to the Greeks. Herder recognizes man's reaction to certain situations with emotion and feeling as a universal quality of mankind, not restricted to any people or any one time. Homer's heroes show feeling in the individual manner characteristic of the Greeks and their age. Herder is especially captivated by the Homeric heroes because he regards their expressions of feeling as genuine, originating within their very souls and hearts. Although he never denies that his own age lacks a display of feeling, Herder consid-

[17] *Ibid.,* I, 94.

ers it far removed from the genuine expression characteristic of
the Greeks, and refers to it with such derisive terms as "ein
Cabinetstück" (III, 34), and "weibliche Ueppigkeit" (III, 37).
Herder wants a genuineness of feeling which lives in the soul and
flows from the heart, rather than feeling which results from a
practicing pen or stilted conventions. Unfortunately, laments
Herder, his own age seems to ignore this type of feeling. "Wenn
es eine Zeit und ein Land gibt, da die Schönheit noch mehr Natur,
noch minder Putz und Schminke: da die Liebe noch nicht Galan-
terie, und die männliche Gabe zu gefallen, etwas mehr als Artig-
keit ist: da wird auch die Empfindung, die Sprache, und selbst
die Träne der Liebe Würde haben, und selbst das Auge eines
Helden nicht entehren" (III, 34). Essentially, Herder's disagreement with Lessing follows the same reasoning present in the
Shakespeare essay. Lessing identifies the peculiar way in which
the Greeks indicate and express feeling, and then seeks to apply
this to every age. While Herder too recognizes the genuineness
of Greek feeling, at the same time not failing to note how this
feeling is expressed, he is more interested in the feeling *per se*,
than how it is expressed. From his own age he expects feeling to
be an outgrowth of the historical and cultural circumstances, as
it was with the Greeks, and to be a genuine reflection of the minds
and hearts of those expressing this feeling.

In the course of his examination of Lessing's *Laokoon* Herder
often finds that he is essentially in agreement with Lessing. When
this is not the case, then it is frequently Lessing's use of broad
generalities which leave no room for exceptions that occasions
the disagreement. One further example, which anticipates the
crux of both writer's works, will suffice to illustrate this. Lessing
observes that Homer creates both visible and invisible beings, but
that painting cannot draw this distinction. To suggest such a distinction at all the painter must use clouds, the origin of which
Lessing sees in Homer. Herder can agree with Lessing's original
statement, but not with the explanation. By means of expertly
chosen examples he shows that Homer's fog or clouds are precisely that and no more. They do not suggest invisibility. By their
very nature Homer's gods are visible, and not invisible, as Lessing

has stated.[18] These gods, for example, can even be seen against their will. A further proof for the necessity of the visibility of the gods can be found in the Greek love of beauty. Why create beautiful gods if they can never be seen? As Haym has observed,[19] here one can see clearly the basic difference in approaches between Lessing and Herder. Lessing sees in Homer a law-giver from whom he can learn the rules for portraying the visible and invisible, while Herder sees in him the creative poet, who by projecting feeling speaks to the soul of the reader.

As a summary of the foregoing we can list four main causes for Herder's disagreement with Lessing: (1) Neglect of the historical; (2) Recognition of the importance of character individuality, but as a representative quality rather than something unique and unchangeable; (3) Statements too general to allow for exceptions; (4) Acceptance of Greek models and rules as standards for his own day and time. All of this is, however, only the means to the end of the main question, which we are now ready to consider.

The main problem which had concerned Lessing, and which also stands in the center of Herder's work, is the determination of the boundaries between poetry and the plastic arts. Lessing designates plastic art *Werk*, literature, music, and dance *Energie*. From these two terms he draws the basic distinctions whereby literature consists of a succession of articulated tones in time, painting and all plastic arts of juxtapositioned bodies in space. Herder, disagreeing with Lessing's narrow limitations, recognizes the *soul*, the sense dwelling in the articulated tones as poetry's most important distinguishing feature and designates *power* as the essence of poetry.

These central distinctions as published by Lessing had practical consequences of considerable importance. As the subtitle of the *Laokoon* makes clear, Lessing's goal was, in the final analysis, to define sharply the respective areas of poetry and painting. Painting *(Malerei)*, it must be understood, always includes sculp-

---

[18]   "Unsichtbar sein, ist der natürliche Zustand seiner Götter." *Laokoön* XII, *Werke* IV, 354.
[19]   Haym, I, 259.

ture for Lessing. Winckelmann, the predecessor of both Lessing and Herder, must be credited with having greatly advanced the understanding and appreciation of the plastic arts, but in so doing he had given these arts first place. Herder does the same in the *Viertes Wäldchen* and *Plastik*, but only temporarily. Lessing, on the other hand, wished to help poetry back to some of its rights.[20] Thus in painting Lessing's distinctions led to the condemnation of allegory and history painting, as well as scenic sequences in one picture, and to speculation about the most fruitful moment;[21] in literature it led to condemnation of enumerative and descriptive poetry, which had enjoyed such tremendous success in the works of Thompson, Brockes, Haller and Ewald von Kleist, and to the rejection of the Horatian *ut pictura poesis*, which for centuries had served as the basis for the comparison of the arts. Herder was fully cognizant of the value of Lessing's ideas, but his historical perspective also indicated to him the dangers inherent therein should they be applied to other times and other poets. It must nevertheless be stressed that, in spite of his many criticisms, reservations, and rebuttals, Herder's primary purpose was to broaden the narrow limits established by Lessing, and not to reject or to attempt to overthrow the main results of the *Laokoon*.[22]

Whether or not we want to admit that Herder's ambition to become the Winckelmann of literature in Germany reached fulfillment in the *Erstes Wäldchen*, it is probably true that this work was the most ambitious and solid treatment of aesthetics that had appeared in Germany. By concerning himself with details and exceptions, as well as with the more general applications, and by deriving his observations from and applying his ideas to the works of specific authors, Herder succeeded in expanding and elaborating upon the broad general statements of Lessing and in producing a work of most penetrating insight into the artistic

[20]   See Markwardt, p. 130.
[21]   Rene Wellek, *A History of Modern Criticism* (New Haven, 1955), I, 161.
[22]   Cf. Irving Babbit, *The New Laokoon* (Boston-New York, 1910), p. 116. "Words do follow one another in time, but not so passively as Lessing states. Three years after Lessing's *Laokoon* Herder pointed out the inadequacy of Lessing's point of view."

problems of the day which were of significance for the future of German arts and letters. In summary of the positions of Herder and Lessing, with particular emphasis on Herder's contribution beyond that of Lessing, Wellek writes: "Lessing tries to restate the neoclassical creed by abandoning its French version and substituting a liberalized interpretation of Aristotle which allowed him to satisfy his desire for ethical realism. He thus upheld the basic principle of mimesis, the concept of rules (however much he wanted to change them), and the view that literary creations is a work of judgement as well as talent." [23] "In Herder the poetics of neoclassicism is, if not dissolved completely, in the process of dissolution. He rejects all its main tenets: the imitation of nature, decorum, the unities, probability, propriety, clarity of style, purity of genre." [24] But even more important than Herder's dissolution of the poetics of neoclassicism is his opening up of new and exciting vistas in the realm of poetry. The position formerly occupied by the static, rational neoclassic poetics is to be filled by a view of literature which is dynamic and soul-oriented. Not only does Herder recognize the soul dwelling in the articulated tones of poetry as its most distinguishing feature, and power as its essence, he further sees inherent in these features the primary purpose of poetry, this by means of its power to project its soul into the soul of man and thereby to aid in its developmental process. In Herder's eyes all true poetry is "eine Geschichte der Menschlichen Seele", (IV, 368), which gives its affinity with all other human souls and enables it to contribute "zur Menschlichen und Christlichen Bildung" (IV, 368).

B. *VIERTES WÄLDCHEN* — SENSUOUS AESTHETICS

The *Kritische Wälder*, like so many of Herder's works, were destined to retain a fragmentary character for some time. Of the projected four *Wäldchen* only three were published in Herder's lifetime. The fourth and last *Wäldchen*, which is considered by some to be Herder's supreme achievement in the field of aes-

[23] Wellek, I, 176.
[24] *Ibid.*, I, 200.

thetics,[25] was not published until 1846, and then, as Suphan has pointed out,[26] in an edition that leaves much to be desired. That the *Viertes Wäldchen* did not see publication until nearly a half-century after his death is undoubtedly one of the tragedies of Herder's life, for as has been so accurately observed, this work "could have changed the entire course of German aesthetics and hence of German art, which at this period was so closely bound up with aesthetic thought".[27] Whether or not one wants to consider it or the *Kalligone* the last word of Herder on aesthetics is immaterial in the final analysis, for the fact remains that we have here a work of first rate importance not only for the limited perspective of Herder's aesthetics, but indeed for the entire aesthetic realm of his day. It is therefore inconceivable that a recent publication which purports to treat Herder's aesthetics can completely ignore this important contribution.[28] That the polemic with Klotz in the *Zweites* and *Drittes Wäldchen* has greatly diminished the effectiveness of these works has already been noted. Not so with the *Viertes Wäldchen*, although it to a certain degree is also a continuation of the polemic against the Klotzian party. Whereas the *Zweites* and *Drittes Wäldchen* are primarily aimed at the leader of the party, Klotz himself, the fourth is directed against the most important of his followers, Friedrich Justus Riedel, whose doctrine of the tripartite division of the soul prompted Herder's first organized excursion into psychology already treated in Chapter I. The *Viertes Wäldchen* is divided into three parts; the first and third are largely concerned with Herder's polemic against Riedel, while the second contains Herder's derivation of the arts from the various senses. Here we can restrict ourselves to an examination of part two.

An important result of the first part of the *Viertes Wäldchen*, which is closely connected with the second, is that man's ideal of beauty and taste are to a great extent dependent upon environmental and psychological factors. As proof of this assertion Her-

[25]   E.g. Haym and Kühnemann.
[26]   *SWS,* IV, iv.
[27]   Clark, p. 88.
[28]   Heinz Begenau in his *Grundzüge der Ästhetik Herders* (Weimar, 1956).

der discusses in detail what various cultures and times have considered beautiful. It must be remembered, he points out, that the soul is in a constant state of flux, always developing and sharpening its powers by means of sensuous impressions. The only aspect of aesthetics which has any claim to absoluteness is natural beauty, and Herder considers feeling for this innate. Artistic beauty, however, which demands most of his attention, is national and is limited to the time and place. Thus one of aesthetics' most important functions is to examine the individual arts and to seek to find the ideal for each individual one. "Es gibt also ein Ideal der Schönheit für jede Kunst, für jede Wissenschaft, für den guten Geschmack überhaupt, und es ist in Völkern und Zeiten und Subjekten und Produktionen zu finden. Schwer zu finden freilich" (IV, 41). Such a statement as this from the pen of Herder may seem both surprising and contradictory, since Herder is often pointed to and cited as the champion of the relativists. The question which arises here is: How can there possibly be one ideal for the beauty of each art or science if the art or science itself is determined by outside factors? A recent publication has concerned itself explicitly with this question.[29] In his essay Otto Mann agrees with Herder's assertion that art is the product of a definite temporal and spacial existence, but disagrees with the usual interpretation of it.[30] Herder has not, he asserts, thereby recognized the immeasurable plethora of art and its differences throughout the ages, which would be relativity. What he has done is to call attention to the unique approach of a transtemporal ideal of art from a temporal perspective. The following statement by Herder himself supports Mann's interpretation:

Der Griechische, der Gothische, der Mohrische Geschmack in Baukunst und Bildhauerei, in Mythologie und Dichtkunst ist er Derselbe? Und ist er nicht aus Zeiten, Sitten, und Völkern zu erklären? und hat er nicht also jedes mal einen Grundsatz, der nur nicht ganz verstanden, nur nicht mit gleicher Stärke gefühlt, nur nicht mit richtigen Ebenmaas angewandt wurde? und beweiset also nicht selbst dieser Proteus von Geschmack, der sich unter allen Himmelstrichen,

[29] Otto Mann, "Wandlungen des Herderbildes", *Deutschunterricht*, X (1958), pp. 27-48.
[30] *Ibid.*, p. 38.

in jeder fremden Luft, die er athmet, neu verwandelt; beweist Er nicht selbst mit den Ursachen seiner Verwandlung, dass die Schönheit nur Eins sey, so wie die Vollkommenheit, so wie die Wahrheit (IV, 40f).

If we are to accept Mann's statement, and Herder's lines just quoted certainly lend their support, then several conclusions are immediately evident. First of all, Herder is no historical relativist, at least not in the same sense that generations of scholars have so labeled him.[31] He recognizes in art only that which is definitely valid, i.e. the fulfillment of certain values. On the basis of this, understanding for him becomes a process of evaluation, for unless certain values are present the work has failed to live up to its ideal, and is therefore unworthy of consideration.[32] Secondly, if there is an element of relativity present, it is not in the object, but in the subject. The basic ideal behind the object remains constant, it is the subject, both in its role as artistic creator and as an aesthetic perceiver which is influenced by outside factors, and is thereby limited. Herder himself once answered a reproach that tones are often dull and confused with this statement: "Das Dunkle und Verworrene ihrer Empfindungen liegt an ihrem Organ, nicht an meinen Tönen: diese sind rein und helle, das höchste Muster einer zusammenstimmenden Ordnung" (XV, 228). By affirming the existence of an ideal in art, i.e. in the object itself, Herder has also largely predetermined the course he pursues in examining the work of art. This is substantiated by his whole line of argument against Riedel's definition of aesthetics. Herder wanted to develop in aesthetics a definite science, to cultivate a definite perspective whereby art can and must be viewed. Since we are primarily concerned with Herder's aesthetic in relation to literature, it might be well to note again the following generally overlooked statement from the first draft of *Brief* 76 of the *Humanitätsbriefe:* "Es giebt nur Eine Poesie, nur Einen guten Geschmack auf der Erde; haben wir diesen nicht, so haben wir gar keinen oder einen falschen. . . . Poesie macht die ganze Natur zur

31 *Ibid.,* p. 43.
32 *Ibid.,* p. 45 Herder's criteria of evaluation are, however, not to be confused with those of Aristotle.

Kunst, die Natur in und ausser uns; die Regel ihrer Kunst trägt sie in sich. Trotz aller Abweichung des Geschmacks ist diese vest und bleibend: denn die Philosophie des Wahren, Schönen und Guten ist nur Eine" (XVIII, 516).

As one writer has expressed it, "Herder versuchte . . . die Welt von der Seele des Menschen her zu verstehen".[33] It is no wonder that in the second part of the *Viertes Wäldchen* Herder is largely concerned with human characteristics, for through them Herder hopes to find the common denominator of the ideal of beauty he is concerned with in the first part of the *Viertes Wäldchen*. His basic approach is both psychological and physiological, with the former receiving most of the emphasis. Since cognition and sensation are not separate, but rather one is derived from the other, Herder rejects the deductive method of Rationalism and with empirical methods traces back the arts to the senses which produce them. The emphasis on the sensuous origins of the arts is only another of the ways he seeks to dethrone the absolutism of reason.

Herder begins with visual perception, for objects of sight are the clearest of all. They are before us, outside of us, and next to us. Since the visual sense presents us only with surfaces and objects removed in space, and since it overwhelms us with many objects at once, it is the most philosophical sense, i.e. it requires the most activity and selection. Because it deals with objects that are superficial and distant, and because the differences between the objects themselves and their colors (which directly affect vision) are so great, sight is also designated the coldest of the senses. That is, it is the least effective. But by the very fact that it provides the greatest number of perceptions, it also determines the terminology for all the senses. "Das Gesicht ist also, das die Bilder, die Vorstellungen, die Einbildungen der Seele allegorisiret, und Schönheit ist fast in allen Sprachen Hauptbezeichnung und der allgemeinste Begrif geworden, für alle feinen Künste des Wohlgefallens und Vernügens. *Schönheit ist das Hauptwort aller Aesthetik*" (IV, 45f). Since the eye sees nothing but the superficial, the art which is derived from it is painting. This is

[33] Benno v. Wiese, *Herder, Grundzüge seines Weltbildes* (Leipzig, 1939), p. 54.

approximately the same result which Herder had already reached in the *Erstes Wäldchen*, except here the juxtaposition on a surface is emphasized more than that of space. An important factor in the perception of visual beauty is the medium through which the sense works in order to perceive. For sight this medium is light. *"Licht ists, das um diese grosse Tafel von Bildern, die vor dem Auge liegt, sichtbar machet: so ists auch eine Lichtmasse, die gleichsam* die ganze Haltung der Malerischen Fläche macht" (IV, 77). It should not be forgotten that light as such plays an important role in the writings of Herder.[34] In several of the theological works light is often mentioned as the medium whereby the earthly is daily reminded of the godly, and the analogy between the creation and the first light of dawn is for Herder one of poetry's most powerful means of calling attention to a daily, divine manifestation to man.

The second gateway to the philosophy of the beautiful is hearing, the sense of music, rhythm, and language. Unfortunately, remarks Herder, our language is extremely poor in suitable expressions for the pleasant in auditory images. These must therefore be expressed metaphorically. This is, of course, partly due to the dominance of sight, but in spite of this the effect of sound penetrates much deeper into the soul of man than does light. "Sie [i.e. the effect of tones] würken durch eine Erschütterung, durch eine sanfte Betäubung der Töne und wellen; die Lichtstrahlen

[34] For this and the following see Hugo Sommerhalder, *Herder in Bückeburg als Deuter der Geschichte* (Frauenfeld-Leipzig, 1945), p. 78ff. Certain similarities between the concepts of Goethe's *Farbenlehre* with those of Herder's on the general subject of light are evident. Cf. Staiger's account in *Goethe* (Zürich, 1956), II, 403-427. Here are a few: In the formulation of his theories Goethe took nature as it is and rejected all attempts to scientifically calculate nature. (p. 406) Adoration of light is prominent with Goethe. He frequently uses it as a poetic image. Light and sun are symbols of a divine revelation. (p. 408) Goethe's color circle is an effort to comprehend all of existence and to portray it in its continuity. (p. 414) (Cf. this with Herder's *Humanität*.) In the *Farbenlehre* Goethe's primary concern was with the world and with man's relationship to nature, and not with individual scientific facts (p. 420). In the historical part of the study Goethe puts German close to Greek. Latin receives a negative characterization (p. 426). Cf. this with Herder's remarks in the *Fragmente* and the Shakespeare essay.

aber fallen, als goldene Stäbe, nur stille auf unser Gesicht, ohne uns zu stören oder zu beunruhigen" (IV, 47). Herder probably had the best knowledge of and appreciation for music of all the literary figures of his time. Even such Kantians as Haym and Kühnemann have readily admitted that here Kant's knowledge in comparison to Herder's was meager indeed. This fine feeling for music would also help to account for Herder's preference of lyrical poetry to drama. Throughout Herder's writings we find passages again and again which are concerned with music. Certain of the qualities with which he deals in these passages are also the same ones which he finds present in lyric poetry. Then too Herder's whole concept of language is linked together with music. Here in the *Viertes Wäldchen* the discussion centers around tones. Herder observes that much had been done to further a science of *Tonkunst*, and that both physics and mathematics are often cited as necessities for any sort of tonal organization. But neither does anything for what Herder calls the "tonartig Schöne". Neither explains how the tones work on or within us. This remark dismisses any considerations which are limited to the external aspects of tonality and gets right down to the crux of the matter by opening the door to a discussion of the role of Herder's psychology.[35] Prerequisite to this, however, is an understanding of Herder's terminology. Two words used here are central: sound *(Schall)*, and tone *(Ton)*. Although sound and tone are related, they are not one and the same. "Der Schall ist nichts anders, als ein dunkles Aggregat der Töne" (IV, 99). "Schall und Ton sind nicht Einerlei: jener ist nur eine dunkle Form der Composition, dieser das Wesen der Tonkunst" (IV, 100f). Thus sound performs a function similar to that of light. It is neither the subject nor the object, but rather the medium whereby these two are brought together so that the actual aesthetic experience can take place. The emphasis in the discussion is on the quality and effect of tones, not sound. When Herder draws a comparison between sight and hearing and assigns to the latter a higher degree of effectiveness he is speaking of the effectiveness of tones, not sound. Accordingly, an important distinction in the effect of each is

[35] See Chapter I.

made: sound only touches and acts upon the outer extremities of man, upon the sense organ which is capable of perceiving it; on the other hand, tones penetrate to the innermost nerves, into the very soul itself. Just as each tone has a source (Herder calls it a body), and each tone differs in accordance with the properties of the bodily mass which produces it, so too do the elements of perception of each tone differ. They differ in two ways, in quality and in type. Of the two the quality is of the greater importance in the psychology and physiology of perception, because it determined whether the sensation from the tone is pleasant or unpleasant. That tone which disturbs and irritates the nerves of our ear is unpleasant; that which harmoniously touches the nerves is pleasant. Since the process whereby a stimulus arouses a pleasant sensation is critical to the aesthetic experience, it will be well to note Herder's description of this process. "Die Nerve wird homogen *angestrengt,* und die Fibern auf einmal mehr gespannet; oder sie wird *erschlaffet,* und die Fibern fliessen allmählich, wie in eine sanfte Auflösung über" (VI, 103). As usual, Herder finds an application of his ideas for his own time and day. Seizing upon the distinction he has made between the effects of sound and tone, he observes that the ancients heard tone, people of his day, however, hear only sound. In the *Fragmente* he had already called attention to the *tönende Worte* of the ancients. In the *Viertes Wäldchen* he further elaborates upon this statement, for here was another chance to point out the basic differences between the ancients and man of his own day. The ancients were close to nature, their reactions and feelings were sharp and pure because they had not been adversely influenced by constant concern with abstract philosophical matters. Since their senses were undulled, they were receptive to the innermost sensation possible through the sense of hearing – tone. But what about most of Herder's contemporaries? What about those who had followed the admonitions of the *Aufklärer?* For them the whole process remained superficial. The aggregate – sound – fell on the organ of hearing, but never penetrated beyond it. For this organ, dulled by the lack of sensitive use, failed to transmit the nucleus of sound, tone, to the soul.

One important proof that hearing is the first and deepest of the senses, the one closest to feeling, is found in language. "Die Natur selbst hat diese Naheit bestätigt, da sie keinen Weg zur Seele besser wusste, als durch Ohr und – Sprache" (IV, 112). The introduction of language at this point requires clarification of Herder's understanding of the relationship of music and language. In the treatise on language Herder attributes the origins of language to man's power of reflection *(Besonnenheit)*. Here he is suggesting that unarticulated tones, a cry perhaps, are the beginnings of language. This fits in with his claim that harmony is not the basis of music. What Herder wants to show, and whether or not he succeeds is open to question, is that language came before music and that man came to music through language. If this is the case, then accented individual tones, e.g. a cry, become the basis for music. Whenever man reaches the stage in language that he momentarily forgets the necessity of thought or feeling and cultivates the tone for the sake of tone, then a step is taken in the direction of music. Singing language, trying to express feeling and passion, and not the song of the bird, becomes for Herder the natural source of music. The language of the ancients was a singing language, a vocal music. Its main components were rhythm, metrics, poetics, and harmony. It was, to use a different terminology, musical poetry.

The third and "lowest" sense which Herder considers is the sense of touch. According to him this sense, although the least known, perhaps deserves to be the best known. At this point in his discussions of this sense he ventures the most daring idea of the *Viertes Wäldchen*: feeling, not sight, gives us our conception of form.[36] "Ich setze also die unleugbare Erfahrung voraus, dass es das Gesicht nicht sey, was uns von Formen und Körpern Begriffe gebe, wie man es durch eine gemeine Meinung annimmt. . . . Ich setze es voraus, dass das Gesicht uns nichts, als Flächen, Farben und Bilder zeigen könne, und dass wir vor allem, was Köperlicher Raum, spärischer Winkel, und solide Form ist, nichts anders, als durchs Gefühl, und durch lange wiederholte Betastungen Begriffe erhalten können" (IV, 49). From this it must

[36] For the first traces of this see *SWS,* I, 399.

logically follow that touch must not be such a low sense after all, as had been the general custom to so designate it. The arts directly affected by this differentiation are painting and sculpture. In the *Erstes Wäldchen* both were considered under the broad term *Malerei*, both produced works for the eye, both worked through colors and figures, both produced that which is juxtapositioned (*nebeneinander*) in space. Here in the *Viertes Wäldchen* Herder begins to make certain basic distinctions between the two. Painting now becomes the art which represents objects according to their exterior. Its area of representation is surface, and the most important factors in this representation are color and light. Never, however, does this art penetrate beneath the surface. It remains superficial. Sculpture is not, however, restricted to surface representations. In no way is it dependent on color as is painting. In *Plastik* (1778), his most developed treatment of this theme, sculpture produces that which stands together *(hintereinander)*. "Das Wesen der Bildhauerei ist schöne Form: nicht Farbe, nicht blosse Proportion der Theile, als Flächen betrachtet, sondern Bildung" (IV, 64). Feeling is incapable of knowledge of that which is represented on a surface, e.g. color. Sight knows nothing of form and content. It is an accepted fact that the blind are incapable of experiencing painting, while through their highly developed sense of touch they can experience the plastic arts.

With the help of what Herder says in *Plastik* we can better determine the far reaching influence of these ideas on Herder's aesthetic. In both the *Wäldchen* and the *Plastik* sight is often referred to as the false sense. Herder does not mean by this that there is basically a flaw in one sense as opposed to another or that this sense is incomplete in comparison with another sense. When he calls sight the false sense he is pointing out that certain external factors influence the sense, its medium for example, and are capable of deceiving the sense itself. One example will serve to illustrate this. A staff in the water presents an untrue image. Anyone who has attempted to hit with a stone an object submerged in water is aware that the object is not where it appears to be. In a sense, our sense of sight has been both distorted and confused. Herder does not feel that the sense of touch is guilty of this distortion. "Das Gefühl ist gleichsam der erste, sichre und treue Sinn, der sich entwickelt" (IV, 79). "Im Gesicht ist *Traum*, im Gefühl *Wahrheit*" (VIII, 9). These qualities put touch in the unique position of being the only sense which can perceive form and figure.[37] If sight is considered a false sense, and touch a true sense, then the art product representative of each of these two senses must necessarily stand in a like relationship with one another, i.e.: "Endlich die Bildnerei ist *Wahrheit*, die Malerei ist *Traum*: jene ganz *Darstellung,* diese erzählender Zauber" (VIII, 17). The eye sees nothing but the surface; painting produces nothing but that which can be represented on a surface. This one-sided representation does not fool us because our experience makes up for what our sense fails to perceive. The essence of sculpture, however, is form, and this can never be perceived by the eye alone. It must be felt. So, as an art form Herder considers sculpture above painting. It is a true representation of the object as it is in all its dimensions. By the same token the sense of touch is placed above the sense of sight. In order to perceive form and figure sight requires the help of feel. Feeling, however, requires no such complement. It is capable of perceiving form without help from another sense.

Herder's derivation of the individual arts painting, music, and sculpturing from the three senses of sight, hearing, and touch, respectively, is of considerable importance to his theory of poetry. For several reasons poetry, which was the most important of the arts for Herder, is conspicuously missing from this triumvirate. First of all there was the important question of language. Because language is the means of expression for poetry it is difficult to fit it into a system of the arts. Language complicates the classification of poetry by assuming for itself qualities of a work of art, on the one hand through the images it creates, on the other through its musical production. But there was also a practical reason why poetry could not be included along with the other

---

[37] Cf. Goethe, from "Römische Elegien": Und belehr' ich mich nicht, indem ich des lieblichen Busens / Formen spähe, die Hand leite die Hüften hinab? / Dann versteh ich den Marmor erst recht: ich denk und vergleiche, / Sehe mit fühlendem Aug, fühle mit sehender Hand.

arts. An appropriate sense was completely lacking. After careful examination Herder comes to the conclusion that it would be impossible to include poetry in any such system anyway, for poetry is the result of not one sense, but an inter-play of all the senses. "Aus allen Sinnen strömen die Empfindungen des Schönen in die Einbildungskraft und aus allen schönen Künsten also in die Poesie hinüber" (IV, 163). Thus among the arts poetry assumes a position analogous to that of the soul among man's faculties. Just as the soul for Herder represents the amalgamation of all of man's faculties into one unified harmonious whole, so is poetry the art form which can best express the harmony and unity of the soul, since by its very nature it is not the result of one, but a combination of the senses. Thus despite the importance of the theory of touch for the remainder of Herder's aesthetic and the burst of enthusiasm of the *Plastik* and *Viertes Wäldchen* for the plastic arts, their reign was short lived, and poetry soon assumed its place as the supreme art form for Herder. "Göttliche Poesie! Geistige Kunst des Schönen! Königin aller Ideen aus allen Sinnen! ein Sammelplatz aller Zaubereien aller Künste" (IV, 166).

The *Erstes Wäldchen* firmly establishes the dependency of Herder's theory of the individual arts upon the soul, while the *Viertes Wäldchen* postulates the psychological and sensuous qualities of the arts and their production. In all aspects, then, Herder's aesthetic is soul-oriented. Whereas Lessing advances a definition of poetry which is eminently valid, his conclusions are largely based on observations of the superficial. Beginning with the same presuppositions, Herder's conclusions are completely soul-centered. The soul of the poetry is its distinguishing characteristic, power is its essence, and its ability to speak to the soul of man establishes its claim to the position as the most important of the arts. Similarly, although each of the arts has its origin in a given sense, and although each sense is ultimately an inherent part of that composite of all of man's faculties, the soul, poetry alone results directly from it. Thus, while according to Herder the soul is at all times a unified harmonious whole, permitting no division into separate faculties, it nevertheless is able to perform a number of individual functions simultaneously. Hence Herder's definition of poetry: "Poesie ist also *vollkommen sinnliche Rede*" (IV, 131). Poetry can so be designated because it alone of the arts is derived not from one sense, but from the combined interaction of all the senses, i.e. the soul. Thus it may be said to be perfect, for its origin lies in the soul. And for Herder, only that which originates in the soul and has affinity with the soul is deserving of this designation.

IV

THE *KALLIGONE*: HERDER'S ATTEMPT
OF A *'SUMMA AESTHETICA'*

A. THE PLEASANT AND THE BEAUTIFUL
AND CRITERIA FOR THEIR DETERMINATION

As was so often the case with Herder's writings, the two works which occupied the last years of his life were occasioned by a polemic with his former friend and mentor Immanuel Kant. Beginning in 1785 with Kant's review of part one of Herder's *Ideen*, the controversy with Kant lasted until Herder's death in 1803, culminating finally in the *Metakritik der Kritik der reinen Vernunft* (1799) and the *Kalligone* (1800), Herder's reply to Kant's first and third *Critiques* respectively.

In the *Kritik der reinen Vernunft*, his epistemology, Kant claimed that reason existed in the human mind as an independent faculty, and as such was capable of criticizing itself. Looking to his psychology and his belief in the human mind as a harmonious whole, permitting no divisions into separate faculties, as he had previously postulated in the *Viertes Wäldchen* in the polemic with Riedel, Herder disputes Kant's claims on the grounds that reason cannot critize itself because it cannot get outside of itself. Reminding us further that "pure" reason, or any other kind of reason is a function of language, and not something transcendent, Herder, in agreement with Leibniz, reiterates the claim that he first made in the *Fragmente* and which he frequently calls attention to throughout his lifetime, that the thought process and language necessarily exist interdependent of one another. "Die menschliche Seele denkt mit *Worten*; sie äussert nicht nur, sondern sie bezeichnet sich selbst auch und ordnet ihre Gedanken mittelst der *Sprache*. Sprache, sagt *Leibniz*, ist der Spiegel des menschlichen Verstandes, und, wie man kühn hinzusetzen darf, ein Fundbuch seiner Begriffe, ein nicht nur gewohntes, sondern unentbehrliches Werkzeug seiner Vernunft. Mittelst der Sprache lernen wir denken, durch sie sondern wir Begriffe ab und knüpfen sie, oft haufenweise, in einander" (XXI, 19). Whereas Herder ascribed man's whole thought process to the soul, i.e., a harmoniously working unified whole, Kant regards it as a function of an intelligible faculty, reason. "Denn er [Verstand] ist nach dem Obigen ein Vermögen zu denken. Denken ist das Erkenntnis durch Begriffe." [1] In his introduction Kant had already written: "Denn ist Vernunft das Vermögen, welches die *Principien* der Erkenntniss a priori in die Hand gibt." [2]

Kant's idea of knowledge *a priori*, which is basic to his epistemology and also to his aesthetic, has often been cited as the primary cause for the inability of the minds of the two philosophers to meet. In his introduction Kant distinguishes between pure and empirical knowledge, and although he never denies the existence of empirical knowledge, he does maintain a difference between knowledge which begins with experience, and knowledge which arises out of experience. Kant makes it clear, however, that the purpose of this word *a priori* is to refer to that knowledge gained entirely without the benefit of experience. "Wir werden also im Verfolg unter Erkenntnissen a priori nicht solche verstehen, die von dieser oder jener, sondern die *schlechterdings* von aller Erfahrung unabhängig stattfinden." [3] Partially because he was an empiricist, and partially because he rejects Kant's division of the human mind into individual faculties, the *Inselbegriffe* of Riedel, whereby the faculty of reason is accorded supremacy, Herder also rejects Kant's idea of knowledge *a priori*. "Sich von sich selbst unabhängig zu machen, d.i. aus aller ursprünglichen, innern und äussern Erfahrung sich hinauszusetzen,

---

[1] Immanuel Kant, *Werke* (in 6 Bänden), ed. W. Weischedel (Wiesbaden, 1957f), II, 110. Quotations from first *Kritik* identified *K.d.V.*, and cited by volume and page. Quotations from third *Kritik* cited as Kant, *Werke*, by volume, page, and paragraph.

[2] Kant, *K.d.V.*, II, 62.

[3] *Ibid.*, II, 46.

von allem Empirischen frei über sich selbst *hinaus zu denken*, vermag niemand. Das wäre ein prius vor allem *a priori*: damit hörte, ehe sie anfing, die Menschenvernunft auf" (XXI, 24). Despite what Herder says here, it must be remembered that Herder's psychology assumed the existence of an innate *a priori* potential within the soul, which to be sure had to be stimulated to growth and development, both from without and within, but which is nevertheless infused into every human soul at the very moment of its creation. Herder's concept differs from that of Kant in that he sees this potential as abiding in the soul, while Kant restricts it to the faculty of reason only. Kant's approach is rational, whereas Herder's is psychological.

In reply to Kant's *a priori* limitations of time and space Herder sets up his own system, the basic of which is being (*Seyn*). "*Seyn* ist der Grund aller Erkenntniss. Wo nichts ist, erkennet nichts und wird nichts erkannt" (XXI, 62). For Kant space and time are purely subjective, while for Herder they are objective forms created by nature. According to Herder's ontology, this being reveals itself through power that is there, i.e., existence, *Daseyn*. From this existence, which is limited in that it is at one place only at one time, the three dimensions of adjacency (*Nebeneinander*), sequence (*Nacheinander*), and influence [4] (*In-und Durcheinander*) are derived. The three senses of sight, hearing, and touch are, respectively, the organs corresponding to these dimensions of being. Through the interaction of sight and hearing, whereby each constantly regulates and limits the other, power is produced. "Die Zeit hat den todten Raum *belebt*, der Raum hat das *Vergangene*, so wie die Zukunft zur *Gegenwart* gemacht, und da beides nicht ohne Kraft geschehen konnte, auch ohne lebendige Kraft nicht vorgestellt werden kann, so *begreift* die Seele, d.i. sie *erfasset, verstehet* in Vielem ein Eins; ein Eins im *Nach –* und *Nebeneinander*, das nicht anders als durch ein Drittes, das *Seyn*, die *lebendige Kraft* entstehen konnte" (XXI, 67). By manifesting itself in all life this power, in turn, becomes organic power, the means whereby the organism, or in the specific case of

---

[4] Robert T. Clark, Jr., *Herder: His Life and Thought* (Berkeley-Los Angeles, 1955), p. 451, notes to Chapter XII, no. 10.

man, the soul, as Herder emphasizes again and again, grows and develops. The organism does not attain totality by mere existence alone, but rather in the purpose of this existence, which for Herder is life, activity, and development to the fullest extent of the innate potential of the soul. Kant, once again, is not interested in the development of the soul, but rather in the expansion of man's rational faculties. Since power, the means whereby the soul grows, manifests itself in organic life, and since organic life is bound to reality, Herder is further strengthening his claim that being, and not apriority, is the basis of all epistemology.

Although more a matter pertaining to aesthetics that epistemology, the question of whether beauty is to be regarded as subjective or objective, or a combination of the two, is dealt with by Kant in his first *Kritik* and is elaborated upon by Herder in the *Metakritik*. As a part of his system of apriority and closely related to his insistence upon the supremacy of reason, Kant declares beauty, indeed any phenomenological realization by man, to be subjective. It is a state or act of the observer. "Wir haben also sagen wollen: dass alle unsre Anschauung nichts als die Vorstellung von Erscheinung sei; dass die Dinge, die wir anschauen, . . . als Erscheinungen nicht an sich selbst, sondern nur in uns existieren können. Was es für eine Bewandnis mit den Gegenständen an sich und abgesondert von aller dieser Receptivität unserer Sinnlichkeit haben möge, bleibt uns gänzlich unbekannt." [5] As we have previously noted in numerous places, beauty for Herder is something both subjective and objective. It is objective because Herder considers man's reason incapable of producing a concept except on the basis of experience. That is, there must be something present, a phenomenon if you will, before there can be any conception. Although Herder believes that an object can be beautiful whether or not there is a subject to perceive it, insofar as human knowledge is concerned he agrees that beauty is also subjective. However, his concept of subjective beauty differs completely from that of Kant: firstly, because he regards this as a process of the soul, and not the intellect; and secondly, because his concept of subjective beauty rests upon his

[5] Kant, *K.d.V.* II, 87.

belief in empathy, whereby the subject "feels himself" into the object being perceived. "Bei jedem wahren Begriff thut die Seele viel mehr als anschauen, sie *erkennet*, sie *eignet sich an*; nur dadurch werden ihr eigentümliche, der Natur, den Sinnen, und sich selbst harmonische, wahre Gedanken" (XXI, 90). Thus for Herder the perception of beauty, or for that matter any other attribute of an object, can never be restricted to any abstract thought or reasoning process. Before leaving the *Metakritik* it is important to note that in every instance where Kant has spoken of the intellect or reason, Herder speaks of the soul. In order to underscore the importance of his treatment of the soul according to the tripartite scheme of phenomenology, development, and perfection, Herder employs a like plan for his treatment of aesthetics in the *Kalligone*. In the first part, entitled "Vom Angenehmen und Schönen", Herder establishes criteria for the determination of the pleasant and beautiful. "Kunst und Kunstrichterei", the second part, is concerned with the means whereby the soul's awareness of beauty can be developed, and the function of the various arts in developing this awareness. Part three, "Vom Erhabnen und vom Ideal", seeks to ascertain what constitutes the sublime and ideal, i.e., the pleasant and the beautiful in their most perfect forms, and to relate them to the attainment of man's ultimate goal and purpose, perfection, *Humanität*.

In words which immediately call to mind similar passages from the *Metakritik* and many of the earlier writings Herder reiterates at the very beginning of the *Kalligone*, in his introduction, the tremendous importance he attaches to language and to the mutual compatibility between thought and expression, a point which is completely overlooked by Kant. "Die Sprache der Menschen trägt ihre *Denkformen* in sich; wir denken, zumal abstract, nur in und mit der Sprache. Habt Ihr zu euren Anschauungen, wie Ihr sagt, eigne Schemate nöthig, so lasst uns unsre Sprache unverwirrt und erfindet euch Ziffern, schematisirt tibetanisch. Der Gesammtgeist aller cultivirten Völker Europas hat Ein philosophisches Idiom: von *Plato* und *Aristoteles* reicht es zu *Locke* und *Leibniz*, zu *Condillac* und *Lessing*. Ein Rottwelsch, das mit Jedermann – verständlichen Worten neue Nebelbegriffe

verbindet, ist und bleibt Rottwelsch" (XXII, 7). With these words
Herder is not only pointing out Kant's failure to take into consideration the importance of language. Even more these words
point to a complete rejection of Kant's entire system, both philosophic and aesthetic, insofar as it is based on reason, which for
Kant was autonomous. In the second and final introduction to
his third *Kritik* Kant openly expresses the need for a reconcilia-
tion between the systems expounded in the two earlier critiques.
In the aesthetic system of the third *Kritik* Kant sees this recon-
ciliation realized.[6] But in his efforts to fill the gap which lay open
between the principles of pure and practical reason Kant only
succeeded in compounding the basic difficulty, insofar as Herder
was concerned. For Kant's arguments completely ignore the objects of aesthetic contemplation and spend all their time discussing the contemplative faculty which, according to Kant, determines their beauty. Herder's reasoning here is essentially the
same as that employed in the *Fragmente* and other earlier writings. A system that is so abstract that it must be built up entirely
upon abstract concepts and expressed in abstract language dis-
regards entirely an important function of language and is so
hopelessly detached from reality that it is devoid of any meaning.

Part one of the *Kalligone* begins with a discussion of the nature of the pleasant, and as Haym puts it, Herder immediately
disturbs the boundaries between the pleasant, the beautiful, and
the good which Kant had drawn with such sure hand.[7] Kant had
said that the most important factor in the aesthetic experience is
judgement, because by it an object is found to be beautiful. Disputing this, Herder maintains that the essential of any aesthetic
experience is feeling. The importance of feeling for Herder's
aesthetic, which has led Jacoby to declare that feeling is its very
starting point, can hardly be over-emphasized.[8] Herder under-

---

[6] For a discussion of this see Katharine E. Gilbert and Helmut Kuhn, *A History of Esthetics* (New York, 1939), p. 328f; Israel Knox, *The Aesthetic Theories of Kant, Hegel, and Schopenhauer* (New York, 1958), p. 11f; Clark, *Herder,* p. 409f.

[7] Rudolf Haym, *Herder,* ed. Wolfgang Harich (Berlin, 1954), II, 749.

[8] Günther Jacoby, *Herders und Kants Ästhetik* (Leipzig, 1907), p. 98.

stands by feeling, as we have already noted, that total faculty of the soul whereby the soul, both consciously and unconsciously, communes with the world.[9] As a result of this position regarding feeling Herder rejects Kant's contention that the pleasant indicates a judgement of the object, and instead makes the pleasant a result of feeling. "Das Angenehme *vergnügt* nicht nur, sondern das Innigst-Angenehme erweitert, kräftigt und stärkt mein Daseyn; das innigst Angenehme ist mein lebendiges gefühltes Daseyn selbst" (XXII, 30). The importance of the soul in this process is not only emphasized by the role which it plays in the appropriation of the pleasant, but also in the effect which the pleasant, once appropriated by the soul, exerts upon it. In Herder's words, the soul is expanded, invigorated, and strengthened by the pleasant. Thus those functions which Kant delegates to the intellect, Herder regards as the prerogative of the soul. For Herder judgement plays only a minor role in the whole process, and this only if the feeling is pleasant, since then the judgement so recognizes it and causes the subject's senses to wish to appropriate this pleasantness. Should however the opposite be the case, and the feeling be unpleasant, then a judgement is pronounced which causes the senses to be repelled by the unpleasantness. "Was, nachdem ich organisirt bin, das Gefühl meines *Daseyns* beängstet, angreift und befeindet, ist unangenehm: was dagegen es erhält, fördert, erweitert, kurz, was mit ihm *harmonisch* ist, das nimmt jeder meiner Sinne gern an, eignet es zu sich und findet es angenehm, gesetzt, dass es auch ein anderweit urtheilender Verstand nicht dafür erklärte" (XXII, 30). A further factor in the aesthetic experience which must not be ignored is taste. Here Herder conceives of taste as a sort of aesthetic watchman. Taste is to make it possible for each individual to pursue his own feeling for pleasantness. That is, taste does not awaken in each subject the same feeling of pleasure or pain. What is pleasant according to the taste of one subject is not necessarily pleasing to the taste of another. The function of taste is to enable the subject to enjoy, and not to judge, as Kant had claimed. "Auch soll das

---

[9] See our discussion in Chapter I, Friedrich Berger, *Menschenbild und Menschenbildung* (Stuttgart, 1933), p. 86, and *SWS*, VIII, 104.

Wort Geschmack uns vom Klügeln zum Geniessen, vom Gehirn auf die Zunge führen" (XXII, 34).

Haym is correct when he states that at the very beginning of the *Kalligone* Herder disturbs the rigid boundaries which Kant had drawn between the three specific types of satisfaction – the pleasant, the beautiful, and the good. "Auch das Sinnlichstangenehme erschien uns also als eine *Mittheilung des Wahren und Guten,* sofern es dieser Sinn fassen konnte; die *Empfindung der Lust und Unlust* dabei war nichts anders, als eben das Gefühl das Wahren und Guten, dass der Zweck des dienenden Organs, nämlich die Erhaltung unsres Wohlseyns, die Anwehrung unsres Schadens erreicht sey" (XXII, 35). Although we can admit the validity of Haym's observation, we can hardly agree with him that this act of Herder's constituted an unwarranted attack on Kant's system and indicated Herder's complete inability to understand the same. Since Kant's whole system was based on the assumption that reason was a separate and distinct faculty, existing as an autonomous unit unto itself, it is not surprising that he also regards the pleasant, the good, and the beautiful as separate attributes, each complete in itself. Herder's system, however, recognizing no such division of the soul into independent faculties, consequently has no room for attributes which pertain to one faculty only. Since for Herder one of the chief characteristics of the soul is its unity and oneness, that which is appropriated by the soul must reflect this same unity, i.e. "Eins aus Vielem". Haym, as well as the preponderance of nineteenth century scholars, was thoroughly schooled in the traditions of Kantian philosophy. Consequently, when faced by other systems or arguments such as Herder's which rest upon presuppositions different from those of Kant's, they are at a loss to draw from them the proper conclusions. They failed to take into account that aesthetics, as the very word itself implies, did not rest upon reason or the intellect alone, but also recognized the important role of the senses and feeling in the aesthetic experience. All of this points to the necessity of exerting extreme care before blindly accepting the judgement of Haym, or anyone else for that matter, without first examining the validity of their claims.

Herder's rejection of Kant's three types of satisfaction is a good illustration of how Haym clearly recognizes the crux of Herder's argument, but fails completely to see its application. Haym has correctly stated that every theory, every idea, and every argument in the *Kalligone* is based on Herder's conviction that beauty must be explained with the object itself in mind.[10] Nevertheless, he is unable to see why Herder cannot accept Kant's distinction of the three types of satisfaction. In the second section of the first part, in which Herder discusses the pleasant in figures, the answer is supplied.

Having once again stated his belief in the unity of the soul, and in the importance of feeling for the aesthetic experience, Herder then turns his attention to a refutation of Kant's analytic according to the four moments of quality, quantity, relation, and modality. According to Kant's aesthetic it is the analysis of the judgement of taste which reveals that required in order to call an object beautiful. According to the first of these four moments, *quality*, the judgement of taste is disinterested. The opening lines of the first part of his aesthetic make it clear that the judgement of taste is contemplative and indifferent to the existence of the object. "Um zu unterscheiden, ob etwas schön sei oder nicht, beziehen wir die Vorstellung nicht durch den Verstand auf das Objekt zum Erkenntnisse, sondern durch die Einbildungskraft (vielleicht mit dem Verstande verbunden) auf das Subjekt und das Gefühl der Lust oder Unlust desselben. Das Geschmacks-urteil ist also kein Erkenntnisurteil, mithin nicht logisch, sondern äesthetisch, worunter man dasjenige versteht, dessen Bestim-mungsgrund *nicht anders als subjektiv* sein kann." [11] Thus as one commentator has put it, Kant "divorces the aesthetic experience from all content and meaning and transforms it into a no-man's land of detached and abstract feeling. His sole concern seems to be to establish the identity of the aesthetic judgement with pure subjective feeling, but feeling – in contrast to the empiricists – dissociated from *sensation*, and also from the socio-ethical prob-

[10]   Haym, II, 750.
[11]   Kant, *Werke*, V, 279, par. 1. Cf. "Daher ist das Geschmacksurteil bloss kontemplativ ...", V, 286, par. 5.

lem of life." [12] Whereas subjective for Kant refers to a faculty within man which is an entity in itself, and which performs one and only one of the functions of the mind, in this case reasoning, without which there can be no determination of the beautiful, subjective for Herder indicates an activity of a unified harmoniously active soul, whereby the soul, in the case of the usual subject, immerses itself within the object and thus partakes of its soul, or, in the case of the artist, animates the artistic creation through the creative act. Herder demands an aesthetic experience in which not only one part of man's personality is benefited, rather one which will contribute to the growth and development of this personality as a whole. In his words, once the object is determined beautiful, there should not only be judgement, but also enjoyment, refreshment, and strengthening for the soul. It should also be added, lest Kant's statement be misunderstood, that while Herder regards the aesthetic experience as an integral part of life, and hence as being of significance in man's day-by-day contacts with his fellow man, he never, under any circumstances, regards the determination of beauty as a social function, which can be carried out according to some general consensus.

According to *quantity*, the second moment: "Das Schöne ist das, was ohne Begriffe, als Objekt eines allgemeinen Wohlgefallens vorgestellt wird." [13] Kant restates here what he has already said in the first paragraph in connection with the first moment that beauty is aesthetic, and not logic. That is to say, for Kant beauty resides in the judgement of taste, and not in the perfection of the object, such as was the case with such aestheticians as Baumgarten, Leibniz, and Wolff. Kant's universality is therefore subjective, and divested of any specific contact with the aesthetic phenomenon. "Folglich muss dem Geschmacksurteile, mit dem Bewusstsein der Absonderung in demselben von allen Interesse, ein Anspruch auf Gültigkeit für jedermann, ohne auf Objekte gestellte Allgemeinheit hängen, d.i. es muss ein Anspruch auf subjektive Allgemeinheit verbunden sein." [14] It is interesting

[12]   Knox, p. 23.
[13]   Kant, *Werke*, V, 288, par. 6.
[14]   *Ibid.*, V, 289, par. 6.

to note how Kant is able to make his case for the universality of aesthetic judgement. The disinterestedness of the satisfaction according to the first moment has established the detached state of mind of the subject. Consequently, since the satisfaction is impersonal and not individual, it may be said that "what pleases me impersonally, pleases me as a member of humanity, and not as a unique individual." [15] Kant sums up the second moment thusly: "Schön ist das, was ohne Begriff allgemein gefällt".[16] On two points Herder finds himself at odds with Kant's second moment. Concept was for Herder, it must be remembered, the representation of the object, i.e., that part of the object which the subject can appropriate for itself. Consequently, in Herder's thinking, Kant's second moment disclaimed the necessity of the object in the aesthetic experience. Secondly, not only does Herder require the presence of an object, he further considers the aesthetic experience an individual, and not universal matter. Since the intensity of the experience is dependent upon the degree of development of the individual's soul, and upon the degree of perfection within the object, no two such experiences can be identical. As Herder concludes: "Das reinste Schöne wird nur den Wenigsten erkannt und geliebt, wie es geliebt werden will, der grosse Haufe haftet am Niedrigen, am Gemeinen" (XXII, 39).

No less an authority than Hermann Lotze,[17] himself strongly pro-Kantian, has made a number of significant comments on Kant's second moment. Although Lotze considers Kant's emphasis on the subjectivity of the aesthetic judgement one of his greatest services, he regards this only as a beginning, and does not think that Kant has gone far enough. Lotze warns against too much emphasis on this subjectivity, however, for should this happen he feels that the aesthetic experience could easily turn into a sort of self adoration with the "I" as the center of the experience to the complete neglect of the object. This idea, of course, is completely in keeping with Kant's doctrine of the su-

---

[15]   Gilbert and Kuhn, p. 335.
[16]   Kant, *Werke*, V, 298, par. 11.
[17]   Hermann Lotze, *Geschichte der Aesthetik in Deutschland* (München, 1868), p. 65ff.

premacy and autonomy of the intelligent, rational man. In what
Lotze says here there seems to be a definite attempt on his part
to modify Kant's position. This is also a point which Herder
takes issue with Kant over, for although Herder never denies the
importance of the subjective aspect of the aesthetic experience,
neither can he accept Kant's theory that completely neglects the
objective nature of the experience. Lotze's argument, the crux of
which seems to be of sufficient applicability here to reproduce
below, is thus more Herderean in tone than Kantian. Lotze evidently realized the vulnerability of Kant's argument on this point
and, instead of dismissing it completely, tried to interpret it in
such a way as to overcome the difficulties. In so doing he has,
perhaps unwittingly, supported the arguments of Herder and all
others who have disagreed with Kant on this vital issue. Lotze
writes:

In Wahrheit ist doch nicht für Kant die Harmonie der Seelenkräfte
das Schöne selbst; sie ist vielmehr die sich selbst geniessende ästhetische Lust; schön ist für ihn wie für den gewöhnlichen Sprachge-
brauch der Gegenstand, dessen Einwirkung auf uns diese Lust erzeugt. Es ist Kants eigne Meinung, was Zimmermann, wie es scheint,
als Bedenken gegen Kant auffürht: wenn auch das Wohlgefallen am
Gegenstand nur die harmonische Thätigkeit unseres Innern ist: der
Grund, der tiefe Thätigkeit anregt, liegt doch in dem Gegenstande
selbst. Aber man hat wohl nicht Recht hinzuzufügen: dieser Grund
liege in dem Gegenstand allein, *nicht* in uns; er liegt vielmehr einzig
darin, dass die Dinge und wir *zusammenpassen*. Es gibt keine Schönheit als solche, ausser in dem Gefühl des Geistes, der sie geniesst und
bewundert; aber der Zusammenhang der Dinge ist so geordnet, dass
er dem Geiste die Formen der Bewegung erregen kann, in denen
jeder Genuss zu Theil wird und der Gegenstand seiner Bewunderung
entsteht. . . . Unter solcher Voraussetzung [i.e. that beauty does not
exist independent] freilich würde die Schönheit wenig Werth haben,
sie würde selbst nur ein Schein sein, wenn sie nicht ausserhalb des
Geistes und bevor er die Welt abbildet, in dieser vollständig als
solche vorhanden wäre, ein möglicher Gegenstand künftiges Genusses
für uns, aber unsere Wahrnehmung nicht bedürftig, um ganz zu sein
wie sie ist.[18]

According to *relation*, the third moment, the judgement of taste

[18]   *Ibid.,* p. 65.

has nothing at its base except what Kant paradoxically terms "purposiveness without purpose". Purpose, he tells us, is the object or cause of a concept, whereas causality of a concept in respect to the object is its purposiveness. Now if purpose were regarded as a reason for satisfaction, then the necessity of admitting an interest would follow, the same interest whose existence Kant has already denied. From this Kant is able to say that the judgement of taste has no subjective purpose. But he is also able to declare that no representation of an objective purpose can determine the judgement of taste, since the latter is aesthetical. All of this means that the judgement of taste, and therefore the determination of beauty, is completely divorced from reality and is regulated to the realm of abstract thought, as indeed Kant emphasizes when he declares in paragraph twelve that "the judgement of taste rests upon *a priori* reasons". Based on this relation of purposiveness without purpose between the object and the subject it further follows that the judgement of taste is pure, that is, it is independent of charm or emotion. "Ein Geschmacksurteil ist also nur sofern rein, als kein bloss empirisches Wohlgefallen dem Bestimmungsgrunde desselben beigemischt wird." [19] On the basis of his emphasis on the purity, i.e., the quality of being *a priori* of pleasure, Kant then formulates his distinction between free and dependent beauty: "Es gibt zweierlei Arten von Schönheit: freie Schönheit (pulchritudo vaga), oder die bloss anhängende Schönheit (pulchritudo adhaerens). Die erstere setzt keinen Begriff von dem voraus, was der Gegenstand sein soll; die zweite setzt einen solchen und die Vollkommenheit des Gegenstandes nach demselben voraus." [20] Such items as Greek decorative designs, foliage for borders on wallpaper, musical phantasies, and objects of nature to which we respond immediately because of their agreeable design without consciousness of their purpose illustrate free beauty. Objects such as horses, churches, palaces, arsenals, and summerhouses belong to the class of adherent beauty because an awareness of the purpose they serve accom-

[19]   Kant, *Werke,* V, 303, par. 14.
[20]   Kant, *Werke,* V, 310, par. 16.

panies our appreciation of their design. One of the problems which this system of distinctions creates, and one which Herder immediately recognized, is that everything that is truly significant or that possesses any meaning for man (human and animal beauty, portraits, sculpture, architecture, e.g.), is excluded from the realm of beauty which is of most importance to Kant's system. This causes Kant to introduce what he calls ideal beauty, which is, so to speak, adherent beauty raised to the highest potency. Ideal beauty is attained by creating a composite image of the item in question and then by reducing this image to a norm. Although according to Kant the imagination accomplishes this by means of a dynamic effect, he does not deny that it would be impossible to arrive at the same result mechanically by simply adding together all the elements and then dividing the sum. In other words, what Herder regards as a psychological process, Kant sees as a rational, mechanical process. And because Herder emphasizes the psychological, ideal beauty must of necessity be an individual matter, dependent only upon the psychological make-up, development, and ability of the individual in question. Kant's process, like all the rest connected with his aesthetic, is not empirical, but entirely *a priori*, taking place within the mind of the subject, with emphasis on the rational and intellectual, rather that the psychological.

According to *modality*, the fourth moment: "Schön ist, was ohne Begriff als Gegenstand eines *notwendigen* Wohlgefallens erkannt wird." [21] As Kant himself tells us, this necessity is of a special kind. It is not a theoretical objective necessity, since then it would be recognized *a priori* that everyone would feel pleasure in any object designated beautiful. Nor is it a practical necessity, because then pleasure would be the necessary result of an objective law and would mean that one unconditionally had to act in a certain way. Therefore, Kant concludes, the necessity is exemplary. ". . . d.i. *eine* Notwendigkeit der Bestimmung *aller* zu einem Urteil, was wie Beispiel einer allgemeinen Regel, die man nicht angeben kann, angesehen wird." [22] Kant goes on to say,

---

[21]   *Ibid.*, V, 324, par. 22.
[22]   *Ibid.*, V, 320, par. 18.

which is of special interest to us, that since the aesthetic judgement is not an objective cognitive judgement, this necessity cannot be derived from definite concepts. Thus in order to facilitate the necessity of judgement of taste Kant presupposes the existence of a *sensus communis*. "Also nur unter der Voraussetzung, dass es einen Gemeinsinn gebe (wodurch wir aber keinen äussern Sinn, sondern die Wirkung aus dem freien Spiel unsrer Erkenntniskräfte verstehen) . . . kann das Geschmacksurteil gefällt werden." [23] This *sensus communis* is essentially different from understanding because it does not judge by feeling, but by concepts. As one commentator has observed, "it merely repeats in a different form what has been said under the second characteristic." [24] Later on in his third *Kritik* Kant further defines the nature of this *sensus communis* and emphasizes two aspects of it which have been of considerable interest to us – its subjective and *a priori* character. "Unter dem *sensus communis* aber muss man die Idee eines *gemeinschaftlichen* Sinnes, d.i. eines Beurteilungsvermögens verstehen, welches in seiner Reflexion auf die Vorstellungsart jedes andern in Gedanken (a priori) Rücksicht nimmt, um gleichsam an die gesamte Menschenvernunft sein Urteil zu halten, und dadurch der Illusion zu entgehen, die aus subjektiven Privatbedingungen, *welche* leicht für objektiv gehalten werden könnten, auf das Urteil nachteiligen Einfluss haben würde." [25] Thus Kant, when faced with his system denying the existence of a communicative phase of the intellect, here specifically that of art, resorts to the *deus ex machina* of the *sensus communis*, just as Leibniz had to resort to "pre-established harmony", when he found that his concept of the monad overemphasized its exclusiveness. Kant is then able to declare that "empirically the beautiful interests only in society". Despite Kant's admission of the *sensus communis*, for him the beautiful remains subjectively determined, whereas for Herder, whose idea of a *geistige Band* is, in some respects, comparable to Kant's *sensus communis*, the beautiful is deter-

[23]   *Ibid.*, V, 321, par. 20.
[24]   Edward Caird, *The Critical Philosophy of Immanuel Kant* (New York, 1889), II, 470.
[25]   Kant, *Werke*, V, 389, par. 40.

mined by the subject, but must first be present in the object. Herder's whole idea of a *geistige Band* emphasizes his belief in the ability of the various objects of creation to commune with one another, and of one object to influence the growth and development of another. Indeed, for the organism to grow and develop as it should, it must be subjected to outside influences, for although the potential for *Humanität* is present in every human being, this potential remains latent until stimulated by outside influences; then it begins to unfold. And those influences which contribute the most to this growth are those which can be characterized as the true, the good, and the beautiful. Kant, however, ascribes empirical attributes to beauty or to the judgement of taste, that all important medium in his aesthetic whereby something is declared beautiful in the first place, in the one case of the *sensus communis* only. Otherwise, as our discussion of the four moments makes clear, Kant's aesthetic is basically a mechanical, subjective, abstract system which is divorced from reality and which gives little or no consideration to the all important work of art itself. Where Kant does come to terms with the meaning of art he will not, or can not recognize its formal, structural, and compositional elements which originate in the soul, and not in the intellect. His one-sided, anti-sensuous position is always inclined to reduce art to the vehicle of mere ideas.

If for Herder there can be no aesthetic experience without an object, then the question immediately arises: what kind of an object? Regarding form, the outward manifestation of the object, the means whereby the object becomes perceivable to the subject's senses, Herder has this to say: *"Wohlgestalt, gefällige Form* der Körper ist eine Verbindung ihrer Theile zu einem Ganzen, zu dem Ganzen, das dieser Körper seyn soll . . . *Wohlgestalt* ist uns eine gefällige Fassung und Zusammenordnung der Theile eines Körpers zu einem Ganzen. Da nun aus Ruhe und Bewegung die Harmonie der Natur zusammengesetzt ist: denn der Körper soll *in sich bestehen,* und die ihn constituirenden Kräfte sollen *aus sich wirken"* (XXII, 47). Thus in order for a form to be beautiful it must possess a certain harmony, that is, as Herder often puts it, there must be "one from many". All of the various parts of the whole must be united in such a way so that the whole can perform its appointed function, so that its own powers may, when stimulated, aid in its development, while at the same time they project themselves outward and stimulate other organisms to growth and development. As Herder tells us, neither the finished form of the whole nor the form of any one of its parts owes its existence to any haphazard or chance occurrence, for it is through this form that the very being, the soul of the object is expressed. The form itself is the result of natural laws revealing themselves corporeally to us as beauty, but before it can be found to be beautiful the form must represent a maximum of its type. "Die sinnliche Wahrnehmung dieses Maximums . . . ist das Gefühl der Vollkommenheit eines Dinges, seiner Schönheit" (XXII, 48). Since for Herder perfection means the harmonious union of all the elements of the object, both outer and inner, it was natural for Herder to reject Kant's differentiation of three kinds of satisfaction. In order for an object to attain perfection it must attain all three of these elements, and not just one. In summary of his findings that objective reality is prerequisite to sensation and perception, Herder writes: "Was empfunden werden soll, muss *Etwas* seyn, d.i. eine Bestandheit, ein Wesen, das sich uns äussert; mithin liegt jedem für uns Angenehmen oder Unangenehmen ein Wahres zum Grunde. Empfindung ohne Gegenstand und desselben Begriff ist der menschlichen Natur ein Widerspruch, also unmöglich" (XXII, 52). Herder's conclusions here in relation to the aesthetic experience are based on those formulated in his psychology. To claim that Herder believes the body is a prerequisite of the soul is to make of him a materialist, as Begenau [26] has attempted to do, and to misunderstand Herder completely. For as we have already seen, it is through the creative power of the soul that the body comes into being. Now although the body is not prerequisite to the existence of the soul, it is prerequisite to its revelation and growth, since it is through the medium of the body that the soul is perceived, and it is through the medium of the body that it establishes sensuous contact with the world about it. This explains why Herder is so insistent on the importance

[26] Heinz Begenau, *Grundzüge der Ästhetik Herders* (Weimar, 1956), p. 20.

of objective reality to the aesthetic experience. The body of the
object for Herder is the gateway to the spirit, and consequently
plays an all important function in the aesthetic experience which
can never be ignored, such as Kant does.

In order for any object to influence the development of an
organism, the attributes of the object must first be appropriated
by the organism. In man, the highest organism and the only one
capable of an aesthetic experience, this appropriation is the task
of the senses, and that part of the object with which the sense
first comes into contact is its form. Repeating much that he had
already previously formulated in the *Viertes Wäldchen* and *Plastik*, Herder distinguishes between the two higher senses, sight and
hearing, and the two so-called base senses, taste and touch, a distinction which for Herder seems to be based solely upon whether
the sense is a direct sense or whether it requires a medium. Hearing differs from sight and touch in that it is concerned solely with
sound, and so plays no role in the appropriation of the phenomenon as such. The same may also be said of taste. Thus the actual
appropriation of the object becomes then a function of either
sight or touch. Sight, it will be remembered from previous discussions, is limited to surface perceptions, e.g. color, whereas
touch is actually able to perceive bodies and shape. But whatever
the sense involved, the most important thing to be borne in mind
is its function in the aesthetic experience. "Die hellste *Synthesis*, ein unwandelbares Eins zu constituiren, ist das Geschäft des
Sinnes" (XXII, 58). Thus the function of the sense is to aid in
bringing about the harmonious unity which is prerequisite to perfection and thus also to the beauty of the object. The sense itself
cannot actually make the object beautiful, but it is the all important gateway through which the subject is able to appropriate the
harmony and the beauty that is present in the object. In the case
of taste and touch this can be accomplished directly without the
intercession of a medium. For sight and hearing however, the
two so-called fine senses, the mediums of light and sound, respectively, are necessary. In summation of this arrangement, Herder
writes: "Statt dass bei den niedern Sinnen Subjekt und Objekt in
der Empfindung gleichsam Eins wurden, fanden wir im vorigen

Gespräch bei unsern feinern Organen, dem Gesicht und Gehör *to metazu*, ein *Medium*, das zwischen den Gegenstand und den Empfindenden trat, jenen, den Gegenstand, ausdrückend und abbildend, diesem, dem Empfindenden, den Aus – oder Abdruck harmonisch zuzählend. Mit Recht nannten wirs also den *Exponenten der Verhältnisse* zwischen Objekt und Subjekt, und bei angenehmen Empfindungen den *Schlüssel ihrer Harmonie*" (XXII, 74).

The theme which determines Herder's disagreement with Kant and his own treatment of various aesthetic questions in the first part of the *Kalligone* is artistic perception, or more specifically, the appropriation of reality through the medium of art. Herder's concern for the object, and for the senses which appropriate the attributes of the object, are all contributions to the development of this theme. Although the artistic creations of man are those which first come to mind when one speaks of the aesthetic experience, they are, of course, by no means the only objects which can play a role in such an experience. Since Herder believes that man's creations must forever fall short of these of the Great Creator, his idea of the object of an aesthetic experience also takes in the various forms within nature, each of which has a beauty and pleasantness all its own. Despite Herder's recognition of the importance of natural beauty, we cannot agree with Nohl's[27] assertion that Herder becomes preoccupied with natural beauty to the neglect of artistic creations and thus brings about an unbridgable gap between his aesthetic theory and practice. Looking about him Herder finds natural beauty on every hand, but regardless of whether the beauty is natural or artistic, the importance of the object in the aesthetic experience lies in its role as stimulant of the concept, that part of the object that the soul is able to appropriate. "In beiden Sinnen waren Licht und Schall weder Objekt noch Subjekt; sie standen aber zwischen beiden, und erzählten Diesem, was an oder in Jenem vorginge, ihm harmonisch oder disharmonisch. Dies erregte Gefühl war *Begriff*, von der Sache, wie durch diesen Sinn der Empfindende sie erlangen konn-

[27] Herman Nohl, *Die Ästhetische Wirklichkeit*, 2nd ed. (Frankfurt, 1954), p. 83f.

te, mithin Wahrheit" (XXII, 75). Herder's belief that beauty always exists in some form, and that this form is inseparable from its concept in the mind of man, is at direct variance with Kant's second and fourth moments. Although each of these concepts may vary from individual to individual, depending upon his own personality and acuteness of sense, they nevertheless are always present. Each concept also contains something of the purposiveness of its form within itself, for in the mind of the subject there is always present some sort of recognition, even if it be unconscious, as to why the object is designated beautiful. Thus the child is attracted to glittering stones for one reason, the minerologist for another. But both find the stones beautiful. Why? Because as Herder explains it, man's perception has been able to appropriate harmoniously for itself the *Maximum* of the object, thus finding the object beautiful.[28] Herder reminds us again and again that the very form of the object gives either a pleasant or unpleasant sensation. For example, slimy objects and creatures, creatures that crawl, objects with no definite form or shape, all produce unpleasant concepts and are repelling to man.[29] But the closer any living object approaches the form of man, the more agreeable it becomes to man, himself the highest organic form, the pattern and measure of all other organic forms. Form attains its position here in Herder's system because of its association with the object, which for him is one of the factors in any aesthetic experience. Kant too, it must also be mentioned, talks a great deal about the importance of form. Suffice it to say at this point, in favor of a more detailed treatment later on, that for Kant form was "pure" form, and as such cannot be compared with Herder's idea of form, which is organic and compositional and subject to dynamic structural and formative principles, and not *a priori* limitations of the sensuous world determined by rational laws.

Three important factors, the sense organ, the object, and the appropriating power determine the distinctness of the aesthetic

[28]   On this concept of the *Maximum* in Herder's aesthetic see Wilhelm Dobbek, "Die Kategorie der Mitte in der Kunstphilosophie J. G. Herders", in *Worte und Werte*, ed. Gustav Erdmann and Alfons Eichstaedt (Berlin, 1961), p. 72f.

[29]   Haym, II, 752 disdainfully calls this Herder's aesthetic of the ugly.

concept. In addition to these factors Herder also establishes three moments of his own which are indispensable to any object or sensation of beauty in opposition to Kant's four moments. "*Wesenheit* des Dinges, *innere Bestandheit und Einheit*, es sey rein in sich oder in constituirenden Theilen, muss daseyn im Objekt, selbst des schönen Traumes. Zweitens. Es muss sich *darstellen*, d.i. reell ausdrücken, empfindbar zeigen. Diese Darstellung, sein lebendiger Ausdruck, muss drittens meinem Organ, wie meiner Empfindungs- und Vorstellungsfähigkeit *harmonisch* seyn" (XXII, 104). Herder's three moments, not unlike Kant's four, are formulated in an attempt to answer two questions which must be the concern of every aesthetician: what is the beautiful, and how is it ascertained? Kant maintained that the concept of beauty originated in the mind of man, and that the formulation of this concept was entirely an intellectual matter. Herder, on the other hand, steadfastly pleads for recognition of the role of the object, and finds the aesthetic experience psychological rather than intellectual. In an effort to elucidate further his position, Herder turns to a historical survey of the ideas of great philosophers of the past. Herder reminds us in answer to his own question concerning the nature of beauty that Socrates said that the beautiful is that lasting quality of the thing itself, its inner form. Recognizing this, Socrates stresses the importance of harmony between the outer and the inner. It was not, however, in the formulation of Socrates, but rather in that of a later thinker, referred to by Herder only as "the philosopher", but in reality Baumgarten,[30] that Herder adopted and made his own concept of perfection.

On the concept of perfection Herder's aesthetic either stands or falls. His concept of perfection, in turn, either stands or falls on his concept of the spirit (*Geist, Seele*). It is not the form of the object alone, but the spirit within the form that is responsible for any sensations of beauty. The subject does not enjoy the form alone, but the essence within the form, its spirit. "Ich geniesse den Wesenhaften Zweck, ich lebe im Geist des Werkes. Im Geist: nicht in der todten Form; denn ohne Geist ist jede Form eine

[30]   Armand Nivelle, *Les Théories Esthétique en Allemagne de Baumgarten à Kant* (Paris, 1955), pp. 30, 35, 70, 255.

Scherbe. Geist erschuf die Form und erfüllt sie: Er wird in ihr gegenwärtig gefühlt; Er beseligt" (XXII, 101). As was clearly established in both the *Viertes Wäldchen* and the *Plastik* Herder's perfection is a perfection with regard to content, not form. The formulation of this objective perfection is "Eins aus Vielem",[31] that is to say, all the various parts of the object have been united into a harmonious whole. Whenever this condition has been met, the purpose of the object has been fulfilled and a concept of it has originated, a concept which according to its very definition is the representation of the object which the subject seeks to appropriate. But despite any perfection in the object itself, unless it be a living organism, it still remains an empty form without the mixture of a spark from the subject. (Aping Kant, Herder gives this empty form the pejorative designation *reine Form*.) Not until that moment when the subject seeks to appropriate for itself the object, does animation of the object take place. That is, through the process of empathy the subject thinks a spirit into the object. From this moment on the aesthetic experience begins, an experience which is based on a complementary exchange between subject and object. The subject seeks to appropriate the object for its own, during which process the object in turn works upon the subject. Written down in one short paragraph,[32] these thoughts are a clear statement of Herder's understanding of the aesthetic experience.

Whereas the spirit is the all important factor in the aesthetic experience for Herder, Kant delegates this position to form, thus precipitating a disagreement of considerable significance in the history of classical aesthetics.[33] Herder never denies the importance of form, but does in the final analysis consider content of greater importance. Both aestheticians frequently talk about the

[31]   *SWS*, VIII, 56f, XXI, 96f, XXII, 267f.
[32]   *SWS*, XXII, 102.
[33]   Franz Schultz writes in *Klassik und Romantik der Deutschen* (Stuttgart, 1952), p. 26f. that with the concept of inner form classical aesthetics either stands or falls. Jacoby says the greatest aesthetic question of the time of Herder and Kant is: "... ob die Schönheit in der Oberfläche der Gegenstände liege oder in Ausdrucke inhaltlicher Vollkommenheit" (p. 67). See also H. A. Korff, *Geist der Goethezeit* (Leipzig, 1957f), II, 423-428.

form, each, however, has his own particular idea of what constitutes form. Form for Herder is the visible outward manifestation
of the spirit of the object, the *Schlaube* of the Shakespeare essay,
that part of the object which is especially subject to temporal and
spacial modifications. Form is important because by means of it
the spirit is identifiable. Kant's concept of form, not unlike his
whole aesthetic, is of a contemplative nature. Form for him signifies the happy relationship of the various parts of those concepts
to be designated beautiful within the mind. True to his desire to
establish beauty as absolute, transcendental, and ideal within the
mind of man, Kant makes all that pertains to content dependent
upon form, or stated in the words of Korff: "Schönheit ist nur
schöne *Form*. Ihr Begriff bezieht sich auf ein allerallgemeinstes
Formprinzip, das von jedem Inhalte unabhängig ist." [34]

Kant centers his discussion of form around its significance for
the judgement of taste, and secondly, for the concept of perfection. Kant tells us that for an object to be determined beautiful
– he uses colors and tones as his examples – it must be regarded
as pure. The purity of the object, in turn, is determined solely on
the basis of its form. "Das Reine aber einer einfachen Empfin-
dungsart bedeutet: dass die Gleichförmigkeit derselben durch
keine fremdartige Empfindung gestört und unterbrochen wird,
und gehört bloss zur Form." [35] Specifically rejecting the possibility
of any augmentation of the form by other attributes of the object,
since the latter would be detrimental and prejudice to good taste,
Kant declares: "In der Malerei, Bildhauerkunst, ja allen bilden-
den Künsten, in der Baukunst, Gartenkunst, sofern sie schöne
Künste sind, ist die *Zeichnung* das Wesentliche, in welcher nicht,
was in der Empfindung vergnügt, sondern bloss, was durch seine
Form gefällt, den Grund aller Anlage für den Geschmack aus-
macht." [36] After further making it clear that this prerogative of
form extends also to those things which serve as the external
complements to the complete object, Kant summarily dispels any
doubts about the position of form in his aesthetic by stating:

[34]   Korff, II, 490.
[35]   Kant, *Werke*, V, 304, par. 14.
[36]   *Ibid.*, V, 305, par. 14.

"Doch in aller schönen Kunst besteht das Wesentliche in der
Form, welche für die Betrachtung und Beurteilung zweckmässig
ist." [37] Although Kant admits that perfection, which he defines as
"objective inner purposiveness", cannot be dismissed without
some consideration, since it does come close to the predicate of
beauty and since certain celebrated philosophers [38] have regarded
it as synonymous with beauty, Kant's position in regard to the
concept of perfection must be a foregone conclusion, since the
paragraph heading in which he discusses this concept bears the
conclusive title: "Das Geschmacksurteil ist von dem Begriffe
der Vollkommenheit gänzlich unabhänging." [39] Whereas for Herder perfection is one of the prerequisites to beauty, since by definition perfection indicates a state of harmony and unity within
the object, without which there can be no beauty, Kant divorces
it completely from beauty and, in his usual manner, considers
perfection a separate and distinct attribute. But the concept of
perfection, that had been one of the main tenets of aesthetics
throughout the eighteenth century, and as is upheld by Herder,
has no place in Kant's aesthetic.

In the second part of the *Kalligone*, section five, under the
heading *Kritische Definition der schönen Künste*, Herder specifically addresses himself to Kant's assertion that "in all beautiful art the essential exists in the form". Herder replies to this
with the following statement, which is one of the most significant
passages of the entire work, and which states one of the most
fundamental theses of Herder's aesthetic. "Dies grosse Krite-
rium der kritischen Kunst, das uns bereits *formelle* Dichter und
Künstler ohne Materie, griechischen Formen ohne Form gegeben, ist selbst die leerste Wortform, die es je gab. Form ohne
Inhalt ist ein leerer Topf, eine Scherbe. Allem Organischen
schafft der Geist Form, die Er belebet: ohn' ihn ist sie ein todtes

---

[37]   *Ibid.*, V, 428, par. 52.
[38]   Kant probably had reference to Baumgarten, but the statement could
just as easily apply to Herder, or for that matter to any of the classical
German aestheticians. See Ernst Cassirer, *The Philosophy of the Enlightenment,* trans. Fritz Koelln and James Pettegrove (Princeton, 1951), p.
338f, esp. p. 341 and p. 342, and Korff, II, 435.
[39]   Kant, *Werke*, V, 306, par. 15.

Bild, ein Leichnam" (XXII, 193f). As is well known, the idea of the importance of both form and content is not new in the *Kalligone*. The strong affirmative statement of the *Kalligone*, which so forcefully expresses Herder's belief in something more than mere lifeless form, stands in contrast to the questioning title of the early publication, *Ist die Schönheit des Körpers ein Bote von der Schönheit der Seele?* (1766). Although Herder fails to reach the concrete conclusions here that are attained in the *Kalligone*, a definite step is taken in this direction when he declares the third and highest level of human beauty to be spiritual charm and grace. It is, after all, this quality which distinguishes human beauty from animal beauty. In the *Fragmente* the emphasis shifts from the human body to language, but the questions posed and and the problems discussed and solved remain the same. Cognizance is joined with feeling, and thought with expression. As Herder himself expresses it, just as a human stands before a viewer and reveals both body and soul, so must language project itself to the listener as a living body.[40] The *Viertes Wäldchen* (1769) presents the problem of form and content in its entirety for the first time. Proceeding in a manner directly opposite that of Riedel, who first establishes his definitions and then forms his system to suit the definitions, Herder first builds up a system and then derives his definition from this system. The treatise on psychology, *Vom Erkennen und Empfinden* (1778), declares that man is a *Seelenmensch (anthropos psuxikos* [41]), and that in this soul is mirrored an image of the divinity. Reiterating again that word and concept must be one, Herder states that the helper of the soul is none other than language. But it is not man alone who can lay claim to this animation, for indeed, all of nature is permeated with organic powers which are comparable to this human soul (*Menschenseele*). *Plastik,* which likewise appeared in 1778, treats the same basic aesthetic problem, but with a slightly different approach. The question this time is not, "Is the Beauty of the Body a Messenger of the Soul?", but rather, "To what extent is the beauty of the body a messenger of the beauty of the soul?"

[40] *SWS,* I, 395, 399.
[41] Cf. I Cor. 2 : 14.

According to the *Plastik*, the beauty of the human body, such as in a piece of sculpture, by no means rests upon conditions of the outward form alone. Instead, beauty is determined by spiritual life.

This helps to explain Herder's position in regard to allegory. Since allegory for him meant the representation of an abstract idea by means of a concrete figure, an allegorical representation has no place for Herder in the fine arts, at least not in sculpturing. If, however, it is a question of one object being represented by another, then Herder would have no objections. For how else, he asks, is the spirit recognized except through the body? But this body is also dependent upon the spirit in order for it to be recognized as beauty. "Nur die *Bedeutung innerer Vollkommenheit* ist Schönheit." . . . "Schönheit ist also nur immer Durchschein, Form, *sinnlicher Ausdruck der Vollkommenheit* zum Zwecke, wallendes Leben, menschliche Gesundheit" (VIII, 56). Both in this passage and the one to follow, two beliefs stand out above all others. First, it must be clear that beauty not only depends upon the harmony of the outer and the inner, of the content with form, but that beauty is inextricably attached to reality and life. Second, that the spirit completely dominates its corporeal manifestation, that it permeates and animates the body. ". . . *dass jede Form der Erhabenheit und Schönheit um Menschlichen Körper eigentlich nur Form der Gesundheit, des Lebens, der Kraft, des Wohlseins in jedem Gliede dieses kunstvollen Geschöpfes*, so wie hingegen alles *Hässliche* nur *Krüppel*, Druck des Geistes, unvollkommene Form zu ihrem Endzweck sei und bleibe" (VIII, 56). As the complete title of the *Ideen* indicates, this work is not primarily devoted to aesthetics, but rather to tracing the development of forms of life in their historical and genetic dimensions through philosophical-historical ideas. Nevertheless, according to Herder's theory whereby man is designated biologically the medial creation (*Mittelgeschöpf*) among animals, at the same time he represents aesthetically the highest being, the ideal of ideals. The preponderance of man's claim to this distinction rests upon the fact that he has been created for a specific purpose, for the development of *Humanität*, which can perhaps best be described as an inner spiritual perfection within man. "Vom Anfange des Lebens an scheint unsre Seele nur ein Werk zu haben, *inwendige Gestalt, Form der Humanität* zu gewinnen und sich in ihr, wie der Körper in der Seinigen gesund und froh zu fühlen" (XIII, 187).

In the *Kalligone* too, man stands at the pinnacle of creation. But even though his beauty as it is represented by the human form becomes the measure of all beauty, this beauty is only the expression of an inner vitality, which is the true and original being of man. Man is conceived by Herder to have an innate sympathy for the well-being and perfection of all creation. Man, this artistic creation (*Kunstgeschöpf*) as Herder calls him, does not possess this sympathy with the rest of creation by accident, but as the result of a "rule of the beautiful", the *geistiges Band* of the *Viertes Wäldchen.* Applying individually to each subject, this rule nevertheless possesses universal application. The rule itself is quite simple, for as defined by Herder it reads: "Von der uns eingepflanzten Regel, *Harmonie, Wohlseyn*" (XXII, 120). Just as the *geistiges Band* is an innate part of man, defying definition and proof, but nevertheless constantly giving proof of its existence in the every day life of man, so too is Herder's rule of the beautiful instilled within man by the Creator at the moment of creation, and must be accepted more by faith than by empirical fact. But here again the validity of this rule is easily recognizable through its effects. In the very center of Herder's view stands the assumption that the absolutes within man, be it perfection, beauty, harmony or pleasure, can never be "purely" perceived, but rather present themselves to us in constant growth and development. It is then the task of our perception to formulate these absolutes from this developmental process. All these symbols of human existence put together result in man's image of the absolute, perfect, and divine, and it is only through the power of that organ of man which possesses endless possibilities of comprehension and combination, namely the soul, that man comes to a realization of these absolutes through active creative participation in the perceptive process. For Kant, however, all of this was a subjective act of contemplation. Visible evidence of man's participa-

tion in this process can be seen in his attempts to create, where
he strives for a certain orderliness and perfection, but does not
always succeed in attaining this goal. But whenever he does, then
the result is a work of art. This in itself distinguishes man from
all other of nature's creatures, for man alone is endowed with
the ability to produce a work of art. Thus in the creative drives
and tendencies within his own soul, in his relationship with nature's creations, and in his desire to model his own creations on
those of nature, man is subject to this "rule of the beautiful".

B. ART AND CRITICISM: THE FUNCTION OF THE VARIOUS ARTS IN THE DETERMINATION OF THE SOUL'S AWARENESS OF BEAUTY

Having once expressed his view on what constitutes beauty, and
how this beauty is perceived by man, Herder next attempts to
establish how man may attain beauty in his own creations, specifically works of art, and what, in turn, the effects of the work
of art should be on his development and growth. But before considering the position of the specific arts in this process, which
Herder calls "den *Kunstgang der menschlichen Natur*" (XXII,
130), he first turns his attention to a comparison of the differences between art and nature. Nature, as seen by Herder, is an
artist with the universe at her disposal, who is able to do whatever she wishes, but conversely only wishes to do that which she
is able. This is possible for nature because she, unlike man, does
not have to be educated to her role as creator, but possesses this
capacity fully developed. The raw materials of nature are at her
beckon and call, and her ability to use these is exemplified by
man, nature's most richly endowed creation. Whether or not this
is apparent to man, each of nature's products has a definite purpose. The purpose which Herder finds has been delegated to man
is that of artist, which allows Herder to say of man: *"Kunst ist
ihm als Menschen natürlich"* (XXII, 140). As used by Herder
here the term "artist" must be considered in its broadest sense
in order to understand its full implications. The term artist here

must be equated with the term creator, and must signify the full utilization of all the powers at man's disposal in the creation of a work of art. But the big question remaining to be answered is: "Aber wie *wird* er Künstler?" (XXII, 128) Unlike nature man does not receive his artistic ability fully developed, nor does he find his materials immediately at hand. Herder supplies the answer to his own question, which is of course education and training. But before he looks directly at the role of the arts in this process, Herder introduces two other factors which he finds are necessary in any true artist: he can, i.e. he can produce a work of art; and he knows, i.e. he is a theorist. Together, these two factors produce the artist, by themselves the former a practioner or artisan, the latter a mere theorist. Kant too had distinguished between "can" and "know", but his results are quite different from those of Herder. Kant recognizes only one necessary quality in the artist, and this that he be able to produce a work of art. To do this, according to Kant, the artist need not operate according to concepts or theories, and he even goes so far as to say that the artist who does work in such a manner is not a true artist.[42]

Since man is an artistic creature, and since art is natural to him, Herder sees man pursuing five free arts: (1) building, (2) gardening, (3) making of clothing, (4) bodily exercise and fighting, and (5) language. These arts are designated free in the sense that they are liberal arts, i.e. *"Was die Menschheit ausbildet, . . ."* (XXII, 130). Kant also employs the term free arts, but free to him means without compulsion. Each of these five free arts, it should be noted, is performed with a definite function in mind, e.g. building for protection, gardening for food and nourishment, etc., and each of them contributes to the growth and development of man. Now although they might be designated handicrafts or sciences, none of these so-called free arts would qualify as an art according to Kant's system. No matter what his environmental or social circumstances, man will pursue these arts according to Herder. But Kant, using his famous example of the man on an island, denies this and maintains that man acts like a man only as long as he remains in a society where this is demanded. The

[42]   Kant, *Werke*, V, par. 43.

basis of these conflicting views of Kant and Herder lies in their conflicting opinions of the relationship of art and nature. Whereas Herder, although not disclaiming certain similarities between nature and the artist, considers the differences greater than the similarities, Kant puts nature and the artist on the same level and says that originality is the essential in the creative act of both. From this observation he then concludes that nature is beautiful only if it is recognized as an art, while it looks like nature. This recognition is an act of judgement, void of any sensation or concept. Herder, however, seeing a definite function and purpose connected with the activities of each of the free arts, not only rejects Kant's determination by an act of judgement, but also views these artistic activities of man as subordinate to the "rule of the beautiful", since all of these activities not only contribute to the well-being of man, but also to his growth and development. "Da alles dies zum *Wohlseyn* der Menschen geschieht, so müssen jeder Bestrebung zur Kunst Bedürfnisse und Triebe, Begriffe und Neigungen zum Grund liegen, ohne welche kein Bestreben Statt findet. Alles Lebendige in der Natur strebet zum *Wohlseyn*, d.i. die Natur sich, sich der Natur harmonisch zu machen: der Mensch allein kann es mit Vernunft und Ueberlegung" (XXII, 142).

If the so-called free arts are worthy of consideration because of their contribution to the "artistic progress of human nature", then how much more true this should be of the fine arts (*schöne Künste*). Kant recognized three fine arts in his aesthetic: the art of speech, the formative arts, and the art of the play of sensations.[43] Kant further distinguishes between two arts of speech, rhetoric and poetry, and his brief discussion of these arts leads Herder to a treatment of the fine arts. Beyond the fact that for both aestheticians poetry was the supreme art form, any similarity in their views ceases.[44] Two important reasons may be cited as the cause for this lack of agreement, and it should be borne in mind that these reasons not only apply here, but indeed to the whole aesthetic systems of both men. First of all, it must be evident that

[43]   *Ibid.*, par. 51.
[44]   See *Werke*, V, par. 53 for Kant's statement of this.

each begins with a different set of premises, which, of course, precludes any similarity of conclusions. And secondly, whereas Kant is a theorist who works almost exclusively in the abstract theoretical realm, Herder is a realist who works almost entirely in the objective realm of art. Again and again in his discussion of poetry and rhetoric Herder calls upon the greats of literature, thereby revealing his close connection with and great knowledge of historical literary tradition. Herder's concept of poetry in the *Kalligone* has not radically changed from that of the *Fragmente*. Poetry is still the mother tongue of the human race and images are still the means whereby the senses and passions speak and comprehend.[45] According to Herder poetry is the result of an interaction between two other beauties, the beauty of sight and the beauty of sound. With the help of language the poet creates representations, i.e., the words cause an image to arise before us which attracts the senses and passions and which is finally apprehended by them. Because he has created his own world into which we must enter if the poetic effect is to be attained, it can be said that the poet attempts to delude us. Poetry creates and forms; it works through what Herder terms "the power of the inner plastic of the soul". That is, the representations, the images which the poet presents to the senses are merely the beginning of a chain reaction because these, by their own interaction within the soul, awaken other images. "Unglücklich ist der Dichter, der nicht mehr Gedanken zu wecken weiss, als er ausdrückt, dessen Gestalten unserm Gemüth nicht wachsen" (XXII, 300). The poet has an obligation to implant within the soul an image which possesses a certain form, or even a propensity to growth and development, but the soul alone can actually accept the stimulation of these images and then create and form totally new images. In other words, the soul brings about the growth which takes place, while at the same time it is contributing to its own growth and development. Thus Herder recognizes the important part in the poetic effect played by our phantasy, that infinite resevoir of images, sensations, and associations which dwells within the soul

[45]   J. G. Hamann, *Werke*, ed. J. Nadler (Wien, 1949f), II, 197; *SWS* XXII, 145. These both have been cited by us elsewhere.

of every man. Or, in the words of the *Kritische Wälder*, poetry
works through its own innate power. Elsewhere Herder wrote:
"Die Dichtkunst ... ist fast keinen Augenblick dieselbe! sie
schaffet, sie *verwandelt*, Figürlich könnte ich ihr Wesen so die
Verwandlung nennen" (VIII, 103). In lines reminiscent of the
early *Sturm und Drang* essays Herder writes: "Der Naturmensch
schildert, was und wie er es sieht, lebendig, mächtig, ungeheuer;
in der Unordnung oder Ordnung, als er es sah und hörte, giebt ers
wieder" (XXII, 146). Even in his old age Herder is still attracted
by the spontaneity and the original power in the poetry of primitive peoples. He describes the early epics of Homer as a series of
images which, one after the other, pass before our eyes and bring
to life the events on the fields before Troy. But, Herder reminds
us, poetry is not mere history, no matter how much history it
might be. History is but a recounting of what has happened,
whereas poetry not only recounts, it represents. Or to use Aristotle's term, it is a *mimesis*. The drama makes use of the same
techniques as the epic, the basic difference here being that the
representations of the drama, i.e. the various scenes, are presented
live on the stage, thus removing the distance between the spectator and the work and causing the spectator to be drawn into the
action. Consequently, as Lessing had already observed in the
Hamburgische Dramaturgie, the drama has a greater potential
effect on the spectator than any other poetic form. Lyric poetry,
the poetry of feeling, though also consisting of a series of images,
differs from the epic and drama in one important respect. Its
images are more subjective, are more a product of the phantasy
of the poet than those of the epic and drama. But whatever the
literary form, Herder concludes, it has a higher purpose than
merely to play with our powers of imagination, as Kant had
stated. Art has become too much a play, an empty shell without
content. In order for poetry to return to its former heights, content, the ability of the poet to influence man, to uplift him, to
educate him, must be restored.

Now if poetry is no mere play, then neither is eloquence. To
the ancient world eloquence signified an inner disposition, as well
as the verbal expression of this disposition. Herder illustrates his

assertion with a number of examples, then characterizes the various epochs in European oratory, and finally concludes with an especially keen analysis of the problems which have beset German eloquence. For Herder true eloquence is, above all else, characterized by the clear presentation of a clearly thought-through content. The characteristics of a great speaker are to be able to say the most with the least, with such understanding that it penetrates directly into the soul of the listener.

The section on the formative arts need only briefly detain us, since for the most part it is but a repetition of the thoughts Herder had written down in the *Plastik* some years earlier. Prominent among these was not only Herder's conviction that the body is the visible manifestation of the soul, but indeed, that the soul is the formative agent of the body. In the *Kalligone* Herder reaffirms this belief in answer to Kant's statement that "plastic is the art which presents corporeally concepts of things as they might have existed in nature". For Herder, Kant's remark not only ignores the most important aspect of the plastic arts, but indeed of any of the formative arts. Plastic is therefore not an art which "presents concepts corporeally", but which presents "bodies animated by spirit". "Der Ausdruck der plastischen Kunst ist *leibhaft*, also auch mittelst leibhafter Formen *geisthaft*, d.i. sympathetisch-wirksam" (XXII, 173). The body is important as the image of the soul, but it must never be lost sight of that the soul is the essence of the body, without which the body loses both its function and significance.

If in Herder's opinion Kant's understanding of the first two arts had shown itself to be inadequate, then he was at a complete loss to characterize his understanding of music. Considering both music and the art of color *(Farbenkunst)* in the same breath, Kant states that their distinguishing attribute is a concern for tone, which he defines thusly, ". . . die Proportion der verschiedenen Grade der Empfindung (Spannung) des Sinnes, den die Empfindung angehört".[46] Kant can never quite make up his mind about how these two arts act, whether they are sensations, or whether they form in themselves a beautiful play of sensations.

[46] Kant, *Werke*, V, 426, par. 51.

In fact, his whole discourse on music can best be characterized by Haym's statement: "Der Musik war allerdings Kant übel begegnet.[47]

On the other hand, not a single member of the literary generation to which Herder belonged could match his penetrating understanding and deep feeling and appreciation for music.[48] The truth of this statement is substantiated again and again. From the tremendous influence which Herder ascribes to the spiritual effect wrought by the wild and primitive songs of the indigenous populace of his native homeland, to his interest in the psychology of music and its use in the home, school, and church, and finally to his recapitulation of the results of the previous discussions on music in the *Kalligone*, one finds nowhere such fascinating accounts of music in the writings of eighteenth century German literature. For Herder every elastic body in nature emits a sound from its innermost being when it is struck. Man becomes a participant in this process for he has compassion *(Mitgefühl)* with any object whose sound comes to him. In itself each tone is individual, each has its own power, and each produces its own effect. These individual tones exist according to a scale, and when harmoniously combined in their comings and goings these tones produce what we call music. *"Alles also, was in der Natur tönt, ist Musik"* (XXII, 180). With this assertion Herder has placed music within the realm of objective nature, from which he consistently draws his knowledge.

In the *Kritik* Kant had written that the feelings of music are produced without, rather than within us. Herder's reply to this is a good example of his understanding of the psychology behind an aesthetic effect. In fact, Herder's whole approach to music might be regarded as an effort to understand music psychologically. In the *Viertes Wäldchen*, the first place Herder makes any significant observation on the nature of music, he writes: "Es gibt dunkle Stellen in der Geschichte der Völker und des Menschlichen Geistes in verschiedenen Zeiten, die sich nicht, als blosse Geschichte verstehen lassen, die oft unverstanden

[47] Haym, II, 756.
[48] Cf. Schultz, p. 210.

verlacht werden, und nur durch gewisse Psychologische Känntnisse Licht erhalten können. So ists mit der Musik der Völker" (IV, 105f). Herder's preoccupation with the psychological aspects of music has prompted Walter Wiora to write: "Im Gegensatz zu Autoren, welche die antiken Musikfabeln wundergläubig nacherzählen oder skeptisch als Kuriostitäten belächeln, geht es Herder um ihr psychologisches Verständnis aus dem Wesen der Musik und der Seele.[49] Thus Herder calls the bucolic songs of the Greeks "Cultur ihrer Seele", (XXIII, 300) and the aesthetics of music "eine *Musikalische Monadologie*" (IV, 114). The songs and melodies of a people are a revelation of their character. "Die Nationalmelodien jedes Volks enthüllten seinen *Charakter*" (XXII, 69). Feelings, Herder claims in answer to Kant, are produced within us; only the sound is produced without. To understand fully why Herder says this we must draw upon his accounts in such earlier works as *Vom Erkennen und Empfinden* and the *Viertes Wäldchen*. Just as light is the medium of the sense of sight, so too is sound the medium of the sense of hearing. This sound is not *a* tone, but an aggregate of tones. The sense of hearing, it should be remembered, is the closest of all the senses to the soul, and music is its most powerful aspect.[50] Music is a spirit, and as such can penetrate directly into the very depths of the soul. " . . . denn sie ist Geist, verwandt mit der grossen Natur innersten Kraft, der *Bewegung*" (XXII, 187). But sound, as the medium and aggregate of the tones, touches only the outer extremities of the soul, in this case the organ of hearing. How then is the inner feeling produced? The process here is essentially the same that we have previously noted in connection with the soul's creative ability to produce images. When a tone penetrates into the soul, the soul responds to the tone. Feelings and sensations are awakened and projected outward. This audible sound, which is a pouring out of the feelings of the resounding object, in turn creates new feelings in the listener, and so continues in a chain reaction. As a result of

[49] Walter Wiora, "Herders Ideen zur Geschichte der Musik", in *Im Geiste Herders*, ed. E. Keyser (Kitzingen, 1953), p. 96.
[50] See *SWS*, IV, 112.

this psychological process Herder compares the creatives powers of music with those of the soul. "Schöpferin bin ich [Tonkunst], und ahme nie nach: ich ruffe die Töne hervor, wie die Seele Gedanken hervorruft, wie Jupiter Welten hervorrief, aus dem Nichts, aus dem Unsichtbare" (XV, 233). These creative powers of music find a further extension in the effects which they exert upon man. "Wir kommen hier wieder in ein lebendiges Feld der Dichtkunst, wo sie *würkte*, wo sie *lebendige That* schuf. Alle Nordischen Völker, die damals wie Wellen des Meers, wie Eisschollen oder Wallfische in grosser Bewegung waren, hatten Gesänge: Gesänge, in denen das *Leben ihrer Väter*, die *Thaten derselben, ihr Muth und Herz lebte*. So zogen sie nach Süden, und nichts konnte ihnen widerstehen: sie fochten mit Gesange wie mit dem Schwert" (VIII, 388f). But the supreme effect which Herder attributes to music is as a humanizing agent of mankind. Music, like poetry, stimulates growth and development of man's soul, and so brings him closer to the attainment of that goal which Herder recognizes as the purpose of life, *Humanität*. "Die Griechen hatten das Wort Humanität nicht: seit aber Orpheus sie durch den Klang seiner Leyer aus Thieren zu Menschen gemacht hatte, war der Begriff dieses Worts die Kunst ihrer Musen" (XVII, 150). "*Durch Musik ist unser Geschlecht humanisirt worden*: durch Musik wird es noch humanisiret" (XVII, 172).

One need only to mention language to see that the tremendous power of the sense of hearing, which Herder rightly calls attention to, is not confined to the art of music alone. Unarticulated tones, a cry perhaps, are the beginnings of language in man. Herder believes that if one can prove that man found music through language, then it follows that individual accented tones are the origins of music. Whenever language reaches the stage that it momentarily forgets the necessity of thought and feeling, and cultivates tone for the sake of tone, then a step has been taken in the direction of music. Singing language, which tried to express passion and feeling, and not the song of the bird, is the natural source of music. The close relationship of language and music is further evident in lyric poetry, which for Herder was the highest and most preferred form of verbal art, and which for him represented a combination of the two elements language and music. "Und da dies Empfindungsreiche Wesen der Musik von jeher so nahe an der Sprache gewesen: so ist hier die *Musikalische Poesie*, über die wir kaum einen Versuch der Theorie, wohl aber mehr Praktische Muster haben, der grosse Vorhof zur Pforte der allgemeinen Musikalischen Aesthetik" (IV, 120). Herder's knowledge and appreciation of music undoubtedly contributed greatly to his understanding and feeling for lyric poetry.

But the power of tone manifests itself in still another manner. Since the tones of music are timed vibrations, they move the body just as feeling moves it. This rhythm finds its expression in dance and in the gestures which accompany dance and music. Especially among primitive peoples these two factors are important companions of music. Through a balanced combination of music, dance, and gesture, and in other instances the word, all moulded together in one expressive art form, the effect is heightened beyond that of the capability of any of these elements individually. Thus the dominance of the soul over the corporeal and material is once again made clear. The spiritual element in the music, the tone, is transmitted directly into physical movement as is expressed in dance and all of its attendant features. The medium (*Schall*) however, unlike the word in language, remains entirely neutral since it is not burdened by the many connotations of the word.

The essential element of poetry for Herder is power, and although he does not apply this concept directly to music, such an application is completely justifiable. Contrary to Kant, who found the frequent changes and repetitions demanded in music distasteful, and one gathers from this that he must never have heard a great work of music, Herder sees the very essence of music in its great variation of tones and accents, in its repetitions, in the varied quality and quantity of its vibrations, in its depths and heights, and in its ability to evoke from the listener feelings and responses of tremendous depth.

To be a critic represented for Herder a position of the highest calling, which not only demanded the utmost integral knowledge and finesse on the part of the individual who followed this calling, but also carried with it tremendous responsibilities. One thing which Herder demanded of every critic was that he have taste, but exactly what this rather nebulous designation taste meant was by no means clearly defined, for different people understood by it different things. Concerning taste, Kant had written: "Das Geschmacksurtheil gründet sich auf einem Begriff . . . aus dem aber nichts in Ansehung des Objekts erkannt und bewiesen werden kann, weil er an sich unbestimmbar und zum Erkenntnis untauglich ist." [51] It should be immediately evident that Herder cannot accept this premise of Kant. Kant says that taste is based on a concept, but a concept that has no relation to the object. Once again he denies the role of the object in the aesthetic experience and places the whole taste process in the conceptual realm of the abstract. This becomes even clearer as one reads on in the paragraph, for Kant, seeking to support his original contentions about how taste works, also claims universal validity for this taste judgement on the grounds that its concept lies in what he terms the supersensible substrate of humanity. The disagreement between Herder and Kant here can be easily seen by calling to mind three points of Herder's aesthetic. First of all, as is well known, Herder sees in the aesthetic experience a two way process between subject and object. For him there can be no such experience unless both are present. Secondly, for Herder the aesthetic concept presupposes the existence of an object. Herder does not recognize abstract conceptual concepts. And thirdly, since for Herder not only the aesthetic, but indeed every realm of human activity is bound to reality, he could neither understand nor recognize Kant's claim of a supersensible substrate of humanity.

In the previous paragraph of the *Kritik* (56) Kant had asserted that "each has his own taste, and yet there is only one taste". Herder finds nothing to disagree with in Kant's statement, but when Kant further contends that each individual taste has universal validity and cannot be disputed, Herder cites Lessing as proof of the falseness of this statement. Lessing writes: "Es ist einem jeden vergönnt, seinen eigenen Geschmack zu haben: und

[51] Kant, *Werke*, V, 445, par. 57.

es ist rühmlich, sich von seinem eigenen Geschmacke Rechen-
schaft zu geben suchen. Aber den Gründen, durch die man ihn
rechtfertigen will, eine Allgemeinheit erteilen, die, wenn es seine
Richtigkeit damit hätte, ihn zu dem einzigen wahren Geschmacke
machen müsste, heisst aus den Grenzen des forschenden Lieb-
habers heraus gehen und sich zu einem eigensinnigen Gesetzgeber aufwerfen. . . . Der wahre Kunstrichter folgert keine Regeln
aus seinem Geschmacke, sondern hat seinen Geschmack nach den
Regeln gebildet, welche die Natur der Sache erfordert".[52] As the
ensuing discussion attempts to bring out, the basic disagreement
here extends over and beyond the specific points dealing with
taste. Rather, it is centered in Kant's denial of the role of the
object in the aesthetic experience and in his insistence that the
judgement of taste is not a judgement of cognition (*Erkenntnisurteil*).

Whereas the remarks on taste noted above were largely directed
against Kant's concept of what he terms the judgement of
taste, Herder now turns to summarizing his own ideas on taste.[53]
Taste for Herder is first of all individual; secondly, it does not
have universal temporal validity since it changes with the circumstances: and thirdly, it cannot be regarded as a principle since it
postulates no reason. Dwelling at length on the confusion and
uncertainty surrounding what is meant by taste, Herder observes
that of all our senses it is the most capricious, for according to
time, place, and circumstances "taste" has designated a myriad
of the most varied possibilities. Herder considers taste one of the
spiritual senses (*geistiger Sinn*). In order for it to perform its
function it must be free from all dulling influences so that it can
correctly react to the stimuli which come into contact with it.
Like any other of the senses, it must appropriate the object, analyse
and test it, and then pronounce judgement on it, not judgement

[52] *Lessings Werke*, ed. Julius Petersen and Waldemar v. Olshausen (Leipzig, n.d.), V, 95f. Cited by Herder *SWS*, XXII, 196.
[53] This is one of Herder's favorite themes. In addition to the account in
the *Kalligone* (XII, 207-219), the reader is also referred to two other
works: *Ursachen des gesunknen Geschmacks bei den verschiedenen
Völkern*, V, 595f, and *Von der Verschiedenheit des Geschmacks und der
Denkart*, XXXII, 18f

that is universally binding, but rather a judgement which reflects the effect of the individual object on the individual subject. If the genius has produced a work of perfection, one in which there is unity and harmony in much, then the taste is likely, but not necessarily, to react favorably. Returning to the same relativism he had expounded earlier, Herder reminds us that taste differs according to the organ, the temperament, and the climate, that habits form taste, which in turn produces models willingly adhered to by man, and that new models in turn change taste, sometimes for the good, sometimes for the bad. As Herder understands it the most important thing is not what "taste" one has, the main thing is to cultivate good taste. And the most important consideration for this is: where does your taste lie? i.e., in what do you find pleasure? Herder is not primarily interested in the outward manifestations of taste any more than he is interested in form to the exclusion of content. For as he observes, good taste can inhabit a humble cottage as well as a splendid palace. Taste, to be deserving of the name, must penetrate into the soul of man and must exert upon this soul a positive formative influence. "In der eigensten Funktion unsrers Lebens, in der uns enganschliessenden Sphäre von Empfindungen, Verrichtungen und Gedanken sollen wir uns Geschmack, d.i. den lichtesten Punkt der verständigsten, leichtesten Wirksamkeit mit Lust und Liebe erwerben: oder alles Schöne fernher gebrachter Wissenschaften und Künste wird Zeitvertrieb und Zeitverderb, eine Trödelei, die wir bald beiseit legen, weil sie uns zuletzt. Das Lesen der Alten selbst, wenn es nicht bis zum innersten Kern dringt und uns zu ihren Gesinnungen in einer ganzen Lebensweise bildet, sondern blos Kennerschaft bleibt, ist auch Ungeschmack" (XXII, 215).

Perhaps it is mere coincidence, but by connecting his thoughts on genius with his investigation of Kant's concept of the universality of the judgement of taste, Herder has achieved a subtle irony, for many of Kant's statements on the nature of genius are difficult to reconcile with those he makes about taste. In paragraph forty-six of the third *Kritik* Kant sums up his concept of the genius in four points: (1) Originality is the most important property of genius. (2) Everything the genius produces must be exemplary. These products must not be imitations and they should serve as standards for others. (3) The genius produces his products by means of some mystical process. He does not know how he arrives at his ideas. (4) Genius prescribes rule to art only, and not to science. By openly admitting that according to his concept of genius the process whereby the genius produces his work must remain inexplicable, Kant only strengthens Herder's belief that his whole aesthetic system is nothing but a hocus pocus. The manner in which Kant contrasts works of art and works of science is also unique. Kant explicitly states, he uses Newton as an example, that no matter how great the scientific discovery or how original, the discoverer cannot be classified as a genius. His explanation for this is that the facts of science can be learned and acquired by experience, but no one can learn how to write poetry. Herder is quick to point out that the genius of man, his human greatness, has revealed itself in all of his inventions, activities, creations, and productions. For as Herder so aptly observes, all sciences and arts have their origins in life and experience, and all stand in the service of mankind. *"Genius* ist ein höherer, himmlicher Geist, wirkend unter Gesetzen der Natur, gemäss *seiner* Natur, zum Dienst der Menschen" (XXII, 205). Just as poetry and music are able to influence the growth and development of man, so too do the other creations or inventions of the genius perform a like function.

Having examined Kant's theories of genius, Herder then turns his attention to his own ideas on the subject. In answer to Kant's four points Herder characterizes the genius according to five points.

(1.) Genie ist *angebohren* ... Es ist *Naturart* (nativum quid), es wirkt also aus sich, aus angebohrnen Kräften, mit angebohrner Lust, leicht, *genialisch.* (2.) Der Genius *schaffet, erzeuget, stellt sich dar* ... Und zwar (3.) War er Genius im Augenblick des *Erschaffens*, als ... der göttliche Funke in ihm schlug ... belebte sein Genius ihn; da war die *genialische* Stunde. (4.) Vollführte er was er begann, so stehet sein Werk *genium* und *genialische* da, ein *Abbild seiner* in Vollkommenheit, oft in Fehlern. (5.) Und eben dass wir in ihr den Naturgeist [i.e. what the genius creates], der hier rein und eigenthümlich wirkte, anerkennen, und uns seines, ihn unsres Geschlechts fühlen: dies macht uns *genialische* Freude. Wir werden *mitgenialisch* (congenial) mit ihm (XXII, 203f).

The above characterization of the genius is not, of course, the first time Herder concerns himself with the genius, for the subject of the genius was one of his favorites, and he returns to it over and over again. Although there are scattered references to the genius throughout the corpus of his writing, three works more than any others, in addition to the *Kalligone*, are directly concerned with genius. These are *Shakespear* (1773), *Ursachen des gesunknen Geschmacks bei den verschiednen Völkern* (1775), and *Vom Erkennen und Empfinden der menschlichen Seele* (1774-78). The first of these treatises on the genius, the Shakespeare essay, was written while Herder was still very much under the influence of Hamann and Young. As Köster has observed: "Hamann und Herder verkündeten den *Gefühlsinhalt* des Wortes Genie." [54] In his role as dramatist Shakespeare becomes the representative of the *Sturm und Drang* man par excellence, and Herder glorifies and contrasts his creative and irrational qualities with those of the reasonable normal man of the Enlightenment.[55] As Herman Wolf has observed in his perceptive essay on Herder's concept of genius, the second of the two works mentioned above, *Ursachen des gesunknen Geschmacks*, takes up a problem which stands in the middle of eighteenth century aesthetical interest.[56] During the seventeenth century and the Age of Rationalism, genius and taste has usually been considered one. This had been the position of Baumgarten and Sulzer, both of whom greatly influenced Herder's concept of genius. But to say as Nivelle [57] has that Herder's definition of genius is identical with that of Baumgarten's or Sulzer's ignores the important fact that

---

[54] Albert Köster, *Die Allgemeinen Tendenzen der Geniebewegung im 18. Jahrhundert* (Leipzig, 1912), p. 21.
[55] See Benno v. Wiese, "Genie und Drama", in his *Herder, Grundzüge seines Weltbildes* (Leipzig, 1939), also our detailed discussion in the following chapter.
[56] Herman Wolf, "Die Genielehre des jungen Herders", *DVJS,* III (1925), pp. 400-425.
[57] Nivelle, p. 246.

in Herder's psychology there was no room for a 'faculty" of tastes such as Sulzer conceived of in the genius, anymore than there was room for a faculty of reason.[58] In the *Ursachen des gesunknen Geschmacks* Herder attempts to resolve the problem created by this faulty psychology by re-examining the relationship of the genius to taste, by seeking to establish whether the two are identical or only psychologically different levels, and by considering what, if any, incongruity there exists in this supposed relationship. After examining the question according to psychological methods, Herder comes to the conclusion that genius and taste are not the same, but rather complement one another. "Genie ist eine Sammlung *Naturkräfte*" (V, 601). *Geschmack ist Ordnung in* dieser Menge" (V, 600f). This essay marks a decided change in Herder's outlook from the Shakespeare, and Wolf, commenting on this change, writes: "Zwar wird das Genie noch der Gottheit Ebenbild, ein Funke von Göttlichkeit genannt, aber wir hören keine dithyrambischen Ergüsse über seine kosmische Bedeutung mehr." [59] The new evaluation of *Vernunft* in this essay is also important, for whereas earlier it was something cold and disrupting, now it is something organizing and ordering in a positive manner. The last of our essays, *Vom Erkennen und Empfinden*, which exists in three versions, those of 1774, 1775, and 1778 respectively, shows a progression in the manner and emphasis placed on the various facets of genius. The version of 1774 contains a lengthy characterology and shows that Herder no longer exclusively emphasizes the emotional and affective in the genius, but, as in the essay on taste, places reason in a new light as something ordering and aiding. In the second version the genius is no longer an exceptional occurrence, but rather a potential inherent in every human awaiting development. In the final version of 1778 the emphasis on characterology is replaced by what might be termed Herder's psychology in a nutshell. It remained for the *Kalligone* to draw all these different ideas together and to present them as a unified whole.

Herder's characterization of the genius in the *Kalligone* ac-

---

[58]   See Clark's discussion, p. 215f.
[59]   Wolf, p. 422.

cording to five definite points shows a definite progression, while
at the same time it emphasizes the spiritual and intellectual attributes so important in the make-up of the genius. As has already been established, Herder did not envisage the genius working exclusively in an abstract conceptual realm as did Kant. Nor
did he think of the genius as one who shuts himself off from
reality and his fellow men to lend some sort of an ivory tower
existence, for the one main purpose of the genius is to serve
humanity. Nevertheless, Herder most certainly recognizes that
the genius is a unique occurrence and, in the final analysis, is the
result of a unique inner disposition, if in degree only, which distinguishes him from other ordinary men. The nature of genius,
as described in the *Kalligone*, can best be compared with the nature of the soul. Genius is an innate condition which reveals itself
through innate powers. As the soul reveals itself through the
creation of a body, the genius reveals itself in the creation of
works of art. Within the genius there glows a divine spark which
animates him and causes him to fulfill his purpose and to create.
The end product of this creative drive stands in the image of
the genius' perfection and bears witness to the growth and development which he himself has undergone. Not only is the condition of the genius himself essentially spritual, i.e. of the soul,
the very purpose he serves is spiritually oriented. Herder writes:
"Geist zu erwecken, Kräfte zu beleben, ist ihr Dienst und der
Lohn ihres Dienstes" (XXII, 206). The product of the genius
therefore not only attests to his own development, but also reaches
out and stimulates the development of others by "awakening
spirit and animating energy" within them. At the same time
recognition of the product of the genius causes us to become
"congenial" with him, which signifies that each, by the power
of his own feeling, enters into the soul of the other. Finally,
this congeniality results in the establishment of a *Naturgeist,*
which serves as a connecting link between all of mankind.

Herder brings this second section of the *Kalligone* to a close
with a brief discussion of the role of the critic. Although the
name of Kant is mentioned nowhere, it is not difficult to see that
much of that said is for his benefit. Contrary to Kant, who main-

tains that the role of taste is to judge, Herder assigns this property to criticism. But by judging Herder in no way infers that this should take place according to hard and fast rules. True criticism is a three way proposition. It must recognize the critic, the one who is criticized, and it must fit the work criticized. Criticism, when properly carried out, enjoys the high purpose of instructing the unlearned masses, and is therefore indispensable to a nation. And what about the critic? Herder's answer is short and to the point: "Wer nicht beleben kann, soll auch nicht tödten" (XXII, 221). Although Herder champions the cause of criticism, he warns against the indiscriminent outbursts of a Gottsched or Klotz or Kant, none of whom, as far as he was concerned, is capable of performing the true function of a critic. But in true criticism, as in art, in taste, and in so many endeavours, Herder recognizes a transcendental quality which is bound by neither time nor place. "Das Reich der wahren Kritik ist nur Ein Reich durch alle Zeiten: Aristoteles und Lessing rücken dirckt an einander, und ernstes Schrittes geht die Kritik fort unter den Völkern" (XXII, 222).

C. THE SUBLIME AND THE IDEAL AND THEIR RELATIONSHIP TO THE ATTAINMENT OF MAN'S ULTIMATE PERFECTION

Both the *Metakritik* and the *Kalligone* have frequently been viewed as a hodgepodge of unrelated ideas and theories, totally dependent upon the very ideas they purpose to refute, in which Herder gives vent to all of his resentments against Kant in unsystematic polemic outbursts. Perhaps some justification for this accusation is to be found in the *Metakritik*, for here Herder was admittedly on foreign ground. But careful reading of the *Kalligone* fails to support such a view, for as one progresses through the work it becomes more and more apparent that Herder recognized a certain few points as basic to any aesthetic system, and since he sees these points revealed in every facet of aesthetics, he consequently returns to them again and again. The third and last part of the *Kalligone* is no exception. Devoted primarily to a discussion of the sublime and the ideal, this section is nevertheless dominated once again by the all important consideration of the form-content relationship, with added emphasis on the meaning of beauty for men and the human task of art.

In his detailed discussion of the sublime Herder shows that it, like the beautiful, is essentially an inner state of the object revealed by its outer form. The sublime furthermore, like the beautiful, is based on a certain measure which has its origin in man's knowledge of things.

These simple assertions contain the principal points of disagreement between Kant and Herder over the sublime. Kant refuses to accept the sublime as one of the forms or manifestations of the beautiful.[60] Comparing the beautiful and the sublime, he asserts that the beautiful rests in the form of the object, while the sublime is found in the formlessness of the object. Beauty generates a feeling of harmony and peace, but in the sublime there is a feeling of overwhelming awe which is incongruous and incompatable to the powers of judgement. Beauty is a direct pleasure, whereas the sublime is the result of a recoil, or as Kant says, it deserves to be called a negative pleasure. This results because the initial reaction to the sublime is one in which the magnitude and immeasurable extent of the sublime causes the imagination to be taxed until it fails. Only when the imagination then falls back upon itself does the feeling of pleasure occur. Disputing this, Herder sees in the sublime the highest form of the beautiful. "Das erhabendste Selbstgefühl ist nur ein Gefühl der Harmonie mit sich und der Regel des Weltalls, mithin das höchste Schöne" (XXII, 239). The sublime for Herder is just as much a result of the perfection and harmony between the form and content as the beautiful. Moreover, only that which is perceptible evidence of Herder's basic principle of "one from many" can be considered sublime. As such the sublime reflects the organic organization of man's soul, a soul which is not only the seat of man's combined powers, both intellectual and sensory, but which itself is the organizing agent of everything perceived and sensed

[60] Kant, *Werke*, V, par. 23 and 29.

by man. The basic meaning of *erhaben* indicates a lifting up, a
striving to new heights. The sublime is, in fact, the apogee of
the soul's dynamic and developmental powers, and requires for
both inception and perception a soul which makes the fullest use
of its inherent potential. Whereas Herder's concept of the sublime is essentially psychological, Kant's is rational and transcendental. Rejecting Kant's claim that the sublime is found in the
formlessness of the object, Herder writes: "Enthalten kann das
Erhabne eben so wenig in einer Form seyn, als das Schöne;
beide werden *an* Gegenständen *empfunden*" (XXII, 243). Later in
the discussion Herder further points out that it is only through
feeling that the sublime can be attained and that the whole process of feeling precludes something to feel, i.e. form.

Kant sees the most important distinguishing feature between
the beautiful and the sublime centered around his concept of
purposiveness. For the most part natural beauty, he concluded,
possesses a certain purposiveness of form. The mere fact of its
purposiveness makes it incapable of doing violence to the imagination. Consequently, only those objects which fail to exhibit a
purposiveness of form and thus excite us without any reasoning
about them can be said to be sublime. In nature this means only
those phenomena which intimate the infinite. This observation
leads Kant to distinguish between two types of the sublime, the
mathematical and the dynamical. The mathematical sublime
refers to that which is absolutely great. It is a category of size.
It is our experience of an object we cannot measure. "The
mathematical sublime is aroused by objects manifesting the dis-
crepancy and disparity between the idea of the absolute great,
of totality, and the importance of sense to satisfy that idea, by
the disagreement or incongruity between the aesthetical judgement of magnitude formed by the Imagination and the judgement
of magnitude formed by Reason." [61] As examples of the mathematical sublime Kant lists the pyramids of Egypt, St. Peter's
at Rome, or the Milky Way. Man instinctively tries to use an
anthropomorphic measure on these, but the extent of such objects
is so great as to defy measure. The second type of the sublime

[61] Knox, p. 57.

is the dynamical sublime. It designates power, a power which defies human measurements. In the first place Kant thinks here of natural phenomena such as clouds, an erupting volcano, the boundless ocean, or a lofty waterfall. But for the aesthetic experience of the sublime to take place it is essential that there be an absence of fear from these objects. Kant claims we can regard these objects as fearful without being afraid of them. That is, one can imagine a case in which he could wish to resist them, and yet all such resistance would be in vain. But be the sublime mathematical or dynamical, it remains a purely subjective process which takes place solely in the mind of the subject.[62]

Herder disputes Kant's theory of the sublime on two basic points: (1) For Herder the sublime is the highest form of the beautiful and as such must possess its basic attributes of harmony and perfection. (2) Just like the beautiful, the sublime is to be found in form, i.e., in the object. Essentially, every major disagreement between Kant and Herder has been centered around these basic points. Lack of agreement here further predestines disagreement in all that follows. Herder finds that he cannot accept Kant's assertion that purposiveness in an object precludes a feeling of sublimity. Indeed, insofar as nature is concerned its phenomena assume true meaning for us only after we understand them.

Gewächse, Bäume, Thiere, in allen Gattungen und Arten, lernten wir in der Natur oder in wahren Beschreibungen kennen; sogar fanden wir sie in Systeme geordnet, und studirten an Allen Ein gemeinsames Naturbild, Einen Typus. "So werden, so wachsen, so sind und entwerden sie (sagen wir uns jetzt), darum sind sie so und nicht anders. Was auf diesem Lebensbaume einer in sich wesentlichen Organization und Naturbildung nicht wächst, ist Tand und Traum." Anerkennend diesen Typus, verfolgen wir ihn durch alle Gestalten; welch ein Erhabenschönes und schönes Erhabene geht in ihm auf! In jeder Pflanze ... wird uns diese lebendige Regel sichtbar (XXII, 237).

Herder sees the sublime everywhere in nature, and although Kant recognizes this too, provided that certain conditions are met, his interpretation of the sublime in nature is completely opposite

[62] Kant, *Werke*, V, par. 28.

that of Herder's. Kant writes: "Aber in dem, was wir an ihr erheben zu pflegen, ist sogar nichts, was auf besondere objektive Prinzipien und diesen gemässe Formen oder Natur führte, dass diese vielmehr in ihrem Chaos oder in ihrer wildesten regellosesten Unordnung und Verwüstung, wenn sich nur Grösse und Macht bleiben lässt, die Ideen des Erhabenen am meisten erregt." [63] Herder's reply is simple, yet forceful: "Das Chaos der Natur sah niemand; absolut genommen ists ein Unbegriff: denn Chaos und Natur heben einander auf " (XXII, 245). Repeatedly Herder emphasizes that his concept of nature is one of order and form, while Kant's is one of chaos and formlessness. And within this order and form there is a constant growth and development. The sublime (*Erhabene*) raises (*erhebt*) man to a higher spiritual level, which for Herder is only possible if the lowest state is organically connected with the highest. For Herder formless concepts are synonymous with no concepts. There is no such thing for him as the absolutely great, for as he states, everything great has measure. Where there is form, it is measurable. "Unvernünftiges kann mir die Vernuft nicht gebieten, meiner Einbildungskraft kein absolut Grosses aufdringen, was kein Begriff ist, kein Ungemessene und Unermessliches ohne Masstab. Dies gehöret der Phantasie, und für diese gab mir die Natur in meinen Sinnen und Seelenkräften so wie Organe des Zusammenstimmenden, so Maasse des Erhabnen. In Ansehung Jenes legte sie mir überall Typen, in Ansehung dieses allenthalben Maasstäbe vor" (XXII, 256). Herder's belief in the measurability of all form quite naturally obviates Kant's concept of the mathematical sublime. Where with one breath Kant cites certain structures as specific examples of the sublime, in the next he denies the existence of the sublime in both nature and art. Herder, however, recognizes the possibility of the sublime in both nature and art. So point by point Herder examines Kant's statements, and point by point he shows why there can be no agreement between his aesthetic and the critical philosophy of Kant.

For many of the same reasons already noted that Herder rejected other points of Kant's aesthetic, he cannot come to terms

[63] *Ibid.*, V, 331, par. 23.

with his concept of the sublime. Herder finds only man's soul capable of grasping the sublime, while Kant sees this as a function of judgement. Whereas for Kant the sublime exists in man's idea of the object, for Herder it exists in the object itself, and before the sublime can be perceived by man's senses and channeled into the soul, the object must give evidence of purpose and the subject of recognition of this purpose. For Kant the sublime is purely a designation of size and mass, both of which are absolutes in themselves, completely independent of the idea of growth and development of both subject and object, which is so important to Herder's understanding of the sublime. So absolute is the sublime for Kant that he considers it supra-sensory, and accessible only by reason. Such a view for Herder is the equivalent of saying that the sublime is beyond the perception of man and hence non-existent.

Up to now the discussion has largely been concerned with determining what objects can be designated sublime and what attributes these objects have. Having made clear his reasons for disagreeing with Kant, Herder now turns to the important consideration of the sublime in feeling. The whole concept of the sublime (*Erhaben*), Herder reminds us, has the basic meaning of uplifted, and is thus associated with objects to which one must be uplifted in order to perceive. Similarly, we speak of a feeling of dread (*entsetzen*) when faced with a view of great depth. Thus Herder defines sublime feelings as follows: "Erhabne Gefühle können keine andre seyn, als die sich wirklich *erhaben*, d.i. vom Niedrigen entfernt, in einer Höhe fühlen . . . Ein *Gefühl des Erhabnen*, oder am *Erhabnen* kann nichts als die Empfindung seiner Höhe und Vortreflichkeit seyn" (XXII, 261). Herder finds nothing in these feelings which suggest a suppression of feeling or a cramping effect such as Kant alludes to. Everything connected with this feeling suggests rather expansion of one's breast, looking upward, striving upward, and elevation of existence. According to his description of the whole process of the sublime Herder is thus able to single out one group of objects which more than any other is responsible for producing feelings of sublimity in man. "Die Kräfte, mit denen die Himmelssphäre auf das

Niedre wirkt, sind uns das höchste Bild *erhabenstiller Einwirkung.* Was also auch in menschlichen Kräften dieser himmlischen Höhe gleich wirkt, nennen wir erhaben, himmlisch, göttlich" (XXII, 263f). Herder also sees a significance in the fact that it is the head, the seat of man's most noble powers, anatomically that part of the body which is most uplifted, that man employs to perceive the sublime. By means of a clever play on words he declares that man himself is a sublime, i.e. uplifted creature, and that the feeling of sublimity is one of his natural characteristics.[64] "Dies Hochgefühl in unserer *erhabnen* Gestalt ist der Charakter der Menschheit" (XXII, 262). But as has already been noted above in connection with the differences between Herder's and Kant's concept of the sublime, the sublime for Herder is, in the final analysis, the highest manifestation of the beautiful. So when Herder finally arrives at his conclusive definition of the sublime, it is essentially the same as that for the beautiful. "Der Analogie der Natur zufolge is also *Erhaben* das, was seiner Natur und Region nach mit Einem Viel, und zwar das Viele in Einem still und mächtig giebt oder wirket" (XXII, 265).

Proceeding next to a discussion of what senses can best appropriate the sublime, Herder concludes that the sense of sight is better able to offer us "mit Einem Viel" than any other sense. This does not exclude, however, the other senses. Consequently, the three art forms first mentioned in which the sublime is revealed are those where sight plays a primary role. These are architecture, sculpture, and painting. Writing about Greek architecture, Herder shows why this art deserves the appellation sublime. "Die griechische Baukunst verband ihr *Eins* mit *Vielem* verständiger, heller, leichter, schöner. Wo der Eindruck des *Einen* mächtiger ist, wird uns das Gebäude *erhabner*: wo das *Viele* uns mehr beschäftigt, *schöner*" (XXII, 267). But no more than the beautiful is contained in the outer form alone, is the sublime.

---

[64]   This is reminiscent of what Herder had said earlier in the *Ideen.* Cf. e.g. *"Die Gestalt des Menschen ist aufrecht*; er ist *hierinn einzig auf der Erde"* (XIII, 110). *"Der aufrechte Gang des Menschen ist ihm einzig natürlich: ja er ist die Organization zum ganzen Beruf seiner Gattung und sein unterscheidender Charakter"* (XIII, 112f).

"Das Erhaben-Schöne, in andern das Schön-Erhabne ist der *Zweckhafte Geist,* der den Bau erfüllt, der im Bau wohnet" (XXII, 267). In statues too the sublime is dependent upon the spirit within the body. "Geformte Bilder stehen leibhaft da, wie vom Geist beseelet; der Geist ist es, der mit dem Wenigsten das Meiste in höchster Natur ausdrückt, er ist der Ausdruck der hohen Alten" (XXII, 268). Mere gazing at a statue alone does not suffice to appropriate the sublime within it. Only through a union of the spirit of the subject with that within the object does the sublime become alive and perform its function of raising the soul of the subject to new, yet unknown heights.

Although for reasons already noted Herder has placed those art forms perceived by sight in first place as sources of the sublime, this does not exclude other art forms. Thus music and poetry are also sources of the sublime. But it must be evident that the objects comprehended and the whole process of comprehension will differ here. This basic difference between art forms in which the sublime is perceived by sight and those in which it is perceived by hearing or by a combination of the two, and the basic difference in the process involved, is exactly the same as already expounded by Herder in the *Erstes Wäldchen* where he distinguishes between the plastic and verbal arts. Whereas sight must perceive the sublime in an object which stands as a finished product with no chance of change, hearing perceives the sublime in power, in a succession and progression, in movement, and in a living effect. Herder wants none of Kant's so-called pure objectivity whereby he claims that poetic images, to be effective, must have the same fixed form as a plastic image. For Herder the sublime is bound together with a striving to achieve the highest form of the beautiful, and to realize this there must be action and progress, not stagnation. He writes: "Mithin ruht das wahre Erhabne eigentlich im *ganzen progressiven* Werk des Dichters" (XXII, 274).

In two short paragraphs in which he treats the moral sublime and the sublime in knowledge, Herder concludes his discussion of the sublime. The same basic ideas that determined his thoughts on the sublime in nature and in art are to be found here. Just as an art object must have measure and purpose, so too moral concepts. They are not empty words, Herder reminds us, but must be pregnant with meaning. "Sitten erfodern Maas; ein moralisches Gesetz ist selbst dem Namen nach nicht leere Form, sondern bestimmte Regel" (XXII, 276). And as is to be expected from what Herder had already said in earlier works, he had no understanding for Kant's ideas of a transcendental Supreme Being.[65] Throughout his writings Herder makes it clear that for him the Supreme Being has revealed Himself to man above all through His son, that He is present in the cosmos, and that He is accessible to man. In a forceful statement in the *Kalligone* he explains why he holds to these concepts. "Eine Heiligkeit, die *über* die menschliche Natur liegt, liegt auch *ausser* ihr: Visionen ins Rein-Uebersinnliche zu einer Bedingungslosen Pflicht aus Bedingungsloser Freiheit nach einem Bedingungslosen Gesetz, das über meine Natur hinaus ist, und nach welchem sie doch als nach einem Unerreichbaren immer hascht und greift, sind Katheder-Erhabenheiten, die nichts als an maassende Schwätzer gebähren" (XXII, 276). Knowledge of the sublime however, be it of art, nature, morality, or the Supreme Being, conforms to one general principle which Herder states at the conclusion of his discussion. "Erhaben im Wissen ist, was mit Wenigem Viel giebt, mich auf einfachen Wegen Viel zu erkennen leitet, hell, mächtig, sicher, nicht aufdringende Worte, sondern Kräfte erweckend in mir und Lust, Liebe, Neigung" (XXII, 281).

The impetus for the polemic in *Vom Ideal des Schönes*, which Herder [66] himself especially esteemed and which has been called the most significant part of the *Kalligone*,[67] is Kant's definition of the ideal of the beautiful. It will be remembered from the discussion above that Kant suggests one way to arrive at the ideal is by purely mathematical and mechanical methods.[68] The result of such a process Kant calls the normal idea, which he defines as the image which serves nature as the archetype for her production of members of the same species. But this normal idea is by no

---

[65]   Cf. *SWS*, XXX, 229 and *Gott, Einige Gespräche*, XVI, 438f.
[66]   Haym II, 763, note 84.
[67]   Begenau, p. 109.
[68]   See Kant, *Werke*, V, par. 17 for his discussion of the ideal.

means the whole archetype of beauty. It is only the form. Kant then further distinguishes between the normal idea and the ideal. Only in the human figure, he claims, can the ideal exist, for here it is an expression of the moral. The true ideal of beauty is thus not expressed by any visible attributes, but is determined by what Kant terms a union of pure ideas of reason with imaginative power. Thus Kant removes his concept of the ideal from the empirical realm into the abstract transcendental, for he denies that the ideal of beauty can be perceived in the object. This proves, he concludes, that a judgement according to such standards can never be aesthetical nor can it be a judgement of taste.

For Herder, however, the ideal of the beautiful is not to be sought in the dark recesses of a reflecting intellect, but as he puts it, in the halls of the gods and geniuses, and the ideals of ancient art. Herder derives the concept *Ideal* from the word *Idee*. Ideal, he says, is the most pure form of a thing. It is the object in its most perfect state. Any art which seeks to corporeally represent the most perfect is automatically drawn to the most perfect of forms, which is the human figure. This "reine Idee der Menschheit", as Herder calls it here, is none other than the upright figure of man, his countenance, forehead and stance, in fact, all the concepts which Herder first introduced and discussed in the *Ideen*. Herder admittedly places a great deal of emphasis here on the outer form of man, but it is clear that of greater importance is that which harmonizes the form. And this is the soul. "Hieraus erklärt sich, was man in ihnen die *hohe Ruhe, die stille Würde*, oder *erhabne Einfalt* zu nennen pflegt und unrecht aus der Sittenlehre holet. Es ist die in diese rein-menschliche Gestaltung gegossene, ihr durchaus einwohnende Seele, der Zusammenklang ihrer Glieder" (XXII, 294). Thus Herder sees the ideal of the Greeks as follows: "Es war die *reine menschliche Gestalt, von allem Thierischen gesondert, ihre eigene Vollkommenheiten ausdrückend in allen Charakteren und Gliedern*" (XXII, 294f). This perfection, of course, presupposes a harmony between the body and the soul and can accordingly be seen in the great works of art of Antiquity and the Renaissance, all of which reveal that supreme idea of man, his genius, his soul. This relation of the genius and soul is the result of an internal process which Herder calls a spiritual echo. "Die Gestalt ging in die Seele des Künstlers und ward in ihr *Idee*; eine die Gestalt darstellende *Geistes-Echo*" (XXII, 297). Man can therefore correctly be called the only creature capable of an ideal for several reasons: (1) Man is the highest form of creation; he is the most spiritual of all forms. (2) He is the only creature able to reproduce this ideal through the medium of art. (3) Man alone of all creatures can determine his purpose and strive toward its fulfillment. Herder sees in this ideal, be it in animate form, through a formative representation, or the images called to mind by the words of a poet, a sort of progression. That is, the figure seems to grow before our eyes. It is not difficult to recognize here Herder's concept of power which he had formulated earlier in the *Kritische Wälder*. All of art strives to attain this dynamism and it is only in this striving that Herder recognizes the immeasurable, the high-flown exuberant (*Uberschwängliche*). Herder thus denies Kant's identification of the moral with the ideal. Each for him is a different concept. The ideal is created, but the moral is fabricated and compiled.

Closely related to the matter of the identification of the moral with the ideal is the question of beauty as symbol of morality. In paragraph fifty-nine of the third *Kritik* Kant declared the beautiful to be a symbol of the morally good, and that it is only in this respect that it gives pleasure. Herder's aversion to allegorical representation is well known, and for the same reasons that he condemns them he cannot see the validity of Kant's argument. By declaring the beautiful to be a symbol of the morally good Kant is using the same technique used by the allegorists. He is saying that an abstract idea is represented by a concrete image. There are several reasons why Herder could not accept Kant's statement. First of all, Herder, in true Platonic tradition, considered the true and the good as identical. Secondly, symbol for Herder means form. It ignores the more important spirit. It is a dulled organ which penetrates no farther than the mere form, i.e., the symbol of an object. Thirdly, any symbolic meaning attached to an object is justified by convention alone. The fact that some consider white a symbol of purity does not give to this symbol universal validity. Fourthly, form is dead. Without the spirit it is lifeless. Therefore only through the manifestation, only when the organic powers within the form act, is it possible to discern the purpose of the object. The morally good can be produced by this action, but it can never be considered as identical with the form of the object.

Now if nature in all her manifestations expresses a spirit through form, art must likewise conform to this principle. In art, however, this becomes a revelation of a special kind. "Gehn alle Künste und Wissenschaften des Schönen auf *Bildung* hinaus, da sie die Empfindung schwingen und beleben, da sie Ideen, Gestalten, Charaktere formen; ist und bleibt *sittliche Bildung* im echten Verstande der höchste Punkt menschlicher Bildung, der alle Seelekräfte umfasst und keine Aeusserung ausschliesst" (XXII, 328). This *sittliche Bildung* is the same thing Herder terms *Humanität* elsewhere.[69] Since it is both goal and purpose of mankind, it can never be absent from a work of art. As Herder puts it, the poet must not be wanting the finger of moral grace. Otherwise, his work is destined to remain common. The dispute here between Kant and Herder is again one of content versus form. Kant sees the moral only in the form, while Herder finds it revealed through the perfection, the harmony between content and form, the effect of the organic power.

Not every art is able to carry out the process of formation and education that Herder deems necessary. The so-called beautiful arts and sciences fail to meet the requirements. Only the formative arts (*bildende Künste*), these which shape and mould the character of man are truly deserving of the appellation "schöne Wissenschaften und Künste". "*Bildend* soll diese Gattung Künste und Wissenschaften werden; den *Menschencharakter* in uns bildend" (XXII, 308). Everything about man can be formed: his members, his senses, his phantasy, judgement, reason and understanding, his likes and dislikes. Man in turn is able to shape nature, human society, even mankind itself. All of this is possible because man knows, i.e. he has science (*Wissenschaft*) and because he can, i.e. he has art (*Kunst*). Herder, like his great fore-

[69] Cf. *SWS*, XIII, 154, 161, 163, 182, 184, 187, 191, and many others.

runners Aristotle, Shaftesbury, Winckelmann, Baumgarten, and Lessing, is working toward and looking forward to a science of the beautiful. This science is not to work through a set of laws, but by its principles and methods is to help man recognize the role of the beautiful and to help him realize his own goal and purpose in life. "Dass hier der Mensch, zu würdigen Zwecken auf richtigen Wegen, in der Gestalt des Reizenden und Schönen nur das Wahre und Gute anstrebe, liebe und wähle, dass er durch kein Hinderniss abgeschreckt, durch jede Schwierigkeit ange-feuert werde, seine Idee immer reiner zu suchen, brünstiger zu verfolgen, ganz zu vollenden; dies ist die bildende *Kunst des Lebens* (XXII, 313). And there is one purpose and goal in life above all others: *"Zur Humanität und Religion ist der Mensch gebildet"* (XIII, 154).

Although the reception which Herder's *Kalligone* received at the hands of various scholars in the nineteenth and twentieth centuries has frequently been commented upon during our dis-cussion, little has been said of its effect on Herder's own con-temporaries. In his conclusions Haym remarks that the *Kalligone* was by far the better work in comparison with the *Metakritik*, but that it nevertheless passed by almost unnoticed.[70] The Kan-tians could quite naturally see no more to Herder's aesthetic that they could in his epistemology, while on the other hand such old friends of Herder as Wieland and Knebel,[71] both no admirers of Kant or his critical philosophy, welcomed the *Kalligone* with words of praise. It is thus of no small significance when some thirteen years later in his eulogy on Wieland we find Goethe [72] expounding the same ideas as those of Herder and expressing grave doubts as to the validity of Kant's system. Since Goethe's words so adequately characterize the basic issues which have dominated our discussion, we bring this discussion to a close with several paragraphs from his speech.[73]

[70] Haym II, 765.
[71] Haym II, 766, notes 87 and 89.
[72] What Goethe says in his speech would tend to discount Haym's belief that Caroline's statement that Goethe's principles were the same as those in the *Kalligone* is of little consequence. See Haym II, 766 and note 88.
[73] Cf. Begenau, p. 140.

Denn sein dichterisches, so wie sein literarisches Streben war unmittelbar auf's Leben gerichtet, und wenn er auch nicht gerade immer einen praktischen Zweck suchte, ein praktisches Ziel hatte er doch immer nah oder fern vor Augen. Daher waren seine Gedanken beständig klar, sein Ausdruck deutlich, gemeinfasslich, und da er, bei ausgebreiteten Kenntnissen, stets an dem Interesse des Tags festhielt, demselben folgte, sich geistreich damit beschäftigte, so war auch seine Unterhaltung durchaus mannichfaltig und belebend; wie ich denn auch nicht leicht jemand gekannt habe, welcher das, was von andern Glückliches in die Mitte gebracht wurde, mit mehr Freudigkeit aufgenommen und mit mehr Lebendigkeit erwidert hätte.

Bei dieser Art zu denken, sich und andere zu unterhalten, bei der redlichen Absicht auf seinem Zeitalter zu wirken, verargt man ihm wohl nicht, dass er gegen die neuern philosophischen Schulen einen Widerwillen fasste. Wenn früher Kant in seinen Schriften nur von seinen grössern Ansichten präludirte, und in heitern Formen selbst über die wichtigsten Gegenstände sich problematisch zu äussern schien, da stand er unserm Freunde noch nah genug; als aber das ungeheure Lehrgebäude errichtet war, so mussten alle die, welche sich bisher in freiem Leben, dichtend so wie philosophirend ergangen hatten, sie mussten eine Drohburg, eine Zwingfeste daran erblicken, von woher ihre heitern Streifzüge über das Feld der Erfahrung beschränkt werden sollten.

Aber nicht allein für den Philosophen, auch für den Dichter war, bei der neuen Geistesrichtung, sobald eine grosse Masse sich von ihr hinziehen liess, viel, ja alles zu befürchten. Denn ob es gleich im Anfang scheinen wollte, als wäre die Absicht überhaupt nur auf Wissenschaft, sodann auf Sittenlehre und was hievon zunächst abhängig ist, gerichtet, so war doch leicht einzusehen, dass wenn man jene wichtigen Angelegenheiten des höheren Wissens und des sittlichen Handelns, fester als bisher geschehen, zu begründen dachte, wenn man dort ein strengeres, in sich mehr zusammenhängendes, aus den Tiefen der Menschheit entwickeltes Urtheil verlangte, dass man, sag' ich, den Geschmack auch bald auf solche Grundfässe hinweisen, und deshalbe suchen würde, individuelles Gefallen, zufällige Bildung, Volkseigenheiten durchaus zu beseitigen, und in allgemeineres Gesetz zur Entscheidungsnorm hervorzurufen.[74]

In paraphrase of Goethe's words it can also be said of the *Kalligone* that its importance for Herder's aesthetic, and aesthetics in general, lies in its efforts to present universal categories for inter-

---

[74] Johann Wolfgang v. Goethe, *Zu Brüderlichem Andenken Wielands, 1813*, in *Weimarer Ausgabe* (Weimar, 1887-1912), XXXVI, 338f.

preting aesthetic experience. Although of considerable importance to an understanding of the *Kalligone*, Kant's thought-structure should not be viewed solely in the light of the polemic which it evokes. On the contrary, Kant's ideas serve the important function of providing a framework to which Herder can attach his own ideas. To decide the merits of the *Kalligone* as Haym does according to whether or not it agrees with Kant's premises is to overlook the main intent of the work. In this last of his major works Herder has successfully drawn together *in nuce* the main ideas expressed in his earlier aesthetic writings. Here one meets thoughts and ideas familiar from reading the *Fragmente*, the *Kritische Wälder*, or the *Plastik*. But here more than any other place in his writings Herder has attempted to put each of these ideas in the proper perspective so that each, while maintaining its own identity, becomes an integral part of an all-encompassing pattern. Herder had no desire to become a dogmatic lawgiver. His conclusions are almost exclusively drawn from observations of life. But whether these come from the nature of the beautiful or its creation, the determination of the beautiful or its human purpose, they all recognize the central function of the soul in the aesthetic experience. Only man's soul is capable of the delicate and complex processes required for the determination of the beautiful, its perception, and its ultimate utilization for the development of man. This is the universal which Herder never tires of proclaiming, and which stretches in an unbroken line from the writings of his youth to those of fulfillment in old age.

V

DRAMA: ART AS AN ORIGINAL MICROCOSM

With the exception of what Weber has termed the pseudo theories of the drama chapter of the *Adrastea*, the bulk of what Herder has to say about drama is found in the short, but succinct, Shakespeare essay which appeared as a contribution to *Von Deutscher Art und Kunst* in 1773. Although we are not primarily concerned with this aspect of the essay, it would be well to remember that its organization falls naturally into seven main sections. A brief introduction and conclusion comprise sections one and seven. Between them there are four main divisions. Sections two and three are devoted to a discussion of Greek drama; section four to the French, who wanted to imitate the Greeks and are accordingly *Affen*; section five, which is the heart of the essay, discusses Shakespeare; and section six is another attack against the French.

Renouncing at the very beginning of the essay the paths already followed by so many who would explain, save, denounce, excuse, worship, deny, translate and berate Shakespeare, Herder, with few words, sets forth his program: "... zu erklären, zu fühlen wie er ist, zu nützen, und – wo möglich! – uns Deutschen herzustellen" (V, 208). Herder wants to understand Shakespeare's innermost creative principles, not for their own sake, but in order that they may be useful (*nützen*), which for Herder means that they would influence the growth and development of man. It is axiomatic for Herder that what is, must act and produce, but in order to understand what is, and how it acts, one must first understand the development of its becoming (*Werden*), the principles behind its genesis. As Herder puts this in somewhat symbolic language: "Der Kern würde ohne Schlaube nicht wachsen, und sie werden auch nie den Kern ohne Schlaube bekommen, selbst wenn sie von dieser ganz keinen Gebrauch machen könnten" (V, 209). With these words Herder has set forth another of his basic principles, which is, that the essential (*Kern*) of any matter can be seen only through its outer manifestation (*Schlaube*), that which the essential, the spirit, has created to represent itself. The critical question for Herder, whether it be in connection with drama, with poetry, with sculpture, or even with music is how to penetrate through this outer shell to the core which lies within it.

The discussion of Greek drama, and especially of Sophocles, which is the subject of the second part of the essay, is to show the separate origins, and thereby the basic differences between the drama of the antiquity and Shakespearean drama. Drama originated in Greece, Herder tells us, in a manner in which it could hardly originate in the Nordic countries. Drama was therefore an art in Greece that it could never be in the Nordic countries. This point is firmly established in the following often quoted, but just as often misunderstood lines: "Also Sophokles Drama und Shakespears Drama sind zwei Dinge, die in gewissem Betracht kaum den Namen gemein haben" (V, 210). Elaborating on this observation, Herder explains that the beginnings of Greek drama can be found in such chance occurrences as time, religious beliefs, political convictions, and the prevalent code of morality. Among the Greeks, however, these are characterized by a unique inner unity, which in the tragedy is revealed in what Herder terms a grandiose "Simplicität der Fabel" (V, 210). To such an extent is this characteristic not only of the drama itself, but even of the raw materials which he utilizes, that Herder says of the Greek poet: ". . . dass der Dichter eher Mühe hatte, in dieser einfältigen Grösse Theile zu entdecken, Anfang, Mittel und Ende Dramatisch hineinzubringen . . ." (V, 211). All of the dramas of Sophocles, whom Herder singles out for special mention, bear this stamp of their unique origins, of the "simplicity of plot", or as Herder refers to it here, "a dramatic picture in the midst of the choir".

The underlying formative principle of Greek drama, which he sees revealed on every hand, is, according to Herder, characterized by a press from simplicity to complexity. "Jene *simplificirten* nicht, denke ich, sondern sie *vervielfältigten*" (V, 211f). Theirs is not an art which makes "Eins aus Vielem", but rather one which develops "Aus Einem ein Vieles". Using the simple impromptus of the dithyrambs as their basis, the Greek poets developed these into a labyrinth of scenes, and while each component of the scene retains its individuality, it was the grandeur of the scene as a whole which reached out and enveloped the spectator. Terming this symbolic revelation of the whole "Wahn des Werdens", Herder states that it was in this manner that the Greeks gave greatness to the dramatic action. Their magnificent tragedies, which Herder significantly calls "masterpieces of the human spirit", must never be regarded as finished products. Since they are in a continual state of coming into being, to be understood the Greek drama must be regarded as the action that it was, for only through the dramatic action does the symbolic succession within the drama appear. The simple dithyrambic sensation is thus replaced by the complex tragic experience, whereby each individual action relates to the whole, thereby emphasizing the conformity of the drama to its basic formative principles. The universal is thus revealed through the individual, while at the same time the individual is never lost sight of.

But just as all has changed in the world since the time of the Greeks, so too have the elements from which Greek drama was created. Customs, beliefs, music, dance, manner of expression – all have undergone change. Thus these elements which the Greek tragedy utilized cannot be imitated in the form in which they presently exist with the expectation of acquiring a drama of the type produced in Greece. The French, however, who more than any other people have sought to take over the place vacated by the Greeks, have attempted exactly this. They have adopted and imitated the outward features of Greek drama, the husk; but for Herder they have never penetrated the core. "Man konnte zwar das Uralte, oder gar von andern Nationen ein Fremdes herbei holen, und nach der gegebnen Manier bekleiden: das that aber Alles nicht die Würkung, folglich war in Allem auch nicht die Seele; folglich wars auch nicht . . . das Ding mehr" (V, 213). Although the French theater has attained a degree of perfection the like of which can hardly be imagined, Herder sees this perfection restricted to the outer shell. The French have successfully adopted the rules and the form and many of the other features, but their drama is still not Greek drama. "Warum? weil im Innern nichts von ihm Dasselbe mit Jenem ist, nicht Handlung, Sitten, Sprache, Zweck, nichts — und was hülfe das Äussere so genau erhaltne Einerlei?" (V, 214). Racine speaks a language of feeling, but one which is several times removed from the source; Voltaire has written beautiful verse, but for Herder this is no verse for the theater, for it fails to fulfill the tragic purpose of the drama such as the Greeks knew it. Borrowing from Aristotle, Herder declares that this purpose is none other than to shock the heart, to excite the soul, and to create a dramatic illusion.

Since in his eyes the French drama fails to accomplish this, it cannot be compared to the Greek drama. The French drama is, to be sure, the shell of the Greek drama, but it lacks spirit, life, nature, and truth. Here we hear the Herder of the *Fragmente* again, who declares that imitations, no matter how skillful, can never hope to attain the same level as the original, nor can they be considered at one with the original. By its very nature poetry is a creation, and hence original, while by its very nature an imitation is something false. Imitations therefore have no place in Herder's ideal of literature. Concerning French imitations he writes: "Das Ganze ihrer Kunst ist ohne Natur, ist abentheuerlich, ist eckel!" (V, 216). Herder's comparison of French and Greek drama serves a twofold purpose: first of all it points out the futility and uselessness of imitations if a literature is to arise which accurately reflects the spirit of the time and people who produce it; and secondly, it emphasizes even more dramatically the genius of Shakespeare, who succeeded, at least for Herder, where the French had failed.

But before turning to the crux of the essay, which of course deals with Shakespeare, it would be well to probe deeper into the basic thoughts which underlie Herder's rejection of the French drama. Since the very drama rejected by Herder has been universally acknowledged to be one of the glories of French literature, this drama must possess some merit, even if it has failed as far as Herder is concerned. On the other hand, according to the criteria established by Herder, it must be apparent that this drama could be designated nothing short of a failure. Whereas the drama of both the Greeks and Shakespeare grew up organically out of folk traditions, that of the French originated at a time when the spiritual heritage of France's great philosophers made itself felt in French literature. As a result, the drama of the French stands on an entirely different level than that of Shakespeare's, or for that matter that of the Greek's. Even so the French drama, consider Racine's *Phèdre*, were often dramas of passion where feeling and life were in evidence at every turn, where the psychological conflicts assumed overwhelming proportions. Nevertheless, Herder sees all this in the French drama as mere mechanics which lack any organic justification. He cannot recognize the principle of honor (*honnête homme*) or external dignity because he finds no psychic bridge between the outer and inner aspects. Although frequently embroiled in psychological conflicts, the characters are never individual personalities, but rather types of a psychological quality. The French were not primarily interested in revealing human souls, but in the presentation of the all encompassing web of fate of a social order which, because of prejudice and rigidity of concept, has become mechanical. In many of the characters of the French drama, e.g. Hyppolytus, it is clear that the spirit and soul of man is no match for the dark powers of fate. This inability of the characters to overcome, or at least to meet fate, is symbolic of a chaotic and incurable world. Herder, however, sees in every aspect of life a certain order, a superimposed theodicy.

This he finds in Greek drama and this he finds in Shakespeare, and it is because of this principle of unity that Sophocles and Shakespeare are designated brothers. These are perspectives, however, which for Herder can originate only in the soul. The soul is the seat of the "spiritual bond" which enables man to communicate with the rest of organic creation, and it is only through his psychic powers that man can approach a supreme order. Herder cannot recognize the *espirit* of the French, or the concept of honor prevalent in the society of the eighteenth century because these for him were superficial perspectives for which the soul has no affinity. In drama Herder looked for a revelation from the deeper levels of the human soul, but in the dramas of the French he found only sentimentalities and matters of outward form. Herder can never reconcile himself to French drama because he expected something from it which it neither had the desire nor the ability to achieve.

Compared with the empty shells of the French dramas, Shakespeare's dramas have little in common. Here is a drama which is not an imitation, but a creation much in the same manner as the drama of the Greeks. Yet here too there are certain obvious differences. As Herder puts it: "*Shakespear* fand vor und um sich nichts weniger als Simplicität von Vaterlandssitten, Thaten, Neigungen und Geschichtstraditionen, die das Griechische Drama bildete . . . *Shakespear* fand keinen Chor vor sich; aber wohl Staats- und Marionettenspiele. . . . Er fand keinen so einfachen Volks- und Vaterlandscharakter, sondern ein Vielfaches von Ständen, Lebensarten, Gesinnungen, Völkern und Spracharten – der Gram und das Vorige wäre vergebens gewesen; . . . er nahm Geschichte, wie er sie fand, und setzte mit Schöpfergeist das verschiedenartigste Zeug zu einem Wunderganzen zusammen, was wir, wenn nicht *Handlung* im Griechischen Verstande, so *Aktion* im Sinne der mittlern, oder in der Sprache der neuern Zeiten *Begebenheit* (evenment) grosses Eräugniss nennen wollen" (V, 218). The external elements of the British drama differ completely from those of the Greek drama. There is nothing here to suggest dithyrambs or choirs, because those have no place among this people. Instead, this people looked to its own history, the spirit of its time, its customs, opinions, language, national prejudices, traditions, likes and dislikes. In the absence of dithyrambs and choirs the British have developed their drama from shrovetide plays and puppet theaters. There can be no question that the drama of the Greeks and that of Shakespeare are two entirely different things,

with scarcely anything in common. Ancient Greece is not six-
teenth or seventeenth century Britain, not to mention such obvious differences as language, customs, etc.

Yet it is not the difference of origins which depends upon the
historical situation that Herder finds astonishing and noteworthy,
but the similarity, even the essentail identity of the inner activity
of the soul. For despite the vast differences between the plays of
the British, and their most illustrious dramatist Shakespeare, and
those of the Greeks, the dramas of the British are just as much
the real thing as those of the Greeks. How and why? Because
their differences are restricted to the shell, the form if you will,
which insofar as the attainment of dramatic purpose is concerned
is not the critical consideration. Within a different shell Shakespeare has nevertheless succeeded in creating the same spirit that
is embodied within the Greek dramas. For Herder Shakespeare
is thus worthy of designation as the new Sophocles: "o Aristoteles, wenn du erschienest, wie würdest du den neuen Sophokles Homerisiren!" (V, 219) Herder's conviction that Aristotles
would "Homerize" Shakespeare as the new Sophocles is simply
an acknowledgement that the true art critic, who remains objective, can not help but immediately recognize the original force of
the poetic spirit, that unchanging norm of all things poetic, regardless of differences of origins, of chance of time and place.
Basic here though is knowledge of the creative, expressive, and
symbolic power of the soul to unite the simple and complex, the
material and spiritual. An experience of the function of the soul,
whether it be according to the principle of one from many, as was
the case with Shakespeare, or many from one, as was the case
with the Greeks, is synonymous with the experience of artistic
power. The important thing is the "how" of the artistic representation, and in principle this must always be the same, for ultimately it has its origins in the human soul. Herder is therefore
not solely concerned with the unique and necessarily different
relationship of the spirit of times and poetic form, of the husk
to the core, but also with the ordering power of the human soul,
which among the Greeks was able to make many from one, in
Shakespeare a one from many.

The remarkable fact revealed by a comparison of the two dramas is not only the similarity of tendencies, though they develop in different directions, but also a direct identity of effect possibilities. "So wars ein Sterblicher mit Götterkraft begabt, eben aus dem entgegen gesetztesten Stoff, und in der verschiedensten Bearbeitung dieselbe Würkung hervor zu rufen, *Furcht* und *Mitleid*! und beide in einem Grade, wie jener Erste Stoff und Bearbeitung es kaum vormals hervorzubringen vermocht! – Glücklicher Göttersohn über sein Unternehmen! Eben das Neue, Erste, ganz Verschiedne zeigt die Urkraft seines Berufs" (V, 218). For Herder the unique in all mankind is revealed in this *Urkraft*, and it is the presence of this quality within the dramas of the Greeks and Shakespeare which makes them worthy of consideration and praise. This is the very quality, however, which Herder misses in the drama of the French.

Addressing Aristotle, who for him is representative of the true critic, of the philosophical aesthete, and speaking of Shakespeare's dramas, Herder exclaims: "Würdest dich freuen, von Jedem deiner Stücke, *Handlung, Charakter, Meinungen, Ausdruck, Bühne* wie aus zwei Punkten des Dreiecks Linien ziehen zu können, die sich oben in Einem Punkte des Zwecks, der *Vollkommenheit* begegnen!" (V, 219) These two allegorical forms, the triangle and the pyramid, are representative of those images of the soul which occur again and again with Herder. The division into three parts and the pyramidal concept of the two lines which intersect at the apex and signify perfection are symbolic of Herder's aesthetic, which he sees as a combination of psychology, mythology, and aesthetics. Herder emphasizes that both Sophocles and Shakespeare, yet each in his own way, are "Vertraute Einer Gottheit" (V, 219). In other words, both possess those two all important qualities which go hand in hand and complement one another: both are geniuses and both are creators. Now although it is specifically Shakespeare who receives the designation genius in the essay, the same can just as well be said of Sophocles or any of the other Greek dramatist. Since the genius himself is a unique occurrence, that which he creates must likewise bear the stamp of originality and individuality. The true genius, however, and Shakespeare is one, is revealed only through the effect of his spiritual powers. He must emulate God, and this Shakespeare does by creating a unity and order in the midst of disorder and diversity, which finally results in the condition of one from many. The originality and individuality which characterize the genius and his creation are therefore only a by-product, but nevertheless an important one, of a judicious management of the powers of the soul on the part of the genius which results then in creative activity. The genius thus becomes the very essence of the combined spiritual powers of man which has something in it of the demoniac and impenetrable. The genius is indicative of human spirit developed to its highest potency. As such he cares nothing for the rules of others or models already extent. Nor is he dependent upon historical development, for the genius can occur at any time or place. The truth of this assertion is easily seen in Herder's comparison of the Greeks with Shakespeare, for had either been dependent upon a historical situation, then neither could have produced the dramas they did at such widely separated times. Not the given historical situation is the decisive factor, but rather the potential inner reaction of the poet to the situation. Despite the great importance which Herder attaches to origins, it is not the origins which determine the poet, but rather the drive toward a predetermined goal. For both Shakespeare and the Greeks this goal is tragedy, not in the generic sense, for as Herder has observed, in this respect the two scarcely have even a name in common, but rather in the sense that true tragedy is symbolic of a universal inner condition of the soul which can occur at any time or place. Herder believes that this condition was present in both the Greeks and Shakespeare because he sees tangible evidence of it in their dramas, and what is even more important, what he cannot see, he feels in his own soul. Furthermore, as his conclusions make clear, Herder also thinks that this condition is present in the dramas of Goethe too.[1]

As we have already had occasion to note elsewhere, there is still another aspect to this matter of genius. For the genius God

[1] Cf. here Otto Mann, "Wandlungen des Herderbildes", *Deutschunterricht,* X (1958), p. 42f.

is the original genius. The creation of the world is thus regarded as an act of genius. This act of creation, which is dependent upon the inner power of genius, and which is not something finished, but rather is constantly and eternally repeated over and over again, is thus recognized as divine. Consequently, that created by the genius is also regarded as divine. In the case of the genius such as Shakespeare this means that within the realm of man he must be just as creatively active as God is in the realm of the universe. Benno von Wiese says that for Herder the image of the genius of mankind merges with the image of the Godhead.[2] Mankind in this sense is an active mirror of the Godhead, however the Godhead is the eternal fount of life from which all geniuses arise in its image. The Godhead is the prototype of the genius. By analogy then the product of the genius is just as much an original creation as the universe is the original creation of God. And so it is with Shakespeare, who is the creator of an artistic microcosm which reflects within it the macrocosm. Herder calls Shakespeare a mortal with divine powers whose original powers enabled him to create something new and entirely different. The new and entirely different which Shakespeare creates is his own world, born out of the spirit of the Germanic North. Just as the Greek dramatists were Greeks writing for Greeks, so Shakespeare is the Nordic dramatist writing for Nordic peoples, which prompts Herder to say: "Ich bin Shakespear näher als dem Griechen" V, 219).

That it is not primarily qualities of individuality or uniqueness which distinguish the true poet, but rather that insofar as these qualities do distinguish him they must reflect certain universalities,[3] is further emphasized by Herder's characterization of Shakespeare's drama as the completion of "Einer Grösse habenden Begebenheit" (V, 220). The distinguishing feature of the Greek drama according to the Shakespeare essay is its action, but the

[2] Benno v. Wiese, *Herder, Grundzüge seines Weltbildes* (Leipzig, 1939), p. 72.
[3] Paul Böckmann, "Der dramatische Perspektivismus in der deutschen Shakespearedeutung des 18. Jahrhunderts, IV. Der Perspectivismus von Individualität und Geschichte bei Herder", in *Vom Geist der Dichtung*, ed. Fritz Martini (Hamburg, 1949), p. 87.

clearest statement of this belief is found in the fourth number of
the *Adrastea,* where Herder theorizes at length about the drama.
Quoting Aristotle on the nature of the drama, Herder explains
drama as: "*Nachahmung einer ämsigbetriebnen, vollständigen
Grössehabenden Handlung*" (XXIII, 349). This is the same definition, it should be remembered, that Herder gives for tragedy in
the third letter of *Ueber ein morgenländisches Drama* (XVI, 93).
In the Shakespeare essay the action (*Handlung*) of the Greek
drama is contrasted with the event (*Begebenheit*) of the Shakespearean drama. "Wenn bei diesem [Greek drama] das Eine einer
Handlung herrscht; so arbeitet Jener [Shakespeare] auf das Ganze
eines Eräugnisses, einer Begebenheit" (V, 219). Exactly what
Herder means by *Begebenheit,* and how it may be determined in
Shakespeare's dramas, has been variously interpreted. Hettner
tries to show that *Begebenheit* means that Herder wanted to epi-
cize the dramatical in Shakespeare.[4] Haym thinks that when Herder contrasts *Begebenheit* with *Handlung* he is comparing the
complexity of Shakespeare's dramas with the simplicity of Greek
dramas.[5] While he agrees with Haym, Weber does not think that
he has gone far enough. Weber concludes that the best definition
for *Begebenheit* is *Vorgang-Komplex.*[6] By accepting what has
been said by Haym and Weber we have a start toward an understanding of Herder's concept of *Begebenheit.* Now it is true that
Herder regards Shakespeare's dramas as infinitely more complex
than those of the Greeks, for Herder points out that one character
type prevailed among the Greeks, while Shakespeare's dramas
contain all types and classes: the Greeks spoke one language, but
Shakespeare speaks the language of all ages and men and becomes
a translator of nature in all tongues. The simple action of Greek
drama, which according to both Aristotle and Lessing resembled
a one time natural occurrence, is for Herder comparable to a
universe in the drama of Shakespeare, for Shakespeare expresses
the whole of natural reality. In short, Herder contrasts the classi-

---

[4] Hermann Hettner, *Geschichte der deutschen Literatur im 18. Jahrhundert,* 5th ed. (Braunschweig, 1909), III, 3, 1, p. 38f.
[5] Rudolf Haym, *Herder,* ed. Wolfgang Harich (Berlin, 1954), I, 465.
[6] Gottfried Weber, *Herder und das Drama* (Weimar, 1922), p. 70.

cal simplicity of the Greek drama with the manifold totality of Shakespeare's drama. But in order to grasp the full impact of the distinction drawn by Herder it is important to note that he does not stop here with these external features. Herder develops his concept of *Begebenheit* from the observation that these "events" have their origins in actual historical occurrences, and not in typical or symbolic "actions", which are individual or which indicate a one dimensional development. "Events" are therefore arbitrary occurrences which transcend the individual and which make no sense until they have been put into some meaningful order by the powers of the poet, what Herder refers to as his *Grösse*. In themselves historical events are not necessarily poetic materials. Only when they are ordered by the poet, only when Shakespeare makes "one from many" are these events moulded into a form that is meaningful and capable of influencing the soul of man. That is what Herder means when he writes: "Da ist nun Shakespear der grösste Meister, eben weil er nur und immer Diener der Natur ist" (V, 222). Shakespeare is worthy of this designation not because he is primarily a dramatist, but because with consummate creative skill he has taken the occurrences and characters provided by the events and shaped them into an orderly whole. Shakespeare's dramas thus become a theodicy, a vindication of the Godhead working in history. In this respect Shakespeare's dramas can be compared with the folksong, for if the folksong is the expression of an individual soul, or the soul of a collection of individuals, a *Volk*, then Shakespeare's drama is the expression of a cosmic soul (*Weltseele*). Each drama must and can be seen as an individual expression, but each one is nevertheless the expression of an individual cosmos in miniature, a microcosm.

The expression of a microcosm as Herder sees it in the plays of Shakespeare becomes a living reality. Contrary to the view of Lessing, Herder does not conceive of the dramatic presentation as a comparison or symbol. All illusionary aspects disappear when he reads (notice, Herder says "reads", not "sees") these plays, and what he experiences becomes reality. "Mir ist, wenn ich ihn lese, Theater, Akteur, Koulisse verschwunden! Lauter einzelne im Sturm der Zeiten wehende Blätter aus dem Buch der Begebenheiten, der Vorsehung, der Welt! – einzelne Gepräge der Völker, Stände, Seelen! die alle die verschiedenartigsten und abgetrenntest handelnden Maschienen, alle – was wir in der Hand des Weltschöpfers sind – unwissende, blinde Werkzeuge zum Ganzen Eines theatralischen Bildes, Einer Grösse habenden Begebenheit, die nur der Dichter überschauet" (V, 219f). Thus as Paul Böckmann has accurately observed, it is the inner perspective in Shakespeare which illuminates the three dimensional unity of man, God, and world that sets his dramas apart from all others. "Shakespeare erscheint erst hier als der unübertroffene dramatische Meister, weil sein Werk jenen inneren Perspektivismus in sich trägt, der auf den Zusammenhang von Mensch, Welt und Gott zurückweist." [7] It must be evident, however, that no matter how much Herder may consider Shakespeare's plays reality rather than illusion, or how real his experience of the play may seem, or how much the event created and developed by the dramatist becomes a self-sufficient event which can maintain its own position within the course of history, that the drama, even if presented on the stage, cannot assume the same proportion as the actual happening with which it deals. Somewhere and somehow, regardless of how unconscious the process is, there must be a connecting link which causes the illusion to seem real. This problem is solved by Herder when he seizes upon the thought that the place where the event unfolds is not the stage, but within the phantasy of the human soul. This thought is touched upon in the final published form of the essay, but is more fully developed in the unpublished draft of the first version. Herder writes here: "Die menschliche Seele gibt der Wolke Körper, dem Körper Geist, und Absicht und Bewegung" (V, 244). This dramatic presentation within the soul is possible because the dramatic happenings within Shakespeare's dramas are not bound by the limitations of time, space, or action, but rather seek to present the world and history on the grand scale in which it really exists. Commenting upon this aspect of Herder's understanding of Shakespeare, which for him represents a significant advance

[7] Böckmann, p. 94.

over Lessing's dramatic sense, Böckmann has this to say: "Je weniger das dramatische Geschehen an Ort und Zeit im engeren Sinne gebunden ist, je mehr es den Einzelmenschen mit Welt und Geschichte in Zusammenhang bringt." [8] The soul thus reacts to these dramas in the same manner that it would experience a natural occurrence. Furthermore, the less the drama itself is limited, the more freely will the soul be able to react to it, and the more real the dramatic presentation will seem. Although he recognized the greatness of the Greek drama, Herder saw this more fully realized in the plays of Shakespeare than in those of any other, while in the dramas of the French he missed this quality completely.

In order to make clear this ability of Shakespeare to take a "Meer von Begebenheit" (V, 220) and, through his genial creative intentions order it into what Herder terms "dunkle kleine Symbole zum Sonnenriss einer Theodicee Gottes" (V, 220), Herder makes no attempt to analyze Shakespeare's dramas in their entirety, but rather concentrates on pointing out the organic cohesiveness of the individual elements of a drama with its form as a whole. Thus he makes the following observations about Lear: "*Lear* . . . in der Ersten Scene der Erscheinung trägt schon allen Saamen seiner Schicksale zur Ernte der dunkelsten Zukunft in sich" (V, 220). In the tragic figure of Othello Herder sees revealed the whole gamut of human emotions. "In *Othello*, dem Mohren, welche Welt! welch ein Ganzes! *lebendige Geschichte der Entstehung, Fortgangs, Ausbruchs, traurigen Endes* der Leidenschaft *dieses Edlen Unglückseligen*! und in welcher Fülle, und Zusammenlauf der Räder zu Einem Werke! (V, 221) Although he recognizes the individual worth of the many scenes in *Macbeth*, he also sees these woven together with consummate mastery into an organic whole. "Ich müsste alle, alle Scenen ausschreiben, um das idealisirte Lokal des unnennbaren Ganzen, *der Schicksals-, Königsmords- und Zauberwelt* zu nennen, die als Seele das Stück, bis auf den kleinsten Umstand von Zeit, Ort, selbst scheinbarer Zwischenverwirrung, belebt, Alles in der Seele zu Einem schauderhaften, unzertrennlichen Ganzen zu machen

[8]   Böckmann, p. 91.

– und doch würde ich mit Allem nichts sagen" (V, 224). And so Herder is able to take one drama after the other and to find in them all, proof of his belief that each of the component parts of the drama mirrors and contains the whole within it.[9] Herder was able to recognize what others had overlooked because his method was synthetic and soul oriented, and not analytic and reason oriented. In so doing he kept within the bounds of his program set forth at the outset of the essay to "feel Shakespeare as he is". To accomplish this, however, it is necessary to commence with the soul of the poet, with the human spirit who has taken these varied elements and moulded into an organized, composite whole. As Herder expresses it: "Tritt näher, und fühle den *Menschengeist*, der auch jede Person und Alter und Charakter und Nebending in das Gemälde ordnete" (V, 220).

Now the source of the events which Shakespeare has so magnificently portrayed and ordered is history, and throughout the essay and the preliminary drafts one finds the words *Begebenheit* and *Geschichte* mentioned side by side. We turn again to these drafts for the best indication of how Herder regarded history and the drama. Both drafts clearly establish the fact that the history motif played an important role for Herder while he was attempting to codify the ideas ultimately expressed in the completed form of the essay. A comparison of what Herder says here about drama and history and what Gerstenberg has to say about the same subject in his eighteenth letter of *Briefe über die Merkwürdigkeiten der Literatur* (1766) is also profitable for an indication of Herder's debt to the ideas of Gerstenberg. Shakespeare brought history to the theater, says Herder, but not as history. The history that Shakespeare presents is "dramatic history", and the use of "dramatic history" as opposed to the use of mere "history" is one of Shakespeare's unique qualities. But the question arises as to what Herder really means when he talks about history and Shakespeare. The term "dramatic history" is introduced in the

[9] Cf. here Eric Blackall's statement about Herder's style in "Herder's Linguistic Theory and His Early Prose Style", *PMLA*, LXXVI (1961), p. 518. "His purpose is to draw attention to component elements, and yet not allow the parts to obscure the whole".

second draft (V, 244), and it does seem to be the preferred expression. In the first draft, however, Herder had written: "Alle Shakespearsche Stücke sind eigentlich Geschichte" (V, 236). Continuing, Herder qualifies his remark and says that this history is not a history of textbooks, but history such as it happens in the grand course of human and world events. In the second draft Shakespeare is called "a painter of history" (V, 245), and in the final published form *Othello* is "living history" (V, 221) and Shakespeare himself "the creator of history and a cosmic soul" (V, 231). Herder was assuredly not thinking of history in the scientific sense, nor was he thinking of the concept of history he developed over a decade later in the *Ideen*.[10] Two paragraphs in the second draft bear out the validity of Dobbek's observation. The first of these deals with the historical illusions which Herder sees being consummated in the soul of man. "Historische Illusion, dünkt mich also, entsteht dem Leser, wenn er in dem Fortfluss der Geschichte das Fortgehende aller Kräfte, die eine Begebenheit hervorbringen, Jede an ihrem Ort, und in ihrem Maasse fühlt, dass er also theils voraus ahndend theils allmählich erfahrend, das Resultat dieser Kräfte in der Begebenheit anschauend erkennet" (V, 244). The goal of the dramatist is to bring about a historical illusion, and to do this he must show the continuous action of all powers in the course of history which produce the all important event. To accomplish this he does not write history, but proceeds like a writer of history. That is, he adapts history in a dramatic way for his own purposes. This is the theme of the second of the two paragraphs. "In eine Geschichte Täuschung zu bringen, ist viel; aber aus ihr Dialog zu machen, zum Dialog Charaktere, aus vollen Charakteren Handlung, aus dieser Dramatische Vorstellung zu machen, wie weit mehr! Wie viel Würkungen der Seele, und wie schnell bewürkt sie das Genie" (V, 245). To the same degree that Herder sees Shakespeare making use of history, he also recognizes Shakespeare as a rich source for the historian.[11] Under these conditions there is no com-

[10]   Wilhelm Dobbek, "Herder und Shakespeare", *Shakespeare Jahrbuch,* XCI (1955), p. 36f.
[11]   Cf. here the recent study by Tom F. Driver, *The Sense of History in*

petition between history and the drama, for drama as history and history as drama mutually illustrate one another. Yet at the same time each maintains its own identity. This unique use of history raises the dramas of the British bard to a level where as creations, albeit poetic creations, they are comparable to *the* creation. The dramatist as creator presides over his creations in the same manner as the Creator presides over *the* creation (S. above, V, 219f). The circle has now been completed. The dramatist is a creator, and his drama a creation, so the stage of the theater becomes a world theater where the characters and events of history pass in review. According to Herder Shakespeare knows only one law, and this he describes thusly: "Als das *Ganze einer Begebenheit mit allen seinen wesentlichen Charakteren, Ursachen, Incidenzen und Hauptfolgen auf die Bühne zu bringen*" (V, 245).

Shakespeare's purpose, in all that he does and says, is to reach out and speak to the soul of the one who comes into contact with his dramas. To do this he must first animate each scene and each act with his own spirit, until the drama becomes so filled with it that any other soul coming into contact with the spirit-filled drama cannot help but be carried away by it. "Der [Shakespeare] hundert Auftritte einer Weltbegebenheit mit dem Arm umfasst, mit dem Blick ordnet, mit der Einen durchhauchenden, Alles belebenden Seele erfüllet, und nicht Aufmerksamkeit, Herz, alle Leidenschaften, die ganze Seele von Anfang bis zu Ende fortreisst" (V, 221). As a result of this effect of soul upon soul Herder can exclaim: "Himmel! wie wird das Ganze der Begebenheit mit tiefster Seele fortgefühlt und geendet!" (V, 221) The human soul alone thus becomes the "eye and point of view" through which we are able to join the individual with the whole, nature with the infinite spirit, and the earthly with the eternal event. In this capacity the soul is the magic key to the "theodicy of God", in which everything has its place, its legality, and its order. By

---

Greek and Shakespearean Drama (New York, 1960). On page 69 the author writes: "The primary connection between drama and history is not the drama's use of historical material as subject matter. It is, rather, in the influence of historical modes of thought upon the patterning of dramatic action."

first grasping the entire event and then bringing it to completion with the power of his soul, which thereby exhibits great versatility, man himself has been raised to the level of the creator by the poet, for by filling man with his own genial spirit the poet makes him capable of seeing symbolically and carrying out the intimated in action and word to that end which transcends the individual. Throughout the essay Herder again and again emphasizes the human spirit which, on the one hand creates and orders, and on the other feels, receives, and completes. "Wenn ein Engel der Vorsehung Menschliche Leidenschaften gegen einander abwog, und Seelen und Charaktere gruppirte, und ihnen Anlässe, wo Jedes im Wahn des Freien handelt, zuführt, und er sie alle mit diesem Wahne, als mit der Kette des Schicksals zu seiner Idee leitet – so war der Menschliche Geist, der hier entwarf, sann, zeichnete, lenkte" (V, 222). Through his creation the poet works upon the soul of man in such a manner that he participates directly in the passions and actions of the poetic creation where, as Herder puts it, "the whole soul is stimulated, cultivated, and transformed". Herder does not mean this in the sense of mere sentimental empathy, but rather as a genuine metamorphosis, whereby art aids in the development and perfection of man. The whole operation must thus be viewed as a formation process of the soul, which creates its own form as its own unique expression.

Although the dramatist makes use of history and is influenced by it, and although the drama – specifically that of Shakespeare – assumes certain features and qualities of history, the finished dramatic product is neither determined by history nor should it be regarded as a product of history.[12] History did not create the dramas of Shakespeare any more than did nature or the cosmic spirit. The creator of these dramas was a man endowed with a creative spirit who, with the materials at his hand, was able to create his own world in miniature. The creators of the Greek dramas were also men – Sophocles, Euripides, Aeschylus – and not history. Nowhere in Herder's writing do we find history des-

[12]   S. Otto Mann, "Wandlungen", and the shorter treatment of this subject in his *Geschichte des deutschen Dramas* (Stuttgart, 1960).

ignated as creator or genius. This designation is reserved for man and is applied only to man. Indeed, the drama and all the other artistic products of man are created by man in a manner which is comparable with nature's creative process, but the fact remains that it is man, and not nature, who is responsible for artistic creation. Nature, just like history, influences the creations of man, but this hardly qualifies it for the designation as their creator. The question arises then: What does Herder mean in those often quoted lines from the philosophy of history? "In gewissen Betracht ist also jede Menschliche Vollkommenheit *National, Säkular*, und am genauesten betrachtet, *Individuell*" (V, 505). Why does he spend so much time in the Shakespeare essay pointing out the differences between Greek, French, and British drama if these differences are not historical and if they do not play a role of prime importance in his final conclusions? And why has the Shakespeare essay been pointed to by generations of scholars as proof of their belief that Herder is a historical relativist?

The differentiation which Herder draws between the "husk" and "core" of the drama and his assertion that Greek and Shakespearean drama are two things which hardly have even a name in common have already been briefly mentioned. The obvious differences between the dramatic products of two widely separated ages and peoples that prompt Herder to this statement are differences found in the husk, not the core. "Dass Zeit und Ort, wie Hülsen um den Kern immer mit gehen, sollte nicht einmal erinnert werden dörfen, und doch ist hierüber das hellste Geschrei" (V, 222). One might also add in a paraphrase of Herder's remark, that the very problem he is suggesting here is still the major stumbling block to an understanding of Herder's essay today. Speaking of Aristotle's canon of time and place, Herder remarks that to force such rules on Shakespeare would be sheer nonsense. The same can be said for any of the other qualities of the drama which are parts of the husk – the choir, the dithyrambs, the unities, the Hellenistic spirit of the Greeks, action versus event, or any other external differences that can be attributed to the influence of time and place. Herder has not hesitated to call attention to these differences, either in the final published form of the essay or in the first two drafts. But, as the lines cited above make clear, this husk, i.e. form of the drama, that part which is historical and which is to a degree determined by external factors, does not grow and develop independent of the core, i.e. content. Since the form does not mature independent of the content, neither can the content occur independent of the form. Furthermore, the content of the drama is no more the result of the form than the core of the fruit is the result of the husk. Consequently, the literary masterpieces we now designate the tragedy of antiquity or Shakespearean tragedy, and which are more a matter of content than form, cannot be said to result primarily from historical growth.

In spite of all his remarks concerning form and individuality in the Shakespeare essay neither is his primary concern. This is not to say, however, that the unique and individual generally connected with form are of no importance at all. As Herder himself points out: "Ists da nicht eben Ort und Zeit und Fülle der äusseren Umstände, die der ganzen Geschichte *Haltung, Dauer, Existenz* geben muss, und wird ein Kind, ein Jüngling, ein Verliebter, ein Mann im Felde der Thaten sich wohl Einen Umstand des Lokals, des Wie? und Wo? und Wann? wegschneiden lassen, ohne dass die ganze Vorstellung seiner Seele litte?" (V, 222) In the symbolic process described here Herder places the main emphasis on the "presentation of the soul", for here also exists that higher totality which transcends individual considerations, for only in human form is the divine intelligible to man. The soul of the poet speaks out of the work itself to the soul of the spectator, thus ordering and uniting everything within the spectator's soul into an indivisible whole. In Herder's metaphor the external and individual features of the drama, which are parts of its form, are only the body of an inner spirit, of the content which is his primary concern. "So sieht man, die ganze Welt ist zu diesem grossen Geiste allein Körper" (V, 225).

Herder wants to evaluate Shakespeare and the Greeks aesthetically, not understand them historically, although at times there does not seem to be a sharp line of distinction drawn between the two activities. Within the art product Herder searches for the fulfillment of certain values, values that can occur at any time or place. Herder's main concern is thus with content *(Gehalt,* not *Inhalt)* rather than form. It would be a mistake to consider only the poet's individual manner of expression, or his own particular style, for the important thing is the whole entity of spirit, and not its individual effects. Herder makes this clear when he says: "Alle Auftritte der Natur an diesem Körper Glieder, wie alle Charaktere und Denkarten zu diesem Geiste Züge – und das Ganze mag jener Riesengott des Spinoza 'Pan! Universum!' heissen" (V, 225f). The inner unity and identity of the soul is the essential consideration. Therefore, even though the forms of Shakespeare and Greek drama may differ greatly, Herder is nonetheless able to say: "Eben da ist also *Shakespear Sophokles* Bruder, wo er ihm dem Anschein nach so unähnlich ist, um im Innern, ganz wie Er zu seyn" (V, 225). On the other hand, although the French have perfected a dramatic form similar to that of the Greeks, they have failed to perfect a content commensurate with this form. Because of this the French are called to account in two of the sections of the essay and are criticized for imitating the form of the Greeks, while neglecting the all important matter of content. Contrary then to the view held by most of the major voices of Herder scholarship, the theme and purpose of Herder's essay is not to emphasize the differences between Shakespeare and the Greeks, but rather to point out their similarity as far as vital issues are concerned.[13] A few of these voices, among them Haym and Hettner, have recognized that Herder saw in the two dramas certain internal common points, but have failed to draw the natural conclusion that all great poetry, no matter what means it may avail itself of, can be called great only if it develops all the powers of the soul and unites them into an organic whole so that universally valid values are thereby attained. Poetry attains the highest perfection whenever it creative-

[13]   The following list will indicate how widespread and established this view is: Hettner, III, 3, 1, p. 39f; Haym, I, 465; Weber, p. 104f.; Friedrich Gundolf, *Shakespeare und der deutsche Geist,* 9th ed. (Godesberg, 1947), p. 183; Johannes Pfeiffer, "Die Erneuerung der deutschen Dichtung im Zeitalter Herders", in his *Über das Dichterische und den Dichter* (Hamburg, 1956), p. 49.

ly experiences the spirit of nature and the universe, which means
that it must not only contain simplicity such as is revealed in the
fate entanglements of Greek drama, or the complexity of world
events as in Shakespearean drama. It must, in addition, recognize
the formative factor of its opposite, which for Shakespeare is the
concept of "one in many", whereby within the "one" a new and
exciting microcosmic realm is symbolically revealed.

So Shakespeare can produce the unity of space and time, which
is lacking in his drama from the very outset, and which Sophocles
found before him in Greek tradition, just as Sophocles was able
to produce the complexity of action, which Shakespeare found
embodied in the traditions of his day. ". . . wenn du eine Welt
hervorbringen kannst, und die nicht anders, als im Raum und
Zeit existiret, siehe, so ist da im Innern dein Maass von Frist und
Raum" (V, 227). In themselves space and time mean nothing for
Herder. They acquire meaning only in relationship to the soul,
and only from the power and freedom of the soul does there result
a measure of them, for it alone can operate without corporeality,
causing time to stand still, or transcending space. Speaking of
time and space Herder writes: "Hast du nie gefühlt . . . was das
also für unwesentliche Dinge, für Schatten gegen das, was *Handlung*, Würkung der Seele ist, seyn müssen? wie es blos an dieser
Seele liege, sich Raum, Welt und Zeitmaass zu schaffen, wie und
wo sie will?" (V, 228) Here is consummated the highest quality
of man, freedom of the spirit, which in the "ordine successi-
vorum und simultancorum of *his* world" is able to create everything needed for *his* perfection and completion.

That the Greek drama and that of Shakespeare possess a common "core", while differing externally, is evident when one
examines the question of dramatic purpose. One of the things
Herder tries to do in the essay is to establish what it is that makes
the Greek and Shakespearean dramas tragedies. According to
Herder the purpose of the tragedy is that already determined by
Aristotle: "Nichts mehr und nichts minder, als eine *gewisse* Er-
schütterung des Herzens, die *Erregung* der Seele in *gewissem
Maass* und von *gewissen* Seiten, kurz! eine Gattung Illusion"
(V, 215). Since drama is able to arouse the soul only according

to the effect produced by the content, the role of the form in achieving the tragic purpose is minimal. In the Greek drama it was not the choir, or the unities, or the dithyrambs which were, in the final analysis, responsible for producing the illusion which affected the soul. They are only the trappings through which the content is revealed. Herder freely admits that, insofar as these outer trappings are concerned, the French have superbly reproduced them. But lacking the proper content, the trappings alone have not been able to produce the tragic effect. "Als Puppe ihm [Sophocles' tragedy] noch so gleich; der Puppe fehlt Geist, Leben, Natur, Wahrheit — mithin alle Elemente der Rührung – mithin Zweck und Erreichung des Zwecks – ist also das Ding mehr?" (V, 216) Shakespeare's dramas, however, though built of different materials, though dealing with different themes, though having their own unique origins, were still able to achieve the same effect as the tragedies of the Greek masters. "So wars ein Sterblicher mit Götterkraft begabt, eben aus dem entgegen gesetztesten Stoff, und in der verschiedensten Bearbeitung dieselbe Würkung hervor zu rufen, *Furcht* und *Mitleid*! und beide in einem Grade, wie jener Erste Stoff und Bearbeitung es kaum vormals hervorzubringen vermocht!" (V, 218) Herder thus sees the possibility of only one tragic motif for all time and all of mankind, but this motif can appear in different forms in any number of different treatments. Since both the dramas of the Greeks and Shakespeare possess this motif, both have a common content.[14] For Herder it was important in determining the artistic excellence of the Greeks and Shakespeare that there be present a sense of harmony between form and intent. In each case the artist had made use of the form which best expressed the cultural presuppositions he affirmed and which best produced the results he desired. Although present in the Greeks and Shakespeare, Herder found this sense of harmony wanting in French dramas.

And so Herder concludes his essay with the observation that the realization of the divine through the free activity of the soul results in a continuent, which however as an earthly phenomenon

[14] O. Mann, "*Wandlungen*", p. 41.

is bound to a one-time corporeality which is inescapably exposed to a gradual wasting away. In Herder's metaphor Shakespeare's dramas are destined to become the "ruins of a Colossus, of a pyramid" which everyone marvels at, but no one understands. All said and done, however, Shakespeare's dramas are and must remain, *"Historie! Helden und Staatsaktion zur Illusion mittlerer Zeiten!* oder . . . ein völliges *Grösse habende Eräugniss einer Weltbegebenheit, eines Menschlichen Schicksals"* (V, 230f). With these definitions Herder has circumscribed the unique, the individual, the characteristic, the time and space bound aspects of Shakespeare's dramas. For although he already considers himself one of the last capable of understanding Shakespeare, and although the course of time brings with it a demand for new forms of expression which Herder is unable to foresee, the essential factor is that human individuality and the complexity of life are fruitfully united and expressed in the realm of the soul. This the Greeks were able to attain, and this Shakespeare attained, and Herder is just as confident that it will be attained in the future, but in what form he is unable to foretell.

With the exception of the Shakespeare essay the only other place where Herder treats drama at any length is in the fourth number of the *Adrastea*. Although written nearly thirty years after the composition of the Shakespeare essay shortly before his death, we find that Herder's theories of drama have changed little here. As in the earlier work Herder points to the basic differences in form between Greek and Shakespearean dramas, he disparages the efforts of the French to imitate the Greeks, he calls upon Aristotle to define Greek tragedy, and he finds the tragic motif realized in the content of the Greek and British drama, the only significant difference being that here a new factor which aids in attaining the goal of the tragedy is introduced. It might be mentioned in passing that in the *Adrastea* the French are not the only ones whom Herder finds have misunderstood the true essence of tragedy. This charge is likewise leveled against his own two countrymen Goethe and Schiller, who according to Herder have wrongly misplaced the emphasis from content to form in their efforts to produce a "classical" drama.

The theme around which Herder develops his discussion of the drama in the *Adrastea* is fate, and this theme becomes the measuring stick by which the drama of all ages is aesthetically evaluated. The Greek drama was built around plots of fate (*Schicksals-fabeln*). "Tragödie ist eine *Schicksalsfabel*, d.i. eine dargestellte Geschichte menschlicher Begegnisse, mittelst menschlicher Charaktere, in menschlichen Gemüthern eine *Reinigung der Leidenschaften* durch ihre Erregung selbst *vollendend*" (XXIII, 355). Still in another place Herder describes the Greek tragedy as: "Einen grossen Kampf menschlicher Leidenschaften unter der höchsten Macht, *dem Willen des Schicksals*" (XXIII, 347). In the plays of Aeschylus, Agamemnon and Orestes, Prometheus and Darius are all subject to the vagaries of fate. And the same can be said for such tragic figures as Oedipus and Philoctetes in the plays of Sophocles. Herder finds, however, that should one of the ancient Greeks suddenly appear and view modern dramas, he would hardly recognize them as such. "Wie Wortreich-stumm, würde er sagen, wie dumpf und Tonlos! Bin ich in ein geschmücktes Grab getreten? Ihr schreit und seufzet und foltert! bewegt die Arme, strengt die Gesichtszüge an, raisonnirt, deklamiret: wird dann Eure Stimme und Empfindung nie *Gesang*? vermisst ihr nie die Stärke dieses dämonischen Ausdrucks?" (XXIII, 347) Enlightened modern-day man does not want to recognize the fate of the Greeks. "Aber Schicksal, und immer Schicksal! Wir Christen und Weise, glauben kein Schicksal" (XXIII, 359). Call it something else then, Herder replies, for admit it or not, we are all subject to fate. "So nenne man's *Schickung, Begebniss, Ereigniss, Verknüpfung der Begebenheiten und Umstände*" (XXIII, 359). Just as in the earlier essay, Herder points to Shakespeare as evidence that the ability to write tragedy as effective as that of the Greeks is also alive in more recent time. Shakespeare becomes the modern propagator of the fate plot of the Greeks. "Was hielt Er [Shakespeare] vom tragischen Schicksal? *Shakespear* schrieb ein Trauerspiel *Hamlet*. Hamlet ist *sein* Orestes" (XXIII, 362). To support his point Herder can point to the many features these two dramas have in common: the murder of the fathers; the sons as avengers of the fathers; one sent by the god Phoebus, the other spurred on by the ghost of his dead father; the implication of the mothers in the plot, etc. So it is too with the other great characters in Shakespeare's tragedies, with Lear, Othello, with Romeo and Macbeth. In his own country Herder can proudly point to Lessing as the dramatist who has revived the fate plot. Two of his dramas are examples, *Nathan*, which Herder calls "eine dramatische Schicksalsfabel" (XXIII, 374f), and *Emilia Galotti*, likewise "eine Fabel des Schicksals" (XXIII, 375).

As Aristotle had already said before him, and as Herder also states, the role of fate or the fate plot is not the primary purpose of the tragedy. It is only a means to this purpose, which, as was also the case in the Shakespeare essay, is to arouse the passions and feelings in man's soul and thereby to produce a catharizing effect. Although it is true that Herder apparently had some difficulty in making up his mind whether this effect was to take place in the persons of the drama or in the spectators, the important thing to note is that it took place within the soul and that only those dramas in which here existed harmony of form, content, and intent could induce this effect. Herder wanted dramas that he could feel and experience, dramas in which he could identify himself with the characters and their fates, feelings, and passions. He wanted a drama in which the phantasies of the soul could actively participate, just as they could react to the songs of Ossian or to the wild songs of his native homeland. No alienation effect for Herder!

By speaking a language of the soul, the great dramas which he praises are able to reveal the innermost workings within the souls of their characters. "O Shakespear! wie kehrst du das Innere hinaus! machst sprechend den stummsten Abgrund der Seele! Alles ist dir Verhängniss und ohne innere Theilnahme doch Nichts Verhängniss" (XXIII, 373). In the Shakespeare essay and for the most part in the *Adrastea* the emphasis is on the drama itself and on the necessity for all tragedy to possess the tragic motif. But at the very end of the discussion in the *Adrastea* Herder introduces another important factor which further supports our claim that Herder uses applied constants in order to aesthetically evaluate and experience art. He writes: "Das Menschenherz bleibt immer dasselbe" (XXIII, 390). In other words, the soul of man has remained basically the same, regardless of the time or people or place or circumstances under which it might be found. For the drama this applies to both the spectators and to the characters of the drama itself. Thus Herder finds the bourgeois tragedy on the same high plane as the heroic tragedies of the Greeks. The former does not constitute a debasement of the latter merely because of the differences in class between the characters. Whether or not the hero dwells in a palace, or wears a robe, or sits on a throne is immaterial. What is pertinent is what he experiences and how he experiences. If these experiences to which fate have subjected him are genuine, if they spring from his heart and soul, then the effect which they produce will likewise be genuine, and the purpose of the drama will be fulfilled.

VI

POETRY, THE DIVINE ART

A. THEORY

The claims of literature, and especially those of poetry, to the designation as the supreme art form, as the highest expression of man's creative ability, were firmly established by Herder in the *Viertes Wäldchen.* "Literature is, according to him, not a merely formal practice of technical skill and special rules, but the highest and most complete expression of the whole personality",[1] "the truest and most characteristic expression and record of the spirit of man".[2] Accordingly, for Herder the greats of the poetic world have contributed more to our knowledge of man than all the greats among philosophers. "ich ... glaube übrigens, dass *Homer,* und *Sophocles, Dante, Shakespeare* und *Klopstock* der Psychologie und Menschenkänntniss mehr Stoff geliefert haben, als selbst die *Aristoteles* und *Leibnitze* aller Völker und Zeiten" (VIII, 171).

Especially in the knowledge of the human soul and the ability to portray the soul of one man for the benefit of another, poets have no peers. "Ein Charakter von *Shakespear* geschaffen, geführt, gehalten, ist oft ein ganzes Menschenleben in seinen verborgnen Quellen; ohne dass ers weiss, malt er die Leidenschaft bis auf die tiefsten Abgründe und Fasern, aus denen sie sprosste" (VIII, 183). The poet not only portrays the souls of others, with each of

---

[1] Martin Schütze, "Herder's Psychology", *The Monist,* XXXV (Oct. 1925), p. 542.
[2] Martin Schütze, *The Fundamental Ideas in Herder's Thought,* serially in *MP,* XIX (1921-22), p. 115.

his creations he also reveals his own soul, while at the same time
he hopes for a soul similarly tuned and receptive to the communication from his soul. "... ein Autor ... giebt mit seinem Buch,
... gewissermaasse einen Theil seiner Seele dem Publikum Preis.
Er offenbaret nicht nur, womit sich sein Geist in gewissen Zeit-
räumen und Angelegenheiten beschäftigte, was er für Zweifel und
Auflösungen im Gange seines Lebens fand, ... sondern er rechnet
auf einigen, vielleicht wenige, gleichgestimmte Seelen ... Mit
ihnen bespricht er sich unsichtbar und theilt ihnen seinen Empfindungen mit" (XIII, 5). A work of literature, in this case the
ode, can thus deserve the designation: "Abdrücke der Seele,
Darstellungen aus der Ansicht der Dinge und den Empfindungen
des Dichters" (XX, 328). In this role as portrayer of the soul
poetry never loses sight of the totality of the soul, and of the three
definite stages through which it must pass, i.e., its initial conception, the growth and development of its inherent potential,
and finally its drive toward perfection. Although the term poetry
has so far been used in the broad sense, as Herder himself frequently uses it, to include all literary genre, he also uses it in a
more narrow sense, to which we now turn, to designate a specific
literary genre, lyric poetry, which for Herder was the most powerful of the literary arts, and the first conceived by man.

Hamann's great service to language was a denial of the rationalistic view which dominated the scene during most of the eighteenth century. Although Hamann too emphasized the importance of the origins of language, his approach remains essentially
mystical and theological. Herder, Hamann's friend and pupil who
traveled paths already blazed by him, chose the literary approach.
"Wer über die Litteratur eines Landes schreibt, muss die Sprache
nicht aus der Acht lassen ... Der Genius der Sprache ist also
auch der Genius von der Litteratur einer Nation" (I, 147). But
this literary approach is dominated by a concern which can rightly be termed one of the hallmarks of Herder's treatment of any
problem. This is the deliberate attempt in all areas which demand
his attention to penetrate directly to origins. Two main reasons
can be advanced for why Herder felt the necessity to return to the
origin of things, and although each of these has its own individual

validity, each nevertheless complements the other and each must be considered in the light of the other. The *Aufklärung* wrote history exclusively from the standpoint of the present. That is, it regarded the past as preliminary to the present.[3] Herder, however, sees the past as both end and means, and is convinced that any time must be seen as a self-sufficient totality in order to be understood.[4] Secondly, Herder employs his quest for origins as a weapon against the *Aufklärung*.[5] By emphasizing sensuous origins Herder hoped to dethrone the absolutism of reason.[6] This is not to say that Herder's approach to the *Aufklärung* and its doctrines is always negative, for the *Reisejournal*, to mention only one of his works, represents a decidedly positive approach.[7] But whenever the *Aufklärung* becomes a purpose and end rather than a means, then Herder opposes it.[8]

In the area of language and literature Herder's first organized efforts to return to origins are his explanations of the origin of language and his characterization of primitive language in the prize essay *Über den Ursprung der Sprache*.[9] Any explanation of Herder's concept of poetry must necessarily go hand-in-hand with a discussion of his ideas on primitive language since Herder, like his friend and teacher Hamann, considered primitive language and poetry as one and the same.[10] Up to this point in our discus-

---

[3]   Hans M. Wolff, "Der junge Herder und die Entwicklungsidee Rousseaus", *PMLA*, LVII (1942), p. 771.
[4]   Wolff, p. 755, *SWS*, XXXII, 86, IV, 364.
[5]   Heinz Peyer, *Herders Theorie der Lyrik* (Winterthur, 1955), p. 12f.
[6]   *Ibid.*, p. 16.
[7]   *SWS*, IV, 364f: "... werde ein Prediger der Tugend *deines Zeitalters*".
[8]   *SWS*, IV, 412: "Alle Aufklärung ist nie Zweck, sondern immer Mittel".
[9]   For a good recent treatment of many of the aspects of Herder's theories which directly concern us here see Eric A. Blackall, *The Emergence of German as a Literary Language* (Cambridge, 1959), Chapter XIV (pp. 451-481), which bears the significant title "The Return to Origins". See also Erich Heintal's introduction to J. G. Herder, *Sprach-philosophische Schriften* (Hamburg, 1960), esp. pp. ix and xv.
[10]   Cf. Hamann's "Poesie ist die Muttersprache des Menschengeschlechts". *Werke*, ed. J. Nadler (Wien, 1949f), II, 179 with Herder's "... denn was war *diese erste Sprache als eine Sammlung von Elementen der Poesie?*" (V, 56).

sion, language has by no means been neglected, and we have seen that in all the major works discussed so far, in the *Fragmente*, the *Kritische Wälder*, and the *Kalligone*, that concern for language has played a major role. In the light of Herder's treatment of and answers to such problems as: what is the relationship of thought and language? what constitutes the being of language and poetry? and which is more important, the word or the connotations and denotations that stand behind it? the importance of language for every subject treated by Herder has been firmly established.[11] Now we are ready to examine still another aspect, that of origins, in preparation for a discussion of Herder's concept of the individual literary genre.

Herder sees three stages in the developing process of language: the first concerns pre-linguistic beginnings; the second, the actual coming into being of language; the third, the development of language up until the present time.[12]

Beginning his prize essay with the words *"Schon als Thier hat der Mensch Sprache"* (V, 5), Herder develops his ideas on the pre-linguistic beginnings of language at the very outset of his treatise. The earliest utterances of man, shared in common with animals, consisted of loud outcries, inarticulated sounds, and individual tones. These utterances were all produced by the reaction of man to feelings, passions, pains, joys, and sorrows. A suffering animal, Herder reminds us, cries out in pain just as did Homer's hero Philoctetes. Using the same image he had employed elsewhere, Herder compares animal feelings to strings which, when struck or plucked, perform their natural function and resound. Already in this pre-stage of language, the cries and tones are audible projections of the inner feelings of the creatures which utter them, if the soul of an animal can be said to possess such. In the fact that every being in nature expresses its feelings, Herder sees revealed a law of nature: "empfinde nicht für dich allein: sondern dein Gefühl töne!" (V, 6) That is, no creature in nature

---

[11]   Cf. here Hermann Hettner, *Geschichte der deutschen Literatur im Achtzehnten Jahrhundert* (Braunschweig, 1909), III, 3, 1, p. 28. S. also Heintel, p. ix and xv.

[12]   Peyer, p. 19.

exists for itself alone. It is predestined that each creature should communicate its feelings to the rest of nature's creation.[13] These utterances, whereby feelings were first communicated, Herder calls language, a language of feeling. *"Diese Seufzer, diese Töne sind Sprache: es gibt also eine Sprache der Empfindung, die unmittelbar Naturgesetz ist"* (V, 6f). Ruefully Herder admits that although vestiges of these natural tones are to be found in all original languages (*Sprachen des Ursprungs*), they are no longer the main component of human language. But the more primitive the language, the more of these vestiges it retains. Although not the roots of languages, according to Herder these vestiges are the sap which gives life to the roots. These outbursts of feeling must not be confused with language itself, nor can they be said to represent the origin of language, for such outbursts are common to all animals, while man alone has developed a true language. Before true language can come into being, the intercession of a specific human capacity is necessary. This capacity Herder terms reflection (*Besonnenheit*). What these outbursts of feeling do indicate is that there is a certain basic medium from which both the language of feeling and true language have drawn nourishment, and that it is only under these certain conditions that either can arise and develop.

The second stage in the development of language was the actual coming-into-being of language. The question of the origin of language was a speculative problem which had greatly occupied the eighteenth century and which had long been a bone of contention among scholars.[14] The importance of Herder's unique

[13] Compare this with Herder's dispute with Kant (*Kalligone — Kritik d. U.*) over the communicable aspects of art in Chapter IV.

[14] Since detailed discussions of the various theories represented are readily available in a number of works, I do not find it necessary to repeat this here. The reader is referred to such works as: Robert T. Clark, Jr., *Herder* (Berkeley-Los Angeles, 1955), p. 130f, Blackall, p. 462f, Gustav Konrad, *Herders Sprachproblem im Zusammenhang der Geistesgeschichte* (Berlin, 1937), p. 18f, Rudolf Haym, *Herder*, ed. Wolfgang Harich (Berlin, 1954), I, 429f. For a recent study which goes far beyond Herder's work or anything done in the eighteenth century see G. Revesz, *The Origins and Prehistory of Language,* trans. J. Butler (London-New York-Toronto, 1956).

contribution to this question has long been recognized by a large number of scholars and scientific linguists. The words of the Danish scholar Otto Jespersen make clear the unique claim to distinction enjoyed by Herder's achievements in an age and field where greatness was conspicuous. "The profoundest thinker on these problems in the eighteenth century was Johann Gottfried Herder, who, though he did little or nothing in the way of scientific research, yet prepared the way for the rise of linguistic science. In his prize essay on the *Origin of Language* (1772) Herder first vigorously and successfully attacks the orthodox view of his age – a view which had been recently upheld very emphatically by one Süssmilch – that language could not have been invented by man, but was a direct gift of God ... Language was not deliberately framed by man, but sprang of necessity from his innermost nature." [15] But Herder not only successfully attacks the orthodox view such as was held by Hamann and restated by Süssmilch, he also contradicts what is known as the sensualist theory developed by Condillac in his *Essai sur l'origine des connaissance humaines* (1746-55), and the mechanistic theory of Rousseau as outlined in his *Discours sur l'inégalité* (1755).[16] Herder's concept of the origin of language is built up around what he terms *Besonnenheit*, the power of reflection. Man alone is in possession of this power and through it he is able to produce language. This power of reflection is not a self-sufficient power or sense or faculty, but rather an aggregate of all of man's faculties, a function of man's soul. *"Es ist die ganze Einrichtung aller Menschlichen Kräfte: die ganze Haushaltung seiner sinnlichen und erkennenden, seiner erkennenden und wollenden Natur; oder vielmehr –* Es ist *die Einzige positive Kraft des Denkens, die mit einer gewissen Organization des Körpers verbunden bei den Menschen so heisst, wie sie bei den Thieren Kunstfähigkeit wird: die bei ihm Freiheit heisst, und bei den Thieren Instinkt*

[15] Otto Jespersen, *Language, Its Nature, Development and Origin* (London, 1922), p. 27.
[16] As Wolff has pointed out (pp. 761-764), Herder is indebted to Rousseau for many of his ideas on language in the *Fragmente*. It is not until the prize essay that we find Herder turning away from Rousseau. For this see Wolff's excellent discussion, p. 773f.

wird" (V, 28-29). Herder reminds us that the difference here
between the power of reflection and the instincts and make-up
of animals is not one of degree or of an addition of powers, but
rather that it represents an entirely individual direction and development of powers. Thus it is by means of the product of these
powers, language, that man is distinguished from animals, for by
its very nature *Besinnung* is a creative power capable of growth
and development, while the drives and instincts of animals are
organically determined, and hardly capable of further development.[17]

But the important question of how this power of reflection
produces language still remains to be answered. Herder explains
it as follows: "Der Mensch beweiset Reflexion, wenn die Kraft
seiner Seele so frei würket, dass sie in dem ganzen Ocean von
Empfindungen, der sie durch alle Sinnen durchrauschet, Eine
Welle, wenn ich so sagen darf, absondern, sie anhalten, die Aufmerksamkeit auf sie richten, und sich bewusst seyn kann, dass
sie aufmerke" (V, 34f). This concentration on one of the many
images which stimulates the senses leads to the isolation and appropriation of characteristics which distinguish it from other
impressions. This reflective characteristic was "Wort der Seele",
and with it language is formed. Using a lamb as an example, Herder shows how this process works and how man thereby finds
language. Man does not react to the lamb as would a ram, or a
wolf, or a lion, all of which are affected by instinct. As soon as
the lamb bleats, the necessary characteristic has been supplied,
for of all the other characteristics of the sheep, it has been isolated and has distinguished itself so as to make the strongest and
most lasting impression on the soul of man. Consequently, when
the sheep appears again, man recognizes him and says to himself:
"Ha! du bist das Blöckende!" (V, 36) Now it is important to

---

[17]   See here esp. *SWS*, V, 34. In his article on Herder and Rousseau already
mentioned Hans Wolff asserts (p. 783) that in reality Herder has not explained the origins of language, but only pointed to the fact that a being
without language cannot be human and that language can simply be seen
as the decisive characteristic of man. From this he deduces that there is
actually no conflict with Hamann's statement that language is "ganz göttlich ... und ganz natürlich".

note here that the whole reflective process is an internal one and
that the characteristic itself is an inner characteristic. Thus the
earliest language, which is a collection of these inner words, is
an inner language of the soul, but a language just as naturally and
necessarily invented by man as the fact that man is man.

That the first words of the soul to become articulated are sound
words, e.g. the bleating of the sheep, leads us to the third of Herder's stages in the development of language. The most important
thing to be noted after the conception of language is the characteristics of this earliest language which is, according to both Hamann and Herder, synonymous with poetry. Herder refers to
these characteristics of primitive language as power elements
(*Machtelemente*), and, as might be expected, the first of these
elements is "tönende Verba" (V, 52). They comprise the very
first words in the vocabulary of man, for they are developed and
collected from all the sounds roundabout man, e.g. the bleating
sheep. Already in the *Fragmente* Herder proclaimed living expression (*lebender Ausdruck*) to be one of the primary features
of primitive language.[18] For a long time among the ancients singing and speaking were one. In both the prize essay and *Vom
Geist der Ebräischen Poesie*, Herder calls special attention to the
importance of Oriental languages. Concerning Hebrew in particular he writes: "Die Wurzeln ihrer Verben . . . sind Bild und
Empfindung und ich weiss keine Sprache, wo die einfache und
leichte Verknüpfung beider so sinnlich und merkbar wäre" (XI,
230). In the same work he terms the elements of poetic language
"Handlung, Darstellung, Leidenschaft, Gesang, Rhythmus" (XI,
225), all of which are dependent upon "tönende Verba". In still
another place in the prize essay where the elements of the first
language are declared to be indentical with those of poetry, Herder
describes them thusly: "Nachahmung der tönenden, handelnden,
sich regenden Natur!" (V, 56)

The second characteristic of primitive language and poetry is
that nouns are derived from verbs. Thus from the verb *blöcken*
is derived the noun *der Blöckende*. This process constitutes the
first step toward abstraction, for it is by means of the nouns de-

18   See especially *SWS*, II, 70ff.

rived from verbs that primitive man is able to personify nature. "Bei den Wilden in Nordamerika z. B. ist noch Alles belebt: jede Sache hat ihren Genius, ihren Geist, und dass es bei Griechen und Morgenländern eben so gewesen, zeugt ihr ältestes Wörterbuch und Grammatik – sie sind wie die ganze Natur dem Erfinder war, ein Pantheon! ein Reich belebter, handelnder Wesen" (V, 53)! In the essay on Hebrew poetry Herder considers animation and personification one of the most important features of early poetry. He points out that in Hebrew poetry this feature is evident on every hand, for the whole language is derived from the roots of verbs. In fact, he knows of no other language where this is any more so the case than in Hebrew.

Another of the important characteristics is the musical quality of man's first language. Already in the *Viertes Wäldchen* Herder had discussed at length the important role played by music in the development of early poetry and speech. This early speech, he says, approximated rough singing, and he comes to the conclusion: "Man sang also, indem man sprach" (IV, 115). This statement is echoed in the prize essay when he writes: "Die Tradition des Alterthums sagt, *die erste Sprache des Menschlichen Geschlechts sei Gesang gewesen*" (V, 57). By repeating the denial already iterated in several of the earlier works that man could not have learned this song, and thereby also speech from the song of a bird, Herder further strengthens his theory that the origin of language lies in man's powers of reflection, which may rightly be considered one of the functions of the soul. The nightingale sings for himself and other nightingales, and not for man. As this early singing language has continued to develop to the present time, its uneven accents, its rhythms, its intonations – in short, all the elements which identified it with song — have undergone a leveling process and have gradually disappeared, until today they are found only in those languages which development has bypassed and which have succeeded in preserving their original qualities. In Herder's view this not only constitutes a loss for language, but for poetry as well, and indicates a turning away from those characteristics which are a direct result of the formative powers of the soul to those which recognize only one aspect of these powers.

A further characteristic of primitive language is its rich imagery. The Hebrew language again serves Herder as model. In the *Älteste Urkunde* he writes: "Man wird viel und mehr als zu viel von *den Zeiten* gehört haben, da es noch keine Bücher und Büchergelehrte gab, da die Sprache des sinnlichen Menschen Bilder und Zeichen, das ist, *Handlungen* waren, und wo man also auch diese *Handlungen*, wenn sie erhalten werden sollten, als solche die sie waren, durch *Bilder und Zeichen* erhielt" (VI, 288). Later on in the same work he refers to Hebrew as an image language ("Bildersprache", VI, 289). Speaking of the origin of Hebrew poetry, Herder asserts: "Dieser ist, wie ich bei den prägnanten Wurzeln ihrer Sprache zeigte, *Bild* und *Empfindung*. Von aussen strömen Bilder in die Seele: die Empfindung prägt ihr Siegel drauf, und sucht sie auszudrucken durch Geberden, Töne, Zeichen" (XII, 6). "Die erste Dichtkunst war also ein *Wörterbuch prägnanter Namen und Ausdrücke* voll Bilder und voll Empfindung" (XII, 7). This ability of the soul to create images, and of the poet to take these images created by the soul and project them to us by the medium of his work, is the subject of the short essay *Ueber Bild, Dichtung und Fabel*, which we have already considered in detail. Through this process the work of the poet then assumes a symbolic character, as Gisela Ulrich has admirably described it: "Indem der Dichter jeden Gegenstand sinnlicher oder eingebildeter Art mit seinem inneren Sinn bezeichnet und diese in seiner Seele gesammelten Ansichten und Bilder in gestaltete Form schliesst, erfolgt eine Umsetzung der Sachen in Bilder, in Worte oder Zeichen. Seine Kunst trägt daher Zeichencharakter. Sie ist Neugestaltung der Welt in Symbol. Der Geist dichtet und verdichtet die Welt der Seele zur Welt der Bilder." [19] This imagery, these symbols and "bold metaphors in the roots of the words" as Herder terms them in the prize essay, were important factors in the feeling that is basic in all primitive language and poetry. As long as they were present and man preserved direct contact with nature, he also maintained his power to empathize with

---

[19]   Gisela Ulrich, *Herders Beitrag Zur Deutschkunde* (Würzburg, 1943), p. 42). Cf. *SWS*, XV, 530.

nature. But as soon as these images gave way to abstractions and allegories for which man had no empathy, then feeling became diluted and weakened and was gradually replaced by abstract metaphysical speculation. This is the state in which Herder finds most of the languages of his day and time, including his own native German. Luckily, however, there still remain a few languages which preserve these qualities, and scattered in among the songs of simple peoples of every nation can be found remnants of the glories of by-gone days which still bear the features of this first language and poetry.

The importance of imagery, and of feeling which is so closely related to it, leads us to still another consideration. Herder adopts G. F. Meier's translation of Baumgarten's adjective *sensitivus*, such as it occurred in the famous phrase "oratio perfecta sensitiva", and says that one of the most important features of a language is that it be *sinnlich*, i.e., close to sense images.[20] According to Herder's system of ages of languages one of the distinguishing features of early language is that it speaks for the eye and ear, for the senses and passions. Regarding the youthful age, which Herder considers a poetic age, he writes in the *Fragmente*: "Die Sprache war sinnlich, und reich an kühnen Bildern" (I, 153). Herder's development of the idea that language must retain its closeness to sense images reaches its climax in the *Viertes Wäldchen*. Here, after examining and refuting Riedel's definition of poetry, Herder is able to advance his own definition: "Poesie ist also *vollkommen sinnliche Rede*" (IV, 131). But as we have already seen, this definition was not original with Herder, and he is quick to admit this himself. Baumgarten had already stated it before him in his *Aesthetica*.

In the *Fragmente* Herder had previously criticized the rationalists philosophers who wished to eliminate synonyms from language. These philosophers considered synonyms so many 'useless servants" and thought of them only as impediments to philosophical thought and expression. Herder, however, considers synonyms

---

[20]   Clark, p. 17. Blackall, p. 452, who apparently agrees with Clark, explains *sinnlich* as a "direct sound-reaction to sense-impressions".

as one of the most important features of this early poetic language.

Although Herder admits that a host of synonyms might present problems to the philosophers, he cannot imagine poetic language without them. "Noch bleiben aber Synonymen! Aber der Philosoph suchte feine Unterschiede in sie zu legen, und sie also als neue, gültige Wörter zu gebrauchen . . . Der Dichter muss rasend werden, wenn du ihm die Synonyme raubst; er lebt vom Ueberfluss" (I, 170). This is another illustration of the difference Herder sees between poetic and philosophical language, on which he dwells at length in the *Fragmente*. The same difference is emphasized again in Herder's review of Bodmer's *Die Grundsätze der deutschen Sprache*, which appeared in the *Allgemeine Deutsche Bibliothek* (IV, 298f). Bodmer favors the delimitation of synonyms, but in his review Herder again points out the basic differences between poetic and philosophical and emphasizes that the poet must necessarily have the vocabulary for a variety of shades of meaning. It is the philosopher, not the poet, who is concerned with conceptual clarity. In the prize essay Herder not only opposes Süssmilch's theory of the divine origin of language, but also his whole concept of language. Prominent among Süssmilch's ideas was his conviction that synonyms are worthless. Herder's defense of the use of synonyms here rests upon his assertion that the more direct man's contact is with sense images, the greater number of synonyms his language will contain.

Closely related to many of the characteristics already discussed is a feature which often complements and unites them. "Geberden, und Accent kommt zu Hülfe, um dies Chaos von Wörten verständlich zu machen" (I, 192). By means of accents and gestures the same fine shades of meaning can be attained that are possible through the use of synonyms. Or even among synonyms it is possible to delegate to them degrees of meaning or importance by varying the accentuation or intonation. While the last two here are purely verbal means of adding to the meaning of language, the use of gestures introduces an entirely new factor, a visible means of aiding verbal expression. As Herder points out both in the *Fragmente* and the prize essay, the close agreement

between word and gesture is a feature of language which fortunately can still be observed in the speech habits of primitive
peoples, but which has all but disappeared in the abstract metaphysical language of most so-called civilized peoples.

Several other characteristics of primitive language and poetry
which Herder discusses at length in the *Fragmente* and which
have already been mentioned in connection with our discussion
of this work should be briefly called to mind. Part six of the first
collection is devoted entirely to a discussion of *Idiotismen*, which
Herder defines as the "patronymic beauties" of a language. These
personal idioms embody the very essence of language and reflect
the national character and way of thinking of the people who
speak it. They are often next to impossible to translate, for they
are unique to a given language. These personal idioms are what
might be termed the genius of the language. This genius is innate
and cannot be acquired through translations or imitations. Once
lost, however, it is difficult to acquire again. The second of these
characteristics discussed primarily in the *Fragmente* is Herder's
much praised treatment of inversions, i.e., free word order, in
section twelve and thirteen of the first collection. With rigid,
stereotyped word order the rationalists aimed for a clear, lucid
exposition of thought, i.e., philosophical thought. But Herder,
more interested in a poetic than philosophical language, wants
inversions, which he says can translate emotional emphasis into
linguistic emphasis.

The characteristics enumerated here thus far all have one thing
in common – they are all external characteristics of language.
They could be seen if the language were written (which of course
primitive language was not), they could be listed in dictionaries,
they could be described in grammars. But what about those even
more important characteristics, which because of their nature
remain unseen and unlisted, but which nevertheless constitute
the very essence of language? Herder tells us that the more original the language is, the fewer the abstractions, but the more the
feelings. The feelings overlap one another and defy any attempts
to classify them logically or orderly. This means "that in primitive languages feelings are not clearly distinguished and concepts

not delineated".[21] In the *Erstes Wäldchen* Herder explains the unique inner condition of poetry by declaring that the "being of poetry is power". Herder was not interested in these external characteristics as ends in themselves, but as means to a greater end. The primary purpose that Herder sees in language is that it should be able to give expression to that inner conglomeration of man which Herder often refers to as his soul. Primitive language is therefore a language of the soul, of feeling, of passion, of perception and sensation. Primitive language reflects man's closeness to and dependency on nature. And although the first language is man's own unique distinguishing feature, it serves as a connecting link between man and other forms of creation and emphasizes his harmony with them.[22] Peyer has summarized this unique condition of language: "Sprache im Ursprung und erste Poesie fussen gemeinsam in der Seinsweise zwischen Zuständlichkeit und Reflexion, in einer Seinsweise, die wir zunächst mit aller Vorsicht als die Empfindung definieren können. Denn das Besondere der Musikalität, der Bilderreichtum, der Reichtum an Synonymen und Inversionen in der Ursprache ist überall Ausdruck der Empfindung, wie Herder ja die Ursprache selber als Sprache der Empfindung bezeichnet." [23] Herder realizes however, that a return to the conditions of primitive language – this is brought out clearly in the short essay "Von den Lebensaltern der Sprache" – would neither be possible nor particularly desirable. Accordingly, although he may dwell at length on the features of this language, his first concern lies with modern languages. Modern language cannot revert to primitive language, but it can, and must, subject itself wholly to the direction of the soul if there

---

[21] Blackall, p. 470.
[22] Cf. *SWS*, XV, 209f.: "Sprache ist das Vorrecht des Menschen, und auch das Siegel, mit dem er sogern alles in der Natur bezeichnet ... Durch die Worte nämlich gewinnet unsere Empfindung gleichsam Form und Gehalt: unser Gefühl wird durch sie ein helleres Bild."
[23] Peyer, p. 27. Cf. Benno v. Wiese, "Der Philosoph auf dem Schiffe" in his *Der Mensch in der Dichtung* (Düsseldorf, 1958), p. 61f: "Die Dichtung wird zu einem Ausdruck der einmaligen Seele, zugleich aber zu einer wirkenden, kosmischen Kraft innerhalb der göttlichen Schöpfung". And p. 65: "Denn die Sprache ist für Herder ... eine positive Kraft der Seele, ein Wörterbuch der Seele."

is to be any true poetry. Thus Herder refers to Klopstock as a speaker of the soul: "Grosser, lieblicher Dichter, du Sprecher der eigensten Empfindungen unsrer Seele, du kannst dein Haupt einst fröhlich neigen" (XXVII, 172). Klopstock, who for Herder was representative of an overthrow of the purely conceptual and reason-determined language of the Enlightenment, is an example of what can be attained poetically, even with modern language, if the soul is permitted to perform its rightful functions. Such tasks as the centralization of all of man's faculties into a unified whole, as serving as the receptacle for all sensations and perceptions, and as actively engaging in creative activities to the developmental benefit of the soul itself and other souls are among these functions.

Where did Herder think that language and poetry which meet these requirements can be found? In a broad sense all *Volksdichtung* possesses these qualities. This *Volksdichtung* was for Herder a poetry of immediacy (*Unmittelbarkeit*). By *Volksdichtung* Herder does not mean the poetry of any certain *Volk*, but rather a poetry which has been experienced inwardly and can express vital energy and life's stream.[24] Consequently, Herder is able to include such diverse works of literature as the Bible, the epics of Homer, the plays of Shakespeare, and common folk songs under the general designation *Volksdichtung*. This was a poetry which, because of its immediacy to mankind, became a vehicle for *Humanität*. It is the expression of a people who act and feel as man should,[25] and it serves as a symbol to these people of their relationship to the Divinity.[26] As Korff has pointed out, since *Volksdichtung* in general, and *Volkslieder* in particular, are direct expressions of the souls of the *Volk* which creates them, only through the understanding of these creative souls can the creations themselves be understood. "Alle Eigentümlichkeiten der Volkslieder,

[24] Franz Schultz, *Klassik und Romantik der Deutschen* (Stuttgart, 1952), I. Teil, p. 184. Elizabeth Blockmann, "Die Deutsche Volksdichtungbewegung in Sturm und Drang und Romantik", *DVJS*, I (1923), p. 428.
[25] Cf. Alexander Gillies, *Herder und Ossian* (Berlin, 1933), p. 124 and *SWS*, III, 34.
[26] Benno v. Wiese, *Herder, Grundzüge seines Weltbildes* (Leipzig, 1939), p. 35.

die den Geschmack des aufgeklärten Menschen beleidigten, erklärte er aus der *Psychologie des Naturmenschen* – der 'wilden', wie er vorzugsweise sagt." [27]
Precisely since Herder saw embodied in the wild and primitive songs of Ossian all of these qualities, both external and internal, his short essay on Ossian is well suited to serve as the starting point of our investigation of his ideal of poetry. As far as Ossian's style was concerned, there was nothing here strange to Herder. The style of Ossian reminded him strongly of the Bible, Homer, and Milton, which prompted Herder to consider Ossian an original genius worthy of consideration in the same class as these other literary greats.[28] For Herder Ossian's songs clearly represented a poetic remnant from a primitive age in which poetry was the expression of the true life of the *Volk*, of nature, and of the power of an innate Divinity revealing Himself in all of human activity.[29] As the account in the travel dairy makes clear, Ossian's poems became an inseparable part of Herder's spiritual existence. His feelings and passions correspond exactly to those of his idol. All the moods of Ossian are relived by Herder as he relives those of no other poet.[30] Herder also sees in Ossian an important representative of *Humanität*. Ossian's portrayal of the Scotch heros acting and feeling like humans enables him to present an incomparable example of human perfection. Indeed, in his description of human nature, noble intentions, pure feelings, and moral characterizations he surpasses all primitive poets, even Homer himself.[31]

At the very beginning of his essay Herder reminds his readers of the quality and type of songs written by the Scotch bard. "Ihnen wollte ich nur in Erinnerung bringen, dass Ossians Gedichte *Lieder, Lieder des Volks*, Lieder eines ungebildeten sinnlichen Volks sind, die sich so lange im Munde der väterlichen Tradition haben fortsingen können" (V, 160). The spirit of the work itself

[27] H. A. Korff, *Geist der Goethezeit*, 4. Auflage (Leipzig, 1957), I, 137.
[28] *SWS*, III, 27f, IV, 320f.
[29] Gillies, p. 32.
[30] *SWS*, V, 169, VI, 136, XVIII, 463.
[31] Gillies, p. 124, *SWS*, III, 34. Herder apparently could not make up his mind whom he honored the most, Homer or Ossian. Cf. *SWS*, XXV, 314.

is sufficient evidence for Herder to dispel all doubts concerning its authenticity.[32] In particular, Herder stresses the lyrical element of the poems, which already at this early date in Herder's life is an indication of which of the poetic genre he considers most perfect. "Nehmen Sie doch Eins der alten Lieder, die in *Shakespeare*, oder in den Englischen Sammlungen dieser Art vorkommen, und entkleiden sies von allem Lyrischen des Wohlklanges, des Reims, der Wortsetzung, des dunklen Ganges der Melodie: lassen Sie ihm blos den Sinn, so so, und auf solche und solche Weise in eine andere Sprache übertragen, ists nicht, als wenn Sie die Noten in einer Melodie von *Pergolese*, oder die Lettern auf einer Blattseite umwürfen?" (V, 161) For Macpherson Herder has only words of praise, for his translations of Ossian have preserved what he considers the original metre, form, tone, rhythm, and melody, and in addition that dark, unnamable quality which flows into man's soul. On the other hand, he is incensed at the efforts of Denis to force the free and easy style of Ossian into the harsh fetters of German hexameter. The Scots, whose songs Ossian recorded, were a wild, free *Volk*, and as such their songs reflect this state of existence. They too are wild, free, lively, full of sense images, and lyrically active. These songs were intended to be sung, to give expression to feeling and passion, and not to be printed in artificial letters or examined by scientific methods. Theirs are creations for the ear, and not the eye, for as Herder has stated in numerous places, music is a purer expression of the soul than the word alone, since in music there is nothing present to distract from the potency of its energy and power. By manifesting itself physically and visably in those two qualities so highly esteemed by Herder in the *Volkslied*, the *Sprünge und Würfe*, this energy gives further support to Herder's belief that art alone possesses the magic key to transform idea into movement, the invisible into the visible, the spiritual into the physical.

For Herder the five nations in North America, i.e., the Iroquois, are a living example of the *Volk* that the ancient Scots

---

[32] A treatment of this question is beyond the scope of this discussion. For the most complete and widely recognized treatment of it the reader is referred to the work by Gillies mentioned above.

must have been. He compares Ossian's songs with the Iroquois songs, which he unfortunately knew only through travel books, and reminds us that travelers who have known both peoples have freely acknowledged their similarities. "Sehen Sie nach, wie viel nach allen Berichten darinn auf lebende Bewegung, Melodie, Zeichensprache und Pantomine ankömmt" (V, 167). In passionate outbursts Herder describes his desire to become one with the people who have produced these wild songs, a desire which was actually consummated in a spiritual, if not a physical sense. "Da will ich die Gesänge eines lebenden Volks lebendig hören, sie in alle der Würkung sehen, die sie machen, die Örter sehen, die allenthalben in den Gedichten leben, die Reste dieser alten Welt in ihren Sitten studiren! eine Zeitlang ein alter Kaledonier werden" (V, 167).

Such wild enthusiasm as Herder exhibits on behalf of these songs smacks of a complete lack of objectivity, and since Herder realizes this, he hastens to assure his imaginary correspondent, who in all probability was Gerstenberg, that this enthusiasm is not based on second-hand knowledge and experience alone, for he himself has had the opportunity to experience personally living remains of these old, wild songs among living people who have adopted neither German customs nor the language or songs. It is fairly certain that Herder refers here to the deeply gripping effect he experienced sometime during the period 1765-66, when for the first time he saw and heard the primitive indigenous Lithuanians, who inhabited the countryside roundabout Riga, perform and sing the songs of their national heritage.[33] This one experience has been shown to have brought about a complete change in Herder's view of poetry and re-evaluation of the place which the songs of primitive people should occupy in literature as a whole.[34] The lasting impression which this experience left in the

[33] For a complete discussion of Herder's early contacts with folk songs see Leonis Arbusow, "Herder und die Begründung der Volksliedforschung im deutschbaltischen Osten", in *Im Geiste Herders*, ed. E. Keyser (Kitzingen, 1953), 129-256, esp. p. 140f. Arbusow's views conflict with those of E. Blockmann, p. 425, who says that Herder first experienced the folk song while on the trip in 1769.

[34] Arbusow, p. 140f.

mind of Herder not only resulted in his own monumental achievements such as the collections of folk songs, but can also be said to mark the beginning of a new era in the development of German literature.

One of the characteristics of primitive language which Herder had particularly stressed in the prize essay was the quality of action imparted to language and speech by the *tönende Verbs*. Agreeing with his correspondent, Herder acknowledges the dramatic quality of Ossian's songs. "Alle Reden und Gedichte derselben [wild people] sind Handlung" (V, 177). Although Ossian's songs do contain this element common to all primitive poetic works, it should be remembered that the outstanding one quality found in Ossian, which more than any other commanded Herder's esteem and response, was lyricism. In his short comparison between Homer and Ossian in the *Horen*, Herder defines the difference between the two poets as follows: "Er ist ein *rein epischer*, Ossian ist, wenn man so will, ein *lyrisch-epischer* Dichter" (XVIII, 454). Herder goes on to say, that in true epic-dramatic style Homer's figures and images are perfectly clear. Everything in Homer goes on right before the eyes of the reader with nothing left to doubt. With Ossian the figures are shrouded in a fog. They are the results of sensations and feelings. So despite the action and the important folksong features *Sprunghaftigkeit und Würfe* that abound in Ossian, his songs are much too subjective and dependent upon the expressions of individual feelings to be counted as dramatic.[35] This is also the reason why, in spite of his great admiration for Homer, Herder ultimately esteemed Ossian even higher.

Herder's enthusiasm for the songs of the Nordic mastersinger, as he termed Ossian, reaches its high point when he announces to his correspondent that he sees in them perfect models in every respect for modern poems.[36] The songs themselves justify their existence for Herder, and their selection as models thus requires no further defense from him. Above all, it is the spirit that fills every song and which emanates from every utterance that com-

---

[35] Cf. here Max Schasler, *Ästhetik, Grundzüge der Wissenschaft und der Kunst* (Leipzig-Prag, 1886), II, 226f and 233f.
[36] Cf. *SWS*, V, 203.

pletely captivates Herder. "Der Geist, der sie erfüllt, die rohe, einfältige, aber grosse, Zaubermässige, feierliche Art, die Tiefe des Eindrucks, den jedes so starkgesagte Wort macht, und der freie Wurf, mit dem der Eindruck gemacht wird – nur das wollte ich bei den alten Völkern, nicht als Seltenheit, als Muster, sondern als Natur anführen, und darüber also lassen Sie mich reden" (V, 181). The presence of this spirit prompted Herder to say some years later in the *Horen* essay, when he had clearly begun to doubt the authenticity of Macpherson's claim, that whether or not the poems are genuine makes little difference. The spirit is the important thing, and Herder never doubts for a moment that the true spirit is embodied in these songs. Now if the spirit is present in the songs and poems, then they will speak to the soul of man. Poetry, Herder tells us, should be the stormiest, surest daughter of the human soul. But in order for the poetry to speak to the soul, the soul itself must be conditioned to its message. The soul must be formed (*gebildet*). Herder fears that most human souls are no longer receptive to the "impromtus" of Homer and Ossian because generations of training have reformed them. His lament is: "Wir sehen und fühlen kaum mehr, sondern denken und grübeln nur; wir dichten nicht über und in lebendiger Welt, im Sturm und im Zusammenstrom solcher Gegenstände, solcher Empfindungen; sondern erkünsteln uns entweder Thema, oder Art, das Thema zu behandeln, oder gar beides – und haben uns das schon so lange, so oft, so von früh auf erkünstelt, dass uns freilich jetzt kaum eine freie Ausbildung mehr glücken würde, denn wie kann ein Lahmer gehen!" (V, 183).

When he surveys his own contemporary literary situation Herder sees two main classes of poets who can produce the type of poetry he has been talking about and hoping for. The first group of poets may even make use of logical content. But they must recognize the existence of presentative, cognitive powers and then contemplate the object and content of their poems until these become as indelibly written in their souls as words printed on a page. Such poets as Milton, Haller, Kleist and even Lessing have written this way. Herder's second group of poets, represented by Klopstock, Gleim, and others, are even closer to Herder's ideal

and to the technique of Ossian. "Fodert sein Gedicht aber Aus-
strömung der Leidenschaft und der Empfindung, oder ist in seiner
Seele diese Klasse von Kräften die würksamste, die geläufigste
Triebfeder, ohne die er nicht arbeiten kann: so über lässt er sich
dem Feuer der glücklichen Stunde, und schreibt und bezaubert"
(V, 184). Ever mindful of the practical aspects poetry and art
have for life, Herder predicts that the poet whose poetry combines
all these elements will have a tremendous influence on young
souls and as much as anyone will help to form these souls so that
they will develop into receptive vehicles for the feelings and passions to which his contemporaries have become so oblivious.
"Eine ganze jugendliche, kindliche Seele zu füllen, Gesänge in
sie zu legen, die, meistens die Einzigen, Lebenslang in ihnen
bleiben, und den Ton derselben anstimmen, und ihnen ewige
Stimme zu Thaten und Ruhe, zu Tugenden und zum Troste seyn
soll, wie Kriegs-Helden-und Väterlieder in der Seele der alten,
wilden Völker" (V, 201).

Although Herder could not foresee this, his own collection of
folk songs was to become one of the most significant contributions
toward fulfillment of this goal. With these folk songs he made
available to the public-at-large visible, concrete evidence of all
he had talked about in the *Fragmente* and Ossian essay. As Carl
Redlich has accurately observed in his introduction to Herder's
poetic works: "Denn darüber kann doch kein Streit sein, dass
die Volksliedersammlung, so weit sie auch hinter dem ihrem Ur-
heber vorschwebenden Ideal zurückgeblieben ist, wegen ihrer
Bedeutung für die gesamte Schriftstellerei Herders und wegen der
Wirkungen, die von ihr ausgegangen sind, die hervorragendste
Stellung unter allen seinen Dichtungen einnimmt" (XXV, vii).
It is also true that Herder's concept of the *Volkslied* did not always maintain a definite, permanent form, but that it often assumed a like identity with what Herder might call a *Nationallied*
or *Bauernlied* or *Nationalgesang*.[37] But by whatever name he
called them Herder saw expressed in these songs and poems the
thoughts and feelings of a definite *Volk* according to their own
unique way. Everywhere that Herder writes about primitive poetry

[37] Cf. *SWS*, XXV, viii and Blockmann, p. 422ff.

he stresses its lyrical, musical rhythms. One could more fully appreciate the full scope of Herder's achievement in rendering the songs in his collection into German texts had he been able to carry out his original intention and publish the original melodies along with the texts. But as it is, something of the original melody can adequately be observed in the rhythm of the verses. The fourth book of the folk song collection is devoted to Herder's collection of Nordic songs. In his introduction to this book Herder raises a question, the answer to which must be obvious to anyone familiar with Herder. Herder observes at the very outset that modern man knows of many more peoples than the ancients. Obviously, however, he cannot personally acquaint himself with all these peoples. *"Wie* aber nun diese Völker, die Brüder unsrer Menschheit *kennen? blos von aussen,* durch Fratzenkupferstiche und Nachrichten, die den Kupferstichen gleichen, *oder von innen?* als Menschen, die Sprache, Seele, Empfindungen haben? unsre Brüder!"* (XXV, 81). No one, Herder continues, even in his own philosophical century will deny the necessity for such knowledge. And one of the best ways to make such knowledge available is through the songs of these peoples. Why? Because such songs not only describe how a people look and what they do, but also how they speak and feel and think, the innermost emotions and processes of their souls. When Herder describes what he foresees as the purpose and goal of a collection of folk songs, he also succeeds in quite accurately characterizing the results realized by his own collections.

Ein Volk *schildern,* heisst eigentlich nichts, als die Sitten und Denkart desselben, so möglich, *durch sich selbst* zeigen: da man aber nicht alles zeigen oder aufzeichnen kann, eben das *ausmerken,* was – nicht am lärmendsten ist, am meisten in die Augen fällt – sondern *am tiefsten sitzt,* gleichsam Geburts-Stamina des Volks enthält und am innigsten *characterisiret.* Wer die Kunst hat, sich dahin *ein zu setzen,* am tiefsten *zu dringen,* am leichtesten zu *zeichnen,* sich und andre ganz damit zu *familiarisen,* des ist *Volks Kenner* und *Zeichner*: das andre sind *Farbenreiber* und *Schmierer* (XXV, 82f).

The task of poetry is not only to portray the soul of man, to show what his morals and manner of thinking are, but also to have an

influence and effect upon these morals. This is the main theme of
the prize essay of 1781, *Ueber die Würkung der Dichtkunst auf
die Sitten der Völker in alten und neuen Zeiten*. This essay complements the prefaces to the folk songs by presenting theoretical
material finally omitted from the prefaces. And strange as it may
seem, it also seems that Herder intended it as a justification for
the folk song collection.[38] Calling upon the ancients as witnesses,
Herder observes that poetry had the strongest of influences on
their morals. Poetry, the daughter of heaven, even had the power
to subdue animals, to animate stones, and to breathe into the
souls of men hate and love, courage and meekness, consolation,
joy and hope. It was poetry that brought coarse peoples under
laws, that encouraged the reluctant to battle and work. And finally poetry was the oldest and, according to tradition, the most effective means of instruction for the formation of the morals
of men and citizens. Three points are to be covered in the prize
essay: (1) a definition of poetry and its effects on the morals of
man; (2) a historical survey of the effects of poetry on the most illustrious nations known, the Hebrews, Greeks, Romans and
Nordic nations; (3) the changes in the effects of poetry in medieval and modern times and the effects of poetry at the present
time. Thus for Herder poetry is "Abdruck unsrer Empfindungen" (VIII, 339), and its purposes are "Abdruck in der Seele [zu
machen]" (VIII, 339), "den Seelen der Menschen einzuhauchen"
(VIII, 334), and "die Seelen der Menschen wieder aufzuschlies-
sen" (VIII, 336), and the ultimate goal of these activities is *"die
Bildung der . . . Volker"* (VIII, 346).

Of primary interest to us here is not Herder's long and sometimes detailed historical survey which he uses to support his remarks, but rather what he has to say about poetry itself. If poetry
is what it should be, Herder tells us, then it must be effective
(würkend). Nature, feeling, whole human souls are expressed
linguistically through poetry, which imprints itself on the souls
of empathic, like-tuned souls. Herder terms poetry an imprint of
perceptions, and the more recognizable and stronger this imprint,
then the truer the poetry is and the more effective it must be. It is

[38] Clark, p. 252.

important to note that it is not the poetry itself, but rather nature, the whole world of passions and actions which lay in the poet and which, expressed linguistically in the form of poetry, produces the effect. In this process language is compared to a canal, the true poet only to a translator. That is, he serves as the bearer of nature into the heart and soul of his brothers. Any effects which his poetry may have are not arbitrary or conventional, but are brought about by natural powers *(Naturkräfte)*. To receive the full effect of these powers man must be a receptive vessel, and the more receptive man is, the greater will be the effect of poetry upon him. The operation of this poetic effect can be compared to a chain reaction, for starting with the poet, it continues on from one individual to another without spending its effectiveness. Since nature, feelings, and passions are so important to the effectiveness of poetry, poetry has enjoyed its greatest period of effectiveness while man was still close to nature, while he still unashamedly expressed his feeling. This was the point, of course, which Herder hoped to illustrate with his folk song collection, and which he now approaches from the theoretical side here. But what is even more important for Herder's aesthetic as a whole is the emphasis which he places on the internal aspects of the effectiveness of poetry throughout the first section of the essay. Herder does not even mention form once. What he is concerned with is that the poetry possess a spiritual quality which not only reflects the disposition of its creator, but also of the people and age to which he belongs. But even should this stipulation be met there is still another requirement if poetry is to be effective, and this is, as we have seen, that man be receptive to poetry. This state of receptiveness is likewise an inner condition which reflects man's whole way of life and his attitudes toward life.

Herder illustrates these theoretical assumptions with examples from history. The effect of Hebrew poetry, which he so highly esteems, he characterizes as divine. God speaks through this poetry and the poetry itself is full of His spirit. Conversely, the poems themselves are directed to God. "Ihn darzustellen, zu preisen und zu offenbaren, das erwählte Volk zu *seinem* Volke, zu einem Volke *Gottes* zu bilden: das allein ist ihre grosse reine Absicht"

(VIII, 344). According to Herder a good deal of the effectiveness of Hebrew poetry can be traced to the fact that in their very beginnings the Hebrews were a poetic people. Witness to this are many passages in the Old Testament. But when the Hebrew culture became diluted by the influences of Hellenism, then the atmosphere which nourished the poetry lost its purity, and the poetry ceased to flourish. A parallel development took place in Greece. Here too Herder thinks that poetry, in its beginnings, was religious in nature, for it shaped the morals of gods and men. And here too it was finally diverse outside influences which brought an end to the golden age of poetry. When one considers the tremendous influences on Herder wrought by the Ossianic songs, it is no wonder that he is especially laudatory of the positive effects of poetry among the Nordic peoples. His discussion of them follows that of the Romans, and Herder finds it a pleasant relief to return to a people for whom poetry did so much. "Wir kommen hier wieder in ein lebendiges Feld der Dichtkunst, wo sie würkte, wo sie *lebendige That schuf.* Alle Nordischen Völker . . . hatten Gesänge: Gesänge, in denen das *Leben ihrer Väter, die Thaten derselben, ihr Muth und Herz lebte*" (VIII, 388). Citing Tacitus as his proof, Herder attributes to the power of the Nordic peoples' songs the ability to withstand the Roman onslaughts. The bards made the national spirit *(Nationalgeist)* of their people indomitable and their morals and customs unextinguishable. In this capacity the bards represented the crux of the national existence. Still another period in Western European history in which poetry played a dominant role was the Middle Ages. Here, under strong Arab influences at a time when there were few books, religion, song, and poetry occupied the very center of life. The previous relationship which Herder saw between poetry and religion easily leads him to see an important role for poetry in Christianity. Herder recognizes a higher purpose for Christianity than producing poets, but at the same time he acknowledges poetry as one of the most important aids which Christianity possesses in the fulfillment of its goals. But in modern time poetry, the child of heaven as Herder calls it, has fallen onto evil days. It has been written in a language which the *Volk* does not understand, and consequently can have little or no effect. Poetry has lost its power. Instead of writing for the *Volk*, one pedant writes for another, one scholar for another. Although this survey of Herder's essay has been cursory, it nevertheless serves to illustrate two important aspects of Herder's theory of poetry. Firstly, it restates with slightly different emphasis what Herder has already made clear elsewhere, namely, that poetry is not only the result of an inner condition of the poet, but that its effectiveness is likewise dependent upon an inner condition within those who read or hear it. Secondly, that to be effective, poetry must be inextricably linked together with all the essentials which concern man, his *Volk*, his religion, his way of thinking, his national ideas and ideals.

The earliest evidence of Herder's interest in poetry and his first efforts to define poetry are found in the two short essays *Fragmente einer Abhandlung über die Ode* and *Versuch einer Geschichte der lyrischen Dichtkunst.* Both were probably written in 1764 and neither was published in Herder's lifetime. Although both contain much in germinal form that has already been discussed in connection with other works, both also contain several features which are uniquely their own. And both are of historical interest because they clearly show how early in Herder's lifetime these matters commanded his interest and attention. At the very beginning of his essay on the ode, and then again at its end, Herder announces the method which he intends to utilize in his investigation. This is the historical method, which for Herder means that the ode must be examined as a never static, but constantly growing and developing organism. Herder observes that most investigations have been concerned with the end product and have given little attention to the vital question of origins. So here, and probably for the first time Herder announces his intention of starting at the beginning and concerning himself with the origins of poetry. This essay is also of particular interest because in it Herder identifies the ode with lyric poetry in general.[39] In the first section of the essay Herder writes: "Das erstgeborene Kind der

[39]　Peyer, p. 54, makes this same observation. He also lists *SWS*, II, 303 as proof of this. Cf. also XXVII, 163.

Empfindung, der Ursprung der Dichtkunst, und der Keim ihres Lebens ist die *Ode*" (XXXII, 62). Now it has generally been recognized that Herder uses his terminology very loosely and that it is almost a necessity to examine each usage individually before its exact meaning can be determined. But it is also an accepted fact that for Herder lyric poetry represented the highest literary genre. This makes it hardly possible that Herder uses the word ode in its narrow sense. This fact is further substantiated by the introduction of the essay where Herder observes that other literary genre have been widely treated, but that the ode has hardly been given any consideration at all. And here one must assume that Herder is referring to critical treatises, for since the appearance of Klopstock's poems lyric poetry in general and the ode in particular had certainly occupied a central position on the German literary scene. But it actually matters little whether Herder uses the term ode in its broad or narrow sense insofar as the connotations which it suggested are concerned. On the one hand the term ode called to mind the perfection of the classical form of Pindar and Horace, either with its song-like quality or its rhymeless, distancing, and solemn treatment of the exalted and sublime. On the other, it signified all the new-found glory of the German lyric in the poetry of Klopstock, which although in many respects was reminiscent of the classical form, in content emphasized the personal, the enthusiastic, and the German. In the poems of Klopstock the soul revealed itself in new creative and expressive heights.

In passing it is interesting to note briefly some of Herder's observations on the nature of the ode in the first of the two essays. Already at this early date the importance which Herder attaches to the soul of an artistic creation is unmistakable. Imitations of Horatian odes, Herder reminds us, have nothing in common with the originals except the form. "Erkennt man aber bei jeder Ode ein antikes Skelet einer Horazischen, so fehlt ungeachtet aller schönen Zusammenpassung einer Seele des schöpferischen Originals; und wir werden selten mehr als einzelne schöne Gedanken auszeichen können" (XXXII, 65). At the same time poetics alone will not assure the creation of true poetry. It is a fundamental principle in Herder's psychology and aesthetics that every organism undergoes development, and although this process of growth and development is, for the most part, desirable, Herder does recognize some negative aspects in it, for the possibility is omnipresent that one of man's faculties might be developed to the detriment of the others. Herder sees an example of this in his own age, where the emphasis on reason has completely overshadowed man's ability to feel and to sense. "Je mehr sich die Gegenstände erweitern, die Menschlichen *Gesites*kräfte sich entwickeln, desto mehr ersterben die Fähigkeiten der sinnlichen Thierseele. Die Ausbreitung der Wissenschaften verengert die Künste, die Ausbildung der Poetik die Poesie; endlich haben wir Regeln, statt Poetischer Empfindungen; wir borgen Reste aus dem Alten, und die Dichtkunst ist todt!" (XXXII, 69). Since imagination plays a role of considerable importance in poetry, it must be evident that the role of the soul is not only a passive one, but that the soul does possess powers of creation all its own, which are critical to the conception of poetry. "Da das enge Reich der reellen Wesen bei uns durch die Bezauberungen der Einbildungskraft sich sehr erweitert hat, so ersetzt auch die Phantasie sehr oft die *wahre* Empfindung, bis der Ankerseil bisweilen zum subtilen Spinnengeweb, was durch die Nadelöhr geht, verlängert wird" (XXXII, 74). The being of poetry is power, and by means of this power poetry comes alive, and reaches out to encompass the whole soul of him who hears and receives its message. "Des eigentlichen Dichters Trieb ist *Wuth*; seine Worte Pfeile; sein Ziel das ganze Herz; dies ist das Götliche unaussprechliche der Dichtkunst" (XXXII, 76). "Die Ode der Natur, die nicht Nachahmung ist, ist ein lebendiges Geschöpf, nicht eine Statue, noch ein leeres Gemälde" (XXXII, 78).

In the midst of his discussion of the ode Herder admits that there is only one living German poet who has succeeded in incorporating into his poetry the elements which he describes in his essay, and which he deems necessary in any true poetry. "Vielleicht ist indessen unter uns nur ein lyrischer Dichter von einer Höhe, die zwischen Affekt und leerer Einbildung schwankt" (XXXII, 75). Although this one lyric poet is nowhere more closely identified, there can be no doubt that Herder had Klopstock in mind when he wrote these cryptic lines. Klopstock, whom Herder names in the same breath with such true poetic geniuses as Shakespeare and Ossian, is the only German poet to merit consistently the designations "genius" and "poet". In the early Riga treatise of 1765, "Haben wir noch jetzt das Publicum und Vaterland der Alten", Herder extolls the name of Klopstock as an example of what a German poet can and should be. In other writings Herder refers to him as "der erhabne *Klopstock*" (V, 80), the "Markgrafen Deutscher Hoheit" (III, 250), and "der Empfindungsvolleste [Dichter] unsrer Nation" (VI, 149). In keeping with his definition of lyric poetry, which he defines as "das schönste Gemälde der menschlichen Sprache" (XV, 532), Klopstock's odes are "Lyrische Gemälde" (I, 209). Speaking of poets who have written religious poetry, Herder writes: "Der Heiligste unter allen, *Klopstock*, und das heiligste Gedicht desselben, *der Messias*" (XXX, 244). In his role as genius Klopstock has taken the German language, moulded it with his creative spirit, emphasized its inherent qualities, and so for the first time in his own age shown that German too is still a proper vehicle for poetic expression. "Die Sprache, der Ausdruck ist Gepräge des physiognomischen Genius, das Kreditiv gleichsam seines Berufs und für uns das Organ seiner neuen Belehrung" (IX, 447). "Aus den Zeiten der Meistersänger, des Opitz und Logau, des Luthers u.s.w. sollte man die Idiotismen sammeln, und insonderheit mehr von Klopstock lernen, diesen Genie in Schönheit und Fehlern, der selbst in der Deutschen Sprache sich dem Schöpfungsgeist anmaasste, und auch diesen Geist der Freiheit eingentlich in Deutschland zuerst ausbreitete: wirklich ein Genie, der selbst in seiner Eccentricität gross ist, und das, so wie Alexander Macedonien, die damalige Deutsche Sprache nothwendig für sich zu enge finden musste" (I, 165). An excellent record of Herder's early, and one might add lasting, enthusiasm for Klopstock can be found in his correspondence with his bride-to-be, Caroline Flachsland, from August 1770 to April 1773. The references here to Klopstock are so numerous that one scarcely reads a letter without finding mention of his name. Caroline becomes Herder's

"Meta", and Herder continually suggests Klopstock's poems to her as suitable reading material, even to the point of sending her copies of these poems which have come to his attention. Of all the poets, Shakespeare and Ossian included, references to Klopstock are more numerous.

But of all the qualities which Herder thought praiseworthy in the poetry of Klopstock one stands out more than any other. Klopstock was a poet of the soul and for the soul. "Leset den Homer, und denn leset Klopstock: . . . dieser spricht, um zu malen, er schildert; und um neu zu seyn: eine ganz andre Welt; die Welt der Seele und der Gedanken, . . .: (I, 167) ". . . ja vielleicht ist sein grosses Talent, die Seele zu schildern, mehr werth, als alles im alten Griechen – . . ." (I, 269). In Klopstock's odes it was these spiritual qualities which attracted Herder's attention and which commanded his esteem. "Klopstock hat in seinen Oden weniger Horazische Züge: . . . allein, bald erhebt sie sich [i.e. the ode] zur Welt der Gedanken und Empfindungen, zu der ihm eignen Kunst, die Seele des Menschen und Christen zu schildern, worinn er eben mit Horaz nicht zu vergleichen ist. Alle seine Oden sind meistens Selbstgespräche des Herzens: . . ." (I, 467). As Adler has pointed out, in his review of Klopstock's odes in 1771 (V, 350ff), Herder "emphasizes above all else their marvelous lyrical quality, especially in these youthful poems in which Klopstock pours forth his whole heart and soul. This universal human spirit he finds breathed through all the poems, but with a different expression in each." [40] Klopstock is thus for Herder another example of the principle that the universal finds expression in the individual, for although Klopstock developed his own inimitable style, he was nevertheless just as able to portray that most important of all universals, the human soul, as Shakespeare before him had done in his dramas. "Da alles Aeussere nur Abglanz der innern Seele ist: wie tief ist nicht der barbarische gothische Shakespear durch Erdlagen und Erdschichten überall zu den Grundzügen gekommen, aus denen ein Mensch wächst, so wie *Klopstock* zu den geheimsten Wellen und Schwingungen einer reinen himmlischen Seele" (VIII, 183f).

[40] Frederick H. Adler, *Herder and Klopstock* (Cleveland?, 1913), p. 52.

If one bears in mind this inclusive definition of the word ode, then it is not difficult to see the essay on lyric poetry as a natural sequence to the ode essay. Again in this essay the first few pages are given over to an explanation of why Herder thinks it necessary to return to the origins of poetry if one hopes adequately to understand it. Poetry is a human art, which is all the more reason why we should investigate it and attempt to reveal its origins. Should these origins lie so far back in history that no documentation has survived, then man must take recourse in hypotheses. This is, of course, the method which Herder adopted. Thus Herder not only attributes the origins of poetry to the dim past, but even its golden age, for this was the age when poetry sang. Believing in the organic growth of things as he does, Herder does not hesitate to challenge the view represented by Lowth and others that, whereas the development of all other arts was a gradual process, poetry was a divine gift and had been perfect from the very beginning. "Keine Empfindung ist *auf einmal* entstanden: sie war im Anfange nicht das, was wie ward; . . . Nach und nach entsprang eine jede Sache; man bekümmerte sich also im Anfange nicht um sie, weil man ihre zukünftige Grösse nicht voraussahe" (XXXII, 89). Herder concedes that the essence of poetry, here in the Old Testament, is divine, but this essence is expressed in a form that is human and which is subject to the same laws of development as any other art. ". . . denn jede Sache wird alsdann gleichsam *sichbar*, und bekommt eine *Gestalt*, wenn sie lange nach ihrem unbemerkten Ursprunge, . . . jetzt zeigt, *dass sie bleiben* wird, . . ." (XXXII, 90). The comparison which Herder sees between the poet as creator and the Great Creator, which was later developed more fully in the work on Hebrew poetry, is also touched on here. One can say that poetry is divine because the poet works in a divine manner. He creates. Finding little good to say about most of the descriptions of poetry he has seen, Herder compares them to a prescription. "Einbildungskraft, Witz, Scharfsinn, Beurtheilung, Gabe des Ausdrucks, jedes nach seinem Maas und so hat der erste Dichter entstehen müssen" (XXXII, 103). But no more than the poet is a mixer of ingredients is he a philosopher, as some would have him to be. "Der Dichter ist

weder ein theoretischer noch praktischer Philosoph, der die Rei-
nigkeit der Vollkommenheit sucht: er ist ein Dichter, der rühren
und Leidenschaften erregen will" (XXXII, 119). This definition
of the poet leads Herder to say of poetry itself: *"Leidenschaft
und Handlung ist die Seele der Dichtkunst"* (XXXII, 122). By
translating the two key words in the definition above "feeling"
and "power", then the completed definition of the *Viertes Wäldchen* can clearly be recognized, for as our discussion has indicated, Herder's basic concept of poetry was to change little
throughout his lifetime.

When considered in the light of some of Herder's more detailed
works on the subject of poetry, then the two short essayistic contributions to part two of the *Terpsichore* can be regarded as compact summaries of Herder's concept of lyric poetry. To be sure,
a good deal is repeated about the quality and importance of language, about the creative act of the poet, etc., that has already
been said elsewhere. Nowhere else, however, does one find
brought together in short, concise statements the various theories
and ideas which Herder had stated about poetry as one does here.
According to the first of the two essays, the eye and the ear constitute the original parents of poetry. "Das *Auge* erfasst *Bilder*;
die Seele erschaffet sich durch dasselbe *Gestalten*: seine Welt ist
das *Nebeneinander*, der *Raum* . . . Das Ohr höret den *Schall*, die
mancherlei *Töne*, durch welche sich die Gestalten in ihrer Bewegung ankündigen; diese *Folge von Empfindungen* giebt die
Seele das Maas der Zeit" (XXVII, 164). These two statements
could well be compared with profit with the definition of the
Viertes Wäldchen. As the union of the two senses sight and hearing emphasizes the sensory aspect of lyrical poetry, which includes
those two characteristic qualities imagery and rhythm, at the same
time it emphasizes the ordering and creative role of the soul. The
particular reference to sight calls to attention the rich imagery of
lyric poetry.[41] Although these images have their beginnings in
those stimulations conveyed to the soul from the eye, the final

---

[41] Cf. this with *SWS*, XXIV, 203 and 253 where Herder emphasizes the
importance of imagery, but warns against assonance and melody for its
own sake.

images are actually creations of the soul, and not the sense of sight. It is likewise the function of the soul to receive the sensations from the ear, and from this plethora of sound to single out the tones which the soul can make further use of. Through its images the soul creates an awareness of space, through the tones which penetrate into it and which it must order, an awareness of time, which in turn points to the musical quality of lyric poetry. Thus the temporal aspect provided by the sense of hearing, together with the special element furnished by sight, puts poetry in the unique position of having qualities from the two most important classes of art, the spacial and the temporal. We can agree then with Herder's definition of lyric poetry as "the most beautiful painting of the human language" (XV, 532), but would wish that he had specified a "living" painting. For there is nothing dead or abstract about lyric poetry. It is a living, dynamic, spontaneous art form which reflects the soul of its creator, while at the same time it attempts to project itself into the soul of the reader or listener. All of these elements taken together lead Herder to define lyric poetry as follows: *"die lyrische Poesie ist der vollendete Ausdruck einer Empfindung, oder Anschauung im höchsten Wohlklange der Sprache"* (XXVII, 171).

By keeping in mind the results of our discussion here and the points already presented in earlier chapters regarding Herder's theoretical utterances on poetry, we now should be able to attain a fairly compact view of his poetic ideal. Although it would be misleading to state that Herder cares nothing for poetic form, it is entirely correct to say that he cares nothing for poetic form *per se*. Poetic form, or for that matter any kind of form, acquires importance only as the outward manifestation of a more important content. The scope of Herder's literary favorites is broad, encompassing such varied types as the Bible, Shakespeare's plays, folk songs, yes even didactic poetry. In form these all differ radically, yet they nevertheless have one important feature in common. In each instance the form has resulted from natural organic growth. This partially explains Herder's passion for returning to origins, for in any organism each stage is of equal importance. The other reason why he returns to origins is to find a poetry not

contaminated by too much sophistication, but which has retained
its originality, simplicity, and vitality. At first glance this may
seem to be an acknowledgement of the so-called primitivistic
point of view, according to which what is oldest and most original
is also the best. As is evidenced by his esteem for Klopstock, Herder cares nothing for origins in themselves unless they serve a
purpose. Herder has established certain criteria for poetry. He
wants it to be "immediate", to sing, to be pregnant with imagery,
to originate in the soul and to speak to the soul, and to have feeling. Of all the poetry he knows, the poetry of origins, what he
terms *Volksdichtung*, best exemplifies these qualities. It might be
argued that in his desire to find poetry that meets his definition
of poetry as "perfectly sensuous speech" that Herder has over-
emphasized its sensuous aspects and feeling, thereby excluding
from poetry any rational content. When one remembers that feeling for Herder is an all-inclusive term, embracing both man's
rational and sensuous faculties, this argument also fades. Herder
never wanted to exclude reason, only to put it into its proper perspective. Poetry must be effective, which for Herder means that
it must appeal to the soul of man, must open up to it new horizons, and stimulate its growth and development. This is possible,
however, only if the poetry itself is spirit-filled, if it has originated
in the spirit of its creator, and is an expression of his innermost
thoughts and emotions. The ultimate goal in the developmental
process of man is *Humanität*, and of all the arts poetry is best
able to bring man closer to this goal.

B. THE POETRY OF HERDER,
"EXKURS ZUR WERKIMMANENTEN POETIK"

Now Herder admits that on the basis of his discussion of poetry
that its form will differ according to the people (*Volk*) who produce it. The difference in language alone is sufficient to support
this statement. But even more important than form is content,
and in lyric poetry, as in every aspect of human endeavours, this
remains constant for Herder. In the second of the two essays he

writes: *"Dem lyrischen Gesange schwebt also ein immer-
wachendes Ideal vor: ein Reichtum der edelsten Gedanken und
Empfindungsweisen im wohlklingensten Ausdruck"* (XXVII,
196). Herder terms this ideal "die Grazie des Lebens" and finds
it dwelling in the lyric poets of all nations. The duty of these
poets is to choose the most beautiful form and the noblest content to express this ideal, for it is not the ideal of one man and
one time, but the eternal ideal of all mankind. Although Herder's
masterful translations and *Nachbildungen* of folk songs and other
poetic works have been received with universal acclaim, his own
original poetic creations have remained practically unknown.
Some of these – mostly the incidental poems – were published
during his lifetime, but the greater number slumbered in obscurity
in Herder's notebooks and private papers until they were finally
published in the monumental Suphan edition.[42] It is to several of
these lyric poems, unpublished in Herder's lifetime, that we now
turn our attention. These same unpublished lyric poems have
recently been pointed to by one scholar as the ideal avenue of
approach to the very core of Herder's personality.[43] The subject of
many of these poems is the human soul, indeed, we can say that
these poems represent a conscious effort on Herder's part to give
expression to the innermost workings of his own soul. Often it
would seem that Herder attempts in them to define those qualities of the soul which, although their existence is generally acknowledged, are destined to remain indefinable. Seeking after a
goal which dwells in the realm of the transcendental, these poems
are full of allusions to a higher identity of man. Expressive in
style, they treat the visible and objective symbolically, whereby
that pertaining to the soul seeks to reveal itself as the connecting
link to an all inclusive whole. Never content to rest within themselves, the poems seem to strive forward in an unending process
of growth and development, until "the complete expression of
a sensation" is attained. A poetry of "ultimate concerns", these

---

[42]   For a detailed discussion see Carl Redlich's introduction to *SWS*,
XXIX, v ff.
[43]   Eduard Spranger, "J. G. Herder: Ahnung und Erfülling", in *Vom Geist
der Dichtung,* ed. Fritz Martini (Hamburg, 1949), pp. 31-48, esp. p. 31ff.

poems are permeated by intellectual presentations, which in spite of their rhythmic linguistic forms, have little in common with the folk song adaptations. As celebrated by Herder in many of these poems, the human soul is often seen as a microcosm.

> Wer bin ich? alles erwacht in mir! mein Geist! ...
> Höhen ... Tiefen! — ich schaudre! ...
>   die nur Gott durchmisst! ...
> Dunkel liegt mein Grund! – Leidenschaft durchfleusst
> ihn unendlich und braus't – braus't – Geist du bist
> eine Welt, ein All, ein Gott, Ich! –
>
>   (XXIX, 258)

This poem is the expression of an inner illumination, of self-discovery on the part of the poet. The answer to the question "Wer bin ich?" is supplied by the dynamics of the awakening spirit, whose potential seems unlimited, since this spirit is like God. ("Geist du bist ... ein Gott.") The spirit does not originate in consciousness, or in reason, but in the dark depths of the soul. First revealing itself as passive, the spirit gradually unfolds into an infinite cosmos. But throughout this whole process, from the moment of the dark awakening until final attainment of universality, and in spite of the enormous tensions generated during this process, the "I" always maintains its human individuality and its original and unique consciousness. A new potential has not been added, only the inherent one expanded. But this is the miracle of man, for simultaneously he is universal, yet individual, in him lies a nothingness of chaos and darkness, yet at the same time the universe, yes even God himself. Man is therefore the beginning and the end of a process which finally unites the antitheses dark and light, nothingness and everything, and the origins of this process, indeed of man himself, are to be found within his soul, where they slumber until awakened and stimulated, both from without and within, to growth and development, until finally the goal of man, perfection, is attained.

While these poems contain many of the qualities which Herder so highly esteemed and praised in folk songs and other works of literature such as the Bible and the plays of Shakespeare, in many respects they fall considerably short of Herder's ideal of lyric poetry. One misses the rich imagery of the Bible, the "Sprünge und Würfe" of the folk songs, and the musical and rhythmic quality of Klopstock's creations. The correctness of Franz Schulz' remarks about the quality of Herder's own poetic creations can, with this in mind, hardly be denied. "Herders Gedichte muten unmusikalisch an. Sie klingen nicht. Ihre Worte und Bilder gehen kaum über das Bereitliegende und Geläufige hinaus. Ihr zarter Schmelz, wo in ihnen nicht leidenschaftliche Jugendlichkeit waltet, liegt im Gedanklichen und in der sinnigen Wendung, die Menschlich-Allzumenschlichem gegeben wird, in dem äolsharfenartigen Mitschwingen von Obertönen und nicht voll zum Ausdruck gekommenen Schwankungen des Denkens und Empfindens." [44] What Schultz has failed to appreciate, however, is that Herder's purpose in writing these poems by no means conforms to the usual pattern of lyric poetry. These poems, and it is significant to note that Herder never published them, were for him both a spiritual confession and catharsis, in which he simultaneously pours out his soul and addresses it. At the beginning of his discussion Spranger has taken note of this fact, and it is likewise of utmost importance for us not to lose sight of it. Spranger writes: "Immer wieder redet er in diesen Gedichten, die niemand um ihres poetischen Wertes willen rühmen und geniessen wird, seine eigene Seele an." [45] Schultz' charge that the poems are unmusical is undoubtedly valid, but should be followed by the remark that their purpose was to express something not at all suited to musical expression, but which, as he himself has correctly observed, is more suited to an intellectual idiom and to the expression of things which, though incapable of making music, all the more reveal the spiritual and sensuous. Since these poems are at once man-centered, man-originated, and man-directed, it can hardly be any wonder that they are expressed in an idea which is "human – all too human". Although Herder may not have succeeded in writing lyric poetry in the strict sense of the word, these poems, with their emphasis on spirituality and feeling, for they originate in the soul, are the expression of the soul, and are writ-

[44]   Schultz, p. 211. S. also p. 210.
[45]   Spranger, p. 31.

ten for the soul, are deserving in every respect of the designation mirrors of the soul.[46]

> Mich sing ich! Welt und Gott ein All! in mir!
> Selbst bin ich Lied, und Welt und Phöbus mir!
>
>   (XXIX, 253) [47]

In an explanatory footnote to one of these unpublished poems – "Der Genius der Zukunft" – written while on the sea voyage in 1769, Herder himself has given several hints as to his frame of mind while writing many of these poems and to the spirituality which he hoped to give expression to in them.

> Der Verfasser glaubt aus langen innigen Bemerkungen seiner Seele, dass aus der Summe der vergangenen Lebenserfahrungen im Grunde des Gemüths gewisse Resultate, Axiome des Lebens liegen bleiben, die in schnellen oder ganz ungewissen Verlegenheiten, wo die kalte Vernunft nicht oder falsch Rathgeberin ist, wie Blitze auffahren, und dem, der ihnen treu folgt, sehr sichre Fackeln seyn können, wo sonst alles dunkel wäre. Er glaubt ferner, dass diese bei gewissen Menschen sehr hoch erhöht werden können, und sehr oft zu sichern Weissagern, Traumgöttern, Orakeln, Ahndungsschwestern erhöht worden sind, und dass fast kein grosser Mann da ohne gewesen, oder zum Ziel gelangt sei: ja er glaubt noch viel mehr, was aber nicht, wie das Vorangemerkte, so nöthig zum Verständniss nachfolgender Ode gereichen möchte, die übrigens zur See gemacht ist, und also in Meeresbildern wandelt. (XXIX, 322)

Significantly, Herder has excluded "cold reason" from playing any role in the process whereby the axioms of life are attained, and instead has delegated to the soul the usual role played by reason. For several reasons the soul is much better suited to perform this function than is reason. The soul acts as a sort of receptacle into which are poured all of man's experiences. Although these may seem to be dormant, they are very much alive, are constantly intermingling with and thereby modifying and expanding one another, until, as Herder puts it, they rise up like a bolt of lightening, revealing the unmeasurable depths of the human soul. It is doubtful, however, that Herder really meant to completely exclude reason from any part at all in such a process.

[46] *Ibid.,* p. 32f.
[47] Cf. this with "An die lyrische Muse", *SWS*, XXIX, 252.

What he wants to do is to exclude the type of reason he specifically designates "cold reason", which is synonymous with Kant's term "pure reason". This type of reason was the embodiment of all cogitative principles which, independent of experience, are present *a priori* in the mind and which possess universal validity. For Herder, however, reason is never *a priori*, but rather is inextricably bound together with all the experiences of the soul.[48] Reason is, in Herder's own words in the fourth book of the *Ideen*, identical with *Humanität*, and like language is one of the features that is uniquely human.[49] Ensuing in and with language, reason is not only one with feeling, but also maintains its individuality instead of succumbing to bland universality. The originality of this reason expresses itself in creative inspiration and in the genius. "Ein mit uns gebohrner Geist, *daimon, vis animi divinior* . . ." (XXII, 202). "War er Genius im Augenblick des *Erschaffens*, als . . . der göttliche Funke in ihm schlug, als in Einem Gedanken sein Werk oder Geschäft ihm ganz dastand" (XXII, 204). "*Genius* ist ein höherer, himmlischer Geist, wirkend unter Gesetzen der Natur, gemäss *seiner* Natur, zum Dienst der Menschen" (XXII, 205). Everything in the soul thus becomes one giant fabric, woven by the Creator Himself, who has created the individual organizations of the universe. But just as Herder compares the creative act of the artist with that of the Great Creator, so too does he identify the soul of man with the soul of the Godhead. The fourth stanza of this poem "Der Genius der Zukunft" is a good statement of this identification as Herder sees it.

> Dich bet' ich an, o Seele! Der Gottheit Bild
> in deine Züge gesenkt! In dir
> zusammengehn des weiten Weltalls
> Erhalterband'! Aus der Tiefe, dir
> aus dem Abgrund webt sich Weltengebäu und sinnst und tastest
> zum Saume des Ends hinan!
> Nur tief umhüllt! in schwangerem Schoos
> mit Wolken umhüllt! in Kluft des erbrausenden Meeres
> da ruht die keimende Nachwelt.
>
> (XXIX, 323)[50]

[48] Cf. *SWS*, VIII, 198, 213, V, 29, 31, 40, 100, XV, 534, XVI, 124.
[49] *SWS*, XIII, 144ff.
[50] Cf. with these statements from the *Reisejournal:* "vom dunkeln Meer

This poem, like Herder's concept of the soul, and like many of his writings, presents through its imagery three distinct, yet intertwined, systems. As an image of the Godhead, the soul is the very point in which the very bands which preserve and maintain being itself come together. This gives way to an image in which is reflected the developmental process of the whole world and a drive to conquer the infinite. Here the soul is pictured as a microcosm, but with all the powers of the macrocosm. Finally, in the pregnant bosom of the soul there lies in germinal form all future development. Being, development of a cosmic system, and final fulfillment in a universe created by the power of the soul, the same three-pronged system we have met elsewhere, remains Herder's concept of the realms within which the soul reveals itself. Since all the images here can be understood as manifestations of a personal "I", the individual and the universal remain of necessity intertwined, so that the individual expresses universality, and the universal individuality. Feeling one's self a creature of God, created in his image, seemingly carries with it the responsibility of immediate development and reception of experiences of the world, in order finally to be able to penetrate to the very brink of infinity and thereby to bring fulfillment to the finite. The powers to do this lie deeply enveloped in the depths of the soul, but once aroused, these powers possess the same might as the roaring sea.

Despite the sea imagery and the ecstatic outbursts of Herder's early *Sturm und Drang* language,[51] the influence of Leibniz is clearly recognizable in this stanza. The soul of man is not only thought of as an image of the Divine Being, but like Leibniz' monads this soul reflects within it the whole universe. Line five of the stanza makes clear the role played in this process by the senses. For Herder the senses are canals through which the macrocosm flows into the soul and thereby becomes an integral part

---

vergangenen Thaten", "in der Seelen Abgründen glänzt der Vorwelt Bild und schiesst weitüber weissagend starkes Geschoss in das Herz der Zukunft".

[51] For a detailed discussion of these early features see Eric A. Blackall, "The Imprint of Herder's Linguistic Theory on His Early Prose Style", *PMLA*, LXXXVI (Dec., 1961), pp. 512-518.

of it. But since the microcosm is but a miniature of the macrocosm, it possesses the same power of creativity which is present
in the macrocosm. Consequently, the images in the soul do not
originate solely from external sources, but are even born within
the soul itself, thus strengthening even further the analogy between the microcosm and macrocosm. This creative power within
the soul is the subject of several of these poems which, like so
many of Herder's creations, remained fragmentary.

> Was ich bin Geist! ich Geist! – so bin ich Gott!
> Ich denk' ich will ich bins! wie Gott, durch den ich bin,
> einst Geister rief aus dem Geisternichts
> und Körper rief aus dem Köpernichts
> ruff ich Gedanken aus dem Gedankennichts!
> ich wills! – es schafft sich Wirkung aus dem Nichts!
> O Gott was gebst du mir! – all deine Welt
> schaff ich dir in mir nach! –
>
>   (XXIX, 230) [52]

Precisely this intimative, fragmentary, and eruptive form is that
best suited to express the cosmic and the universal, which is Herder's main intent, and for which ordinary words, expressions, and
images will hardly suffice. How shall language give a half-way
satisfactory portrayal of the inner creative act which is the subject of this poem? How can the power be named which can transform the superhuman and godlike into the realm of the earthly
and manlike? The only answer is Herder's stammering excla-
mation: "O Gott was gabst du mir!"

Reminiscent of the Barock lyrics of Fleming, Gryphius, An-
gelus Silesius, and especially those of the great Protestant poet
Paul Gerhardt, with a subtitle which seems to mean nothing more
than Barock, and with the typical Barock motive of the transitory nature of life in the last stanza, the three stanzas of the following poem are a visible reminder of the soul: its origins, its
growth and development, and its final perfection. Indeed, the
more of these poems one reads, the more apparent it becomes
that Herder's most genuine work is built around one eternal
theme, the soul and its three stages of development.

[52] Cf. *SWS,* XXIX, 8.

Fragment eines Lobgesanges an die Menschliche Seele.
nach Altdeutscher Manier!

Statt Luft – und Himmelswesen
preis' ich die Menschenseele!
Die Schöpferin! Erlesen
hat sie in dunkler Zauberhöle
sich einen Erdenleib, und ward
in Herrlichkeit und Schöne
der Götter offenbart!

Nimm, was die Menschenseele
für neuen Sinn ersonnen!
Und fleuch aus deiner Höle
zu wandeln unter Stern' und Sonnen!
Und kehr' hinab und sieh und sprich,
was Grösseres du gesehen,
die Sonnen, oder dich.

Was dir ein Erdball dünket,
der Leib, den du ernährest,
der todt zu Staube sinket,
wenn du zu neuen Reichen kehrest –
ist eine Welt, von ihr vereint
und herrlich Kunstgebildet,
was dir ein Erdklos scheint.

(XXIX, 312) [53]

Along with this emphasis on spirituality there is a further re-markable feature about many of these poems. It is impossible not to recognize in them the very same ideas which Herder develops more fully later and then makes the subject of some of his greatest works. This is the case with a poem which, although it was neither dated nor entitled by Herder, was probably written as early as 1764 and bears the title "Der Mensch" in the Suphan edition. The similarity of the major theme of this poem with what Herder says some twenty years later in the *Ideen* is unmistakable. The subject of the poem is man, and its opening lines are devoted to an enumeration of the various types of man which the poet wishes to exclude from discussion in his poem. Although many of the human types listed in these lines figure prominently in, and con-

[53] Cf. XXIX, 375f: "Die Menschenseele", and I, 472f.

tribute significantly to Herder's overall concept of man and his purpose and function, they are all ignored in this poem and are only mentioned because Herder thereby is able to heighten the climatic effect reached when he finally does introduce the man whom he celebrates here. Thus it is not the man who embodies within himself the various facets of creation, nor man who stands at the pinnacle of creation and has dominion over it, nor man who emulates the creative act whom the poet has chosen as his subject. These types and many more are all disregarded in favor of the man whom Herder describes in the short, eight line stanza.

> Den Menschen der Natur, den keiner je gesehen
> und jeder in sich fühlt, und jeder wünscht zu sehen
> und niemand such zu seyn: den Menschen ohne Kunst
> voll Seele ohne Witz, gut ohne Göttergunst,
> voll Menschheit ohne Scham, voll Wahrheit ohn Vergnügen –
> Den Sing' ich. Sey mein Lied, wie, den du singst, Natur!
> blos durch Empfindung wahr, schön, durch die Wahrheit nur. –
>   (XXIX, 255) [54]

The man celebrated here by Herder also has many features in common with the type of man celebrated by Hamann and Rousseau. Once again the influence of the Barock is apparent in the form of the poem and in the almost didactic comparison of the individual virtues, which are linked together by the preposition *ohne*. Such key words in Herder's description as "soul", "good", "mankind", and "truth" are further emphasized by the ryhthmic movement created by this duality, a movement in which it seems as if all external and transitory attributes are cast off. What remains is nothing perceptible in the rational sense, only that "blos durch Empfindung wahr". The thought content of the poem is released from the inner being of man, that part of man which each desires to know, but which each must be content to feel within him through the elucidation of contrasts, until only that which can no longer be grasped conceptually, but which is basic – being remains. Beauty and truth become interchangeable, symbolic of the fact that the world of concepts has given way to

[54] Cf. also *SWS*, I, 474 and 547. Herder cites lines from this poem in XXX, 30.

a world of feeling, being, and creation. The man identified here is the same man that Herder calls for again and again in the *Fragmente* and other early works, and as late as the *Kalligone* he is the type of man Herder contrasts with Kant's man of reason. Herder seems to realize, however, that the man he celebrates must necessarily remain an ideal, but an ideal for which man must continually strive.

Another of Herder's unpublished poems, a work consisting of sixty-nine four line stanzas in which Herder has achieved a fine lyrical quality absent in many of his poetic creations, is an excellent statement of Herder's thoughts on the creation, the position of man relative to the creation and the Creator, and the importance of feeling, the soul, and the spirit. This poem bears the title "Die Schöpfung", and more than the first half of it is devoted to a poetic account of the creation before man is created. These forty odd stanzas are only an introduction to the main part of the poem, which is concerned with the creation of man. Here again as in "Der Mensch" the similarity with the main ideas of the *Ideen* is remarkable, although "Die Schöpfung" was written in 1773, some ten years before the first part of the *Ideen* appeared in 1784. Man is presented as the highest form, as the goal and purpose of creation. But as soon as Herder introduces man he makes it clear that it is not because of his form alone, but rather that it is due to his spirit, his capacity to feel, which distinguishes man from the rest of creation and enables him to claim distinction as the goal and end of the creative process.

> Nein! o nein! Du nicht das Ziel
> seiner Schöpfung, nur Gefühl,
>
> (XXIX, 442)

The culmination of the process of creation, which Herder describes in five stanzas of the poem, is represented as a search for a creature in which can be united the dual roles of creator and created. This creature must not only reflect in itself the spirit of the creation, but by projecting the creative spirit within it must also carry on the creative work already begun. Then, and only then, can this highest order of creation, man, be said to exemplify its creator.

> Nein! die Schöpfung, itzt am Ziel
> harret, schweigt noch! – Ihr Gefühl
> wandelt in sich, und vermisst
> was Geschöpf und Schöpfer ist;
>
> Suchet Einen, der mit Geist
> *schmeckt* und was er *ist, genuesst,*
> suchet, der mit Gottesblick
> alle Schöpfung stralt zurück! –
>
> In sich, von sich. Und selbst ich
> in sich stral' und väterlich
> von sich stral' und walte frei
> und wie Gott ein Schöpfer sei! —
>
> Sieh den suchet, jetzt am Ziel
> Gottes Schöpfung, wirft Gefühl
> in sich dess, was sie vermisst,
> und der Mensch – der Gott – er ist!
>
> Neu Geschöpf, wie nenn ich dich! –
> Gott der Schöpfung, lehre mich –
> Doch ich bin, ich bin es ja,
> dem dies Gottesbild geschah! –
>
> (XXIX, 443)

The next three stanzas leave no doubt as to the position of man once this animation has been accomplished. Man is like God, he is in His image, but a spiritual, not a physical image. Man is free, he possesses a soul which creates, acts, feels like the soul of Jehovah Himself.

> *Ich wie Gott!* Da tritt in mich
> Plan der Schöpfung, weitet sich,
> drängt zusammen und wird *Macht!*
> endet froh und jauchzt: *vollbracht!* –
>
> Ich wie Gott! Da tritt in sich
> meine Seel' und denket Mich!
> schafft sich um und handelt frei,
> fühlt, wie frei Jehovah sei.
>
> Ich wie Gott! Da schlägt mein Herz
> Königsmuth und Bruder-Schmerz.
> Alles Leben hier vereint,
> fühlt der Mensch sich aller Freund!
>
> (XXIX, 443)

With the exception of the last five stanzas, the remainder of the poem is given over to an exposition of man's place as Herder sees it in the order of things. Scarcely any of the more important ideas concerning man, the soul, or the universe are lacking here in this poetic interpretation. Despite the risk of some repetition these should be enumerated. Because of his soul and his power to feel and sense, man can say that creation reached its climax in him. The third stanza reaffirms the statements of other poems that man is representative of creation as a whole. He is a microcosm. In this same stanza the important service performed by the senses as intake canals of the soul prepares the way for the important lines of the fifth stanza, "Und ward Bild, Gedank und That/ und ward Mensch". These lines are reminiscent of Hamann's cryptic "Rede, dass ich dich sehe", and should be compared with Herder's treatment of this same general idea in *Ueber Bild, Dichtung und Fabel*, where Herder writes: "*Bild* nenne ich jede Vorstellung eines Gegenstandes mit einigem Bewusstseyn der Wahrnehmung verbunden" (XV, 525). As the highest form of creation man is also the most harmonious of creatures. Within him all powers of the soul are united into a harmonious whole with the Great Creator and the universe. In two of the stanzas the Herder of the *Ideen* and *Kalligone* is easily recognizable. Herder here stresses the contribution made by the anatomical features of man to his preeminence in the order of creation. The following stanza is in close agreement with what Herder says about language in the *Älteste Urkunde*. In both the poem and the prose work the influence of Hamann can clearly be seen as Herder contradicts much of what he had said earlier about language in *Über den Ursprung der Sprache*. And in the last two stanzas Herder calls attention to the immortality and timelessness of God and likewise of the human soul by comparing them to an inexhaustible sea.[55] At the same time Herder is attaining that special type of immortality peculiar to the poet which he talks about in the short essay *Über die menschliche Unsterblichkeit*. This is the immortality which man achieves through the works he leaves to poster-

[55] See esp. *SWS*, XIII, 170 and Haym II, 239-246 for a complete discussion of immortality.

ity and, for the poet, is an immortality of the word. Due to the relative inaccessibility of the poem, I have reproduced these stanzas below.

Fühlt sich Sinn voll Mitgefühl
bis zur Pflanze, bis zum Ziel
aller Menschengöttlichkeit,
feint sich liebend weit und breit,

Immer tiefer, höher. Ich
bins, in dem die Schöpfung sich
punktet, der in alles quillt
und der Alles in sich füllt! –

Bis zur letzten Schöpfung hin
fühlet, tastet, reicht mein Sinn!
Aller Wesen Harmonie
mit mir – ja ich selbst bin sie!

Bin der Eine Gottesklang,
der aus allem Lustgesang'
aller Schöpfung tönt' empor
und trat ein in Gottes Ohr,

Und ward Bild, Gedank und That
und ward Mensch. Der Schöpfung Rath,
Mensch, ist in dir! Fühle dich
und die Schöpfung fühlet sich! –

Fühle dich, so fühlst du Gott
in dir. In dir fühlt sich Gott,
wie ihn *Sonn'* und *Thier* nicht fühlt,
wie er-sich – in sich – erziehlt! –

Schweig', o hohe Harmonie
meiner Seelenkräfte! Sie
fasst die Welt nicht. Gottes Bild
tief verhüllt und tief enthüllt,

Was ich *bin.* – Da wölbst du dich
meine Stirn, so breitet sich
jener Himmel, schaut ihn an
Gottes Licht und Wolkenbahn!

Und was dies mein Haupt versteckt,
ist im Himmel dort verdeckt,
und was dies mein Auge spricht,
spricht Jehovahs Angesicht.

Leben athmet hier und Geist,
der Jehovahs Othem heisst.
Sprache schaffet dieser Mund,
so schuf seines Herzens Grund

Gott im Worte für uns hin! –
Und so tief als Gottes Sinn,
reicht auch Menschliche Natur
immerdar auf Gottes Spur.

Uns ein unerschöpflich Meer!
Ewigkeiten strömtens her,
Ewigkeiten strömtens hin,
was Gott ist und was ich bin.

(XXIX, 444f)

The ideal which Herder places in the center of his own lyric poetry is no exception to the ideal which he sees in the true lyric poetry of all nations and all time. Indeed, it is the same ideal which Herder seeks in every aspect of life and which he finds best exemplified in man, in his form, his capabilities, his powers of speech and reason, but above all in his total inner spiritual condition, which according to Herder is eternal and immutable. All of these features Herder tries to bring together and express with one word, *Humanität*. "Ich wünschte, dass ich in das Wort Humanität alles fassen könnte, was ich bisher über des Menschen edle Bildung zur Vernunft und Freiheit, zu feinern Sinnen und Trieben, zur zartesten und stärksten Gesundheit, zur Erfüllung und Beherrschung der Erde gesagt habe: denn der Mensch hat kein edleres Wort für seine Bestimmung als Er selbst ist, in dem das Bild des Schöpfers unsrer Erde, wie es hier sichtbar werden konnte, abgedruckt lebet. Um seine edelsten Pflichten zu entwickeln, dörfen wir nur seine Gestalt zeichnen" (XIII, 154f).

CONCLUSION

This study has attempted to show that not only the content, the *what* of Herder's observations, but also the *why*, the presuppositions and the unique manner of critical approach to the object are of importance to an understanding of Herder's aesthetics. Thus it is no accident when the structural scheme of many of his writings is patterned after the same three stages which are characteristic of the development of the human soul. It is not by chance that in the *Plastik* Herder declares that even the seemingly dead statue is imbued with a spirit which exists in a like relationship to the form of the work of art as man's soul does to his body. Nor is it coincidental that Herder conceives of the work of art as the creation of man's soul, as a visible manifestation of the soul's creative power, just as he likewise considers the body the creation of the soul and its means of sensuous contact with the universe about it. All of these observations rest on Herder's concept of the human soul, and on his conviction that aesthetics can best be understood by the application of certain psychological principles. The same unity and harmony which is characteristic of the human soul as is postulated in the *Viertes Wäldchen* is the dominant feature of any work of art according to the Shakespeare essay, but especially of literature, which Herder considered the most complete expression of man's whole personality. Those same dynamic qualities of the soul which receive special emphasis in *Vom Erkennen und Empfinden* and which are indicative of the soul's powers to grow, to develop, and to create, are especially esteemed by Herder as basic traits of the folk song in the Ossian essay and in his other enthusiastic treatments of folk poetry. Just as Herder assigns to man's soul dominance over the body, so too does he see the soul, the content of the work of art, as more important than its form. Thus in the *Fragmente* it is the spirit of the word, and not its form which is of prime importance to the proper development of German. In the *Viertes Wäldchen* and *Plastik* it is the feeling of inner perfection and harmony which produces beauty in a statue, in the Shakespeare essay it is similarity in content which makes Sophocles and Shakespeare brothers, and in the *Kalligone* Herder's emphasis of content in the arts is one of the distinguishing features of his system from that of Kant. Herder wrote in 1774: "Geist wirkt auf Geist, auf Kraft und nicht aufs hölzerne Phänomenon, den Körper" (VIII, 253). Since Herder's primary concern is for the content of the work of art, then it must follow from the above that only man's own inner powers are capable of perceiving this content. This inner power of perception and sensation for Herder is the human soul. Consequently, Herder admonishes the critic to feel himself into the soul of the work of art he examines, he pleads for the poet to speak to the soul of his reader, and he longs for a reader who has conditioned his soul so that it will be receptive to the message of the poet, for only the soul is capable of grasping universals, only through a union of the souls of the subject and object can the aesthetic experience take place.

Herder's methods have revealed far more than the subjects or the contents of his thoughts, that which he could and wanted to see. They have gone beyond the polemic nature of many of the writings to his innermost convictions and intentions. His works have also been examined in the light of their structural peculiarities, and have been seen to be unique, organic works of art in which the structuring, the development of certain ideas, the adoption of certain aspects of criticism, the choice and suggestion of examples, etc. reveal definite principles of composition and organization, an inner method of presentation which says much more than mere rational concepts could ever express. Herder is not only concerned with emphasizing the existential aspects of art and their immediate effects, for he sees in aesthetic criticism one of the best means of gaining deeper insights into the nature and destiny of mankind. Art never exists for its own sake alone, but is for Herder always a sense-developing power of man in order for him to be able to recognize the essential, the good, the beautiful and the divine in the human realm and to give expression to it. The truth and validity of that which is human are also ultimate concerns in art. Precisely for this reason he who has the deepest insight into the being and destiny of man also has the best understanding and taste in art. All art, but especially poetry, is a way to the development of man, to a consciousness of man in regard to his most inner and ideal powers. Aesthetics for Herder is not only a special science based on mechanical rules as it was for Baumgarten, or abstract views of the possible dependent upon monads, entelechy, and atoms as it was for Leibniz, or a human endeavour dominated by the power of judgement such as it was for Kant, but rather a comprehension, movement, and development of the *whole* man. Aesthetics is a part of the *Humanitätsideal* as it developed in German thinking toward the end of the eighteenth century. Aesthetics is a science of the innermost genetic powers and of organized God-given formative powers. Aesthetics is a doctrine of the soul.

Because of the psychological depths, the anti-rationalistic elements, and the relationship to general human presuppositions which Herder includes in his aesthetic, a comparison with other aesthetic systems is difficult. Herder must have felt this himself, since he often builds his own foundations upon a critical or polemic framework. Within this framework the ideas of another give impetus, direction, and perspective to his own thoughts. In such cases one must not be misled by the polemic balast, but rather must view it as an aid in helping Herder's own ideas stand out more clearly. We have seen in the *Erstes Wäldchen* how, by using the ideas of Lessing in the *Laokoon*, Herder develops an awareness of the historical and recognition of the importance of character individuality, how he is able to expand the narrow boundaries Lessing assigns to the individual arts into perspectives more fruitful for their production and appreciation, and how he shows that one standard or model cannot universally be applied. In the *Viertes Wäldchen* Herder's concept of the unity of the soul, its functions and its unique developmental structure are built upon what he terms Riedel's "faulty psychology". And finally, we have seen in the *Kalligone* how Herder draws together the many facets of his concept of aesthetics as a soul-centered, soul-oriented science in reference to Kant's reason-centered aesthetic.

The choice of Schiller for the purposes of this concluding comparison is especially suitable for several reasons. Although Herder never engaged in a direct polemic with Schiller as he did with Lessing, Kant, and others, his disapproving views of Schiller's aesthetic are well known.[1] To a large extent this was due, of course, to his association of Schiller's ideas with those of Kant, whose theses, both epistemological and aesthetic, he had emphatically rejected in his last two major works. Nor is there any reason to question Herder's conviction that in the realm of aesthetics Schiller followed closely in the path of Kant. Although Schiller cannot be described as "a mere disciple of Kant", he was, in Wellek's words, his "first and still cautious follower".[2] Indeed, Schiller himself freely acknowledges his debt to Kant in the first letter of *Über die ästhetische Erziehung des Menschen,* where he writes: "Zwar will ich Ihnen nicht verbergen, dass es grösstenteils Kantische Grundsätze sind, auf denen die nachfolgenden Behauptungen ruhen werden." [3] Even excluding Schiller's association with the ideas of Kant, a comparison of Herder's ideas with those of Schiller seems profitable with regard to their concepts of the nature of man, the function and purpose of art, the importance and character of man's developmental process, the relationship of form and content in the aesthetic experience, and the ultimate goal of man and the role played by art in man's drive toward this goal.

[1] See Rudolf Haym, *Herder,* ed. Wolfgang Harich (Berlin, 1954), II, 656f, 699f, and Robert T. Clark, Jr., *Herder: His Life and Thought* (Berkeley-Los Angeles, 1955), p. 373f.
[2] Rene Wellek, *A History of Modern Criticism* (New Haven, 1955), I, 232.
[3] *Schillers Werke,* ed. R. Boxberger (Berlin-Stuttgart, n.d.) in *Deutsche National-Litteratur,* 129 Band, *Schillers Werk* XII, 1. p. 218. All citations from this text. Hereafter cited according to page in the text.

Aesthetics for Herder can never be considered a rational manipulation of change or a complex "education" of man by art as it is for Schiller in his *Über die ästhetische Erziehung des Menschen*. Rather, art for Herder is a direct, alive, active, and convincing revelation of human being in its concrete, historical, and fateful possibilities. A universal concept of life corresponds to a finished concept of the totality of man, such as it is given in the human soul. Individuality here is only an expression of the psychic aspects of man, and not a subjectivity such as was developed by Schiller and those who looked to his writings later in the nineteenth century. Schiller saw art as the unity of man's intellectual powers, Herder as the unity of all his powers. On the one hand Schiller applies his aesthetic to concepts such as freedom, dignity, self-determination, salvation of the supreme in man against the ravages of time and environment, intensification of morality, and intellectual self-genesis. On the other Herder sees in art a direct, universal, and natural development of the human soul, a creation out of the entirety of his existence. Like Herder, Schiller too wanted a free and perfect man, but unlike Herder, Schiller, because of his belief that the modern poet was divided in himself and in conflict with society, wanted to re-establish him "sentimentally" and to restore him through art, instead of fashioning (*bilden*) him "naïvely" and allowing him to come into his own according to his innate potentials.

Speaking of Schiller's concept of man, Benno v. Wiese has recently written: "Was in Gott Einheit ist, wird im Menschen zur Zweiheit." [4] In other words, Schiller conceives of man as some sort of dualistic being. Man is a split personality. In the twelfth of his *Ästhetische Briefe* Schiller postulates his theory of the two opposing forces within man, of the *Stofftrieb* and the *Formtrieb*. The thoughts expressed in this letter are characteristic of Schiller's ideas on the double nature of man, that he is sensuous and spiritual, subjective and objective, naïve and sentimental, aesthetic and ethical. Schiller is always working with opposites. Such Kantian antitheses as the physical and the moral, the natural and the ideal, and the phenomenal and the noumenal are common-

[4] Benno v. Wiese, *Schiller* (Stuttgart, 1959), p. 488.

place in Schiller's writings. The problem to which Schiller addresses himself in the thirteenth letter is how to restore the unity of man destroyed by the concept of the two opposing forces in the preceding letter. Instead of doing this, as one might expect, by adding another force which will bridge the gap between the two opposing forces *Formtrieb* and *Stofftrieb*, Schiller introduces a new and surprising concept as mediator, culture. Thus it becomes the task of culture, i.e. of art and beauty, as the eighteenth letter makes clear, to heal the split in man's personality between man and nature, between man's intellect and his senses. But despite the mediative efforts of culture, beauty, and art, despite the introduction of the concept of a *Spieltrieb* as the unification of the *Formtrieb* and *Stofftrieb*, and despite Schiller's intimations in the thirteenth letter and elsewhere that in their drives toward opposite goals the two forces neutralize one another, man remains a creature with a twofold nature. "Aber was heisst denn ein blosses **Spiel,** nachdem wir wissen, dass unter allen Zuständen des Menschen gerade das Spiel es ist, was ihm vollständig macht und *seine doppelte Natur* auf einmal entfaltet" (p. 264, emphasis supplied). This finds further support in the eighteenth letter where Schiller declares: ". . . der Abstand zwischen Materie und Form, zwischen Leiden und Thätigkeit, zwischen Empfinden und Denken unendlich ist, und schlechterdings durch nichts kann vermittelt werden" (272).

Such an admission from the pen of Herder would be impossible. Indeed, Schiller's whole system of *Triebe* and mediative efforts are rendered superfluous by Herder's fundamental belief in the unity of man's soul. "Wie schön wird eben damit die Menschliche Seele! Einheit im Grunde, tausendfache Mannichfaltigkeit in der Ausbildung, Vollkommenheit in der Summe des Ganzen" (IV, 34). As we have already made clear in Chapter I, this is Herder's basic disagreement with Riedel in the *Viertes Wäldchen*, and this is the one point he reiterates over and over again in every one of his works whenever he deals with the human soul or matters pertaining to psychology. ". . . denn die Formen der Seele sind überall Eins" (VIII, 113). "Kurz, alle diese Kräfte sind im Grunde nur Eine Kraft . . ." (VIII, 196). Moreover, this unity of the soul is one of man's distinguishing characteristics and one of his foremost claims to his own unique place within the overall cosmic scheme of things. Only through this unity of the soul, with all his powers and faculties working together in harmonious unity, has man been able to lift himself up to his present level. "Sie [die Sinne] stellen ihr [die Seele] alle ein Mannichfaltes vor, wo ihr Macht und Amt gegeben wird, daraus ein Eins zu machen" (VIII, 239).

Not only does Schiller conceive of man as having a twofold nature, he also explicitly states that of the two active forces within him, i.e. the sensuous and the reasonable, the reasonable force is the dominant one. This is expressed in a footnote to the thirteenth letter. "Sobald man einen ursprünglichen, mithin notwendigen Antagonism beider Triebe behauptet, so ist freilich kein anderes Mittel, die Einheit im Menschen zu erhalten, als dass man den sinnlichen Trieb dem vernünftigen unbedingt unterordnet" (p. 256). Herder's reaction to a statement such as this would be the same as his reaction to similar assertions representative of the *Aufklärung*. Since man's soul is a unified, harmonious whole, no single one of his faculties can assert dominance over another. This is not to deny the importance or the place of reason, which Herder never did, but merely to place it in the proper perspective along with the rest of man's faculties. In fact, reasonableness is characteristic of the total direction of man, but is never a power or faculty that assumes dominance over man. ". . . die Vernunft [ist] keine abgetheilte, einzelwürkende Kraft, sondern eine seiner Gattung eigner Richtung aller Kräfte . . ." (V, 31). This same concept of reason that assumes dominance over the sensuous for Schiller is also the determinant of beauty. Schiller writes in the tenth letter: "Dies scheint einen Begriff der Schönheit vorauszusetzen, der eine andere Quelle hat als die Erfahrung" (249). Later in the same letter Schiller speaks of "dieser reine Vernunftbegriff der Schönheit", and "dem reinen Begriff der Menschheit". In a letter to Körner dated 25 October 1794 he wrote: "Das Schöne ist kein Erfahrungsbegriff, sondern vielmehr ein Imperativ." [5] We can thus agree with Wil-

[5] Quoted by Herbert Cysarz, *Schiller* (Halle/Saale, 1934), p. 168.

helm Böhm when he says: "Der 10. Brief ist die eindrucksvolle Ankündigung der Absicht, die Schönheit als einen reinen Vernunftbegriff abzuleiten." [6] Commenting on this concept of Schiller's, Benno v. Wiese writes: "Es geht ihm um den 'reinen Vernunftbegriff der Schönheit', der seinem Wesen nach mit dem Begriff der ganzen Menschheit identisch ist. Diesen Begriff [ist] in einem Prozess des Philosophierens zu realisieren, . . ." [7] Such methods, such concepts, such intentions are completely foreign to Herder's aesthetic. In the *Kalligone* he categorically establishes his position in regard to any concept of "pure reason". Previously he had already written in the *Metakritik*: "Sich von sich selbst unabhängig zu machen, d.i. aus aller ursprünglichen, innern und äussern Erfahrung sich hinauszusetzen, von allem Empirischen frei über sich selbst *hinaus zu denken*, vermag niemand" (XXI, 24). A belief in the subjective and objective nature of the aesthetic experience is one of the cornerstones of his aesthetic. "Seyn ist der Grund aller Erkenntniss. Wo nichts ist, erkennet nichts und wird nichts erkannt" (XXI, 62). To be sure, there is an *a priori* force in the soul of man, but this is his inherent potential. Only through his experiences, however, only by means of contact through his senses with the world about him, does man develop this potential. "Kein Erkennen ist ohne Empfindung, . . . (VIII, 236).

Closely related to Schiller's concept of *Vernunft* are his concepts of morality, form, and freedom. In the twenty-third letter Schiller writes: "In einem wahrhaft schönen Kunstwerke soll der Inhalt nichts, die Form aber alles thun; denn durch die Form allein wird auf das Ganze des Menschen, durch den Inhalt hingegen nur auf einzelne Kräfte gewirkt" (286). This statement stands in marked contrast to Herder's well-known declaration of the *Kalligone:* "Im Geist; nicht in der toten Form; denn ohne Geist ist jede Form eine Scherbe" (XXII, 101). By referring back to the series of letters beginning with the third letter we can see clearly that Schiller identifies his concept of form with his con-

[6] Wilhelm Böhm, *Schillers "Briefe über Die Ästhetische Erziehung Des Menschen"* (Halle/Saale, 1927), p. 37.
[7] v. Wiese, p. 486.

cepts of morality and reason. As Böhm has commented: ". . .
die Moral, – Vernunft, . . . ist blosse Form . . ." [8] Comparing
Schiller's position in regard to the determination of beauty with
that of Goethe and Homer, which, by the way, would also apply
to Herder, Cysarz has written: "Schön ist nicht nur die geist-
durchströmte Sinnlichkeit, die Sinnlichkeit Homers und Goethes,
sondern auch die Sittlichkeit . . ." [9] If form is morality and reason,
it is also freedom. In the eleventh letter Schiller writes: ". . . und
so hätten wir denn fürs erste die Idee des absoluten, in sich selbst
gegründeten Seins, d.i. die Freiheit" (250). In his *Freiheit und
Form* Cassirer has forcefully described this relationship: "Als
die reine Form aller Geistigkeit überhaupt aber hat Schiller nun-
mehr die Idee der Freiheit erkannt." [10] For Herder freedom could
hardly be absolute being, founded in itself, since he recognizes
no such phenomenon as absolute being. Rather, what Schiller
views as the result of absolute being, Herder ascribes to the developmental qualities of the soul and his belief in a dynamic
creation. Thus Herder is able to write: "Die Seele kann nichts
thun, als dass sie würke. . . . Dies ist das Phänomenon der
Menschlichen Freiheit . . ." (VIII, 245). The soul's activity Herder describes as: "Freiheit im Erkennen und Wollen, der Abgrund und Gottesschatz unsrer Seele" (VIII, 294). Herder's cryptic "Wo Geist des Herrn ist, da ist Freiheit" (VIII, 295), points
to his firm belief that man, the only one of God's creations imbued directly with His spirit, is free to develop his innate potential. "*Der Mensch ist zu feinern Trieben, mithin zu Freiheit
organisiret*" (XIII, 142). Man is not born in a state of perfection,
but it is his prerogative, indeed his duty, to attempt to attain such
a state.

Geist Gottes hiess bekanntermaassen von den ältesten Zeiten her
bewegende mächtige Naturkraft, jene *lebendige Regung* die den Geschöpfen Leben mittheilt, die durch Wirksamkeit ihr Leben erhält,
ihre Kräfte stärkt und födert. *Geist Gottes* hiess ihnen in menschlichen Seelen *jede edelste Kraft*, wenn sie sich in vollem Genuss

[8]   Böhm, p. 33.
[9]   Cysarz, p. 192.
[10] Ernst Cassirer, *Freiheit und Form* (Berlin, 1922), p. 444.

ihres Daseyns auf die vorzügliche *Tendenz* des Menschen, immer vollkommener zu werden, heller im Verstande, reiner im Herzen, kräftiger im Willen, von innerm Vorwurf frei, der Gottheit nahe, ihr verwandt, nach ihr gebildet (XXX, 229).

The concept of freedom gains its importance for Schiller's aesthetic when one considers the second letter, where Schiller calls art "eine Tochter der Freiheit" (219), and states that it is beauty "durch welche man zu der Freiheit wandert" (220). As we have already seen, Herder is able to avoid this complicated system of concepts in his aesthetic by assigning all of these functions to the soul. Just as the soul of man is of greater importance than his body, so too the content of the work than its form. By empathy the subject is able to project his soul into the soul of the object. The experiences, the knowledge gained from the aesthetic experience, influence the soul of the subject and aid in its development on the way to *Humanität*. In Herder's aesthetic art and beauty are parts of a formative process, or to paraphrase Schiller, what might be termed a *Bildungstrieb*. Such a force, however, is lacking in the aesthetics of Schiller. In summary of this Cassirer writes: ". . . dass jedoch für Schiller die Freiheit der Oberbegriff ist, unter den er die Gesamtheit aller Form und Bildung befasst, während für Goethe die 'Bildung' das allgemeinste Prinzip ist, von dem aus er das Sittliche, und somit die Freiheit selbst, noch als eine besondere Energie zu deuten sucht." [11]

Schiller does not recognize in art and beauty a formative or pedagogic value which will aid man in his climb toward perfection and *Humanität*. Rather, as the title of his work indicates, he wishes to educate man aesthetically. The ultimate goal of this process is explained in the twenty-third letter. ". . . es giebt keinen andern Weg, den sinnlichen Menschen vernünftig zu machen, als man denselben zuvor ästhetisch macht" (288). Herder has no desire to make the sensuous man reasonable. Indeed, he regards his state of man, as it was generally thought of in his time, as a false state. "Der Zustand unsrer kalten Besonnenheit ist ein künstlicher . . ." (XV, 534). Because of his concept of the function of beauty Schiller can refer to it as "die zweite Schöpferin"

[11] *Ibid.*, p. 453.

(283). Beauty may stimulate, it may awaken, it may aid in forming a potential already present, but for Herder it can never create. The designation "Second Creator" he assigns to the artist, specifically the poet, who creates his own microcosm in a manner analogous to the creation of the macrocosm. "Indem er alles nennt, und mit seiner Empfindung auf sich ordnet, wird er Nachahmer der Gottheit, der zweite Schöpfer, also auch *poietes*, Dichter" (XII, 7). For Schiller beauty is deserving of the designation he gives it because it creates the aesthetic, and hence reasonable state of man, thus leading sensuous man to duty and reason and preparing him for his place in a universe which is reasonably ordered. Art and beauty thus assume a tremendous civilizing role. They heal "the wounds of civilization, the split between man and nature and between man's intellect and his senses. Art makes man whole again, reconciles him with the world and with himself." [12] As Cysarz has observed: "Die Schönheit knüpft das Band zwischen Seele und Weltall." [13] Now though it may be argued that Schiller ultimately arrives at a concept of man as a unified, harmoniously organized whole which does not differ radically from Herder's idea of man, there can be little doubt that the manner in which he finally reaches his conclusion is completely at odds with Herder's basic assumptions. The fundamental premise of Herder's psychology, that man's soul exists in God-given indivisible unity, that all of its forces, powers, and faculties are organized into a harmoniously functioning whole, that the soul maintains contact with other souls and the whole of creation through its own power, i.e. the *geistige Band*, and that the soul possesses its own inherent potential for growth and development, which only awaits activating influences and stimuli before it begins to function, all obviate any concepts of art as a unifying agent or beauty as man's link with the rest of creation. That which is a complete whole in the moment of its conception has no need for further completion. To be sure, Herder assigns to art and beauty a significant role in the developmental process of man. The basic state of man he presupposes, however, even before art

---

[12] Wellek, p. 233.
[13] Cysarz, p. 177.

and beauty begin to make their influence felt, is a final state for Schiller, reached only after art and beauty have "educated" him.

This brief discussion of several points of Schiller's and Herder's aesthetic should emphasize further the tremendous importance of Herder's unique psychological approach to his aesthetic. More than any other factor it is this approach which enables him to reveal new and startling perspectives of aesthetic evaluation, to exert such tremendous influence on the future development of literature and aesthetics, and to assure a permanent place for his ideas in any history of aesthetics. Schiller's terminology is Kantian, and so differs radically from Herder's. But his methods, although influenced by Kant and thus different than Herder's, are his own. His conclusions, or perhaps better the conclusions he hopes and attempts to reach, are often surprisingly similar to those of Herder. Similarity of conclusions, however, is not enough for Herder. Methods and terminology are not something secondary, but are of basic importance in his aesthetic, for by the use of his own terminology and the application of his own methods Herder is able to open up new perspectives in the realm of aesthetics. "Wie schön wird eben damit die Menschliche Seele: Einheit im Grunde, tausendfache Mannichfaltigkeit in der Ausbildung, Vollkommenheit in der Summe des Ganzen. ... Alles soll aus Einem gebildet, und zu mannichfaltigen Vollkommenheit erhoben werden" (IV, 34).

A SELECTED BIBLIOGRAPHY

A. BIBLIOGRAPHICAL WORKS

In addition to the standard bibliographies of Goedeke, Körner, Kosch, and Eppelsheimer the reader is referred to the following two comprehensive Herder bibliographies:

Berger, Dieter, "Herder-Schrifttum 1916-1953", in *Im Geiste Herders*, ed. Erich Keyser (Kitzingen am Main, Holsner-Verlag, 1953), pp. 268-305.

Clark, Robert T., Jr. *Herder: His Life and Thought* (Berkeley and Los Angeles, University of California Press, 1955). pp. 455-478.

B. EDITIONS AND CORRESPONDENCE

Goethe, Johann Wolfgang, *Weimarer Ausgabe*, 143 vols. (Weimar, H. Böhlau, 1887-1912).

Hamann, Johann Georg, *Sämmtliche Werke*, ed., J. Nadler, 6 vols. (Wien, Verlag Herder, 1949f).

Herder, Johann Gottfried, *God, Some Conversations*, ed. and trans. with notes and introduction by Frederick Henry Burkhardt (New York, Veritas Press, 1940).

——, *Kalligone*, ed. Heinz Begenau (Weimar, Hermann Böhlaus Nachfolger, 1955).

——, *Sprachphilosophische Schriften*, ed., Eric Heintel (Hamburg, F. Weiner, 1960).

——, *Sämmtliche Werke*, ed. B. Suphan *et al.*, 33 vols. (Berlin, Weidmannsche Buchhandlung, 1877-1913).

Kant, Immanuel, *Kant's Critique of Judgement*, trans. with notes and introduction by J. H. Bernard, 2nd ed. rev. (London, Macmillan and Co., 1914).

——, *Werke*, ed., Wilhelm Weischedel. 6 vols. (Wiesbaden, Insel Verlag, 1957f).

Lessing, Gotthold E., *Werke*, ed. Julius Petersen and Waldemar v. Olshausen. 25 vols. (Leipzig, Bong & Co., n.d.).

Schauer, Hans, ed., *Herders Briefwechsel mit Caroline Flachsland.* I (August, 1770, to December, 1771) (Weimar, Verlag der Goethe-Gesellschaft, 1926); II (January, 1772, to April, 1773) (Weimar, Verlag der Goethe-Gesellschaft, 1928).

C. SPECIAL STUDIES PERTAINING TO HERDER

Adler, Frederick H., *Herder and Klopstock* (Cleveland?, 1913). (Diss. Illinois)

Arbusow, Leonis, "Herder und die Begründung der Volksliedforschung im deutschbaltischen Osten", in *Im Geiste Herders,* ed., E. Keyser (Kitzingen am Main, Holzner-Verlag, 1953), pp. 129-256.

Auerbach, Eric., "Vico und Herder", *DVJS,* X (1932), pp. 671-686.

Begenau, Heinz, *Grundzüge der Ästhetik Herders* (Weimar, Hermann Böhlaus Nachfolger, 1956).

Blackall, Eric A., "The Imprint of Herder's Linguistic Theory on his Early Prose Style", *PMLA,* LXXVI (1961), pp. 512-518.

Blättner, Fritz, "Das Shakespearebild Herders", in *Vom Geist der Dichtung,* ed., Fritz Martini (Hamburg, 1949), pp. 49-64.

Böckmann, Paul, *Der dramatische Perspecktivismus in der deutschen Shakespearedeutung des 18. Jahrhunderts,* IV. "Der Perspektivismus von Individualität und Geschichte bei Herder," in *Vom Geist der Dichtung,* ed. Fritz Martini (Hamburg, 1949).

Chrobok, Paul, *Die ästhetischen Grundgedanken von Herders Plastik in ihrem Entwicklungsgange* (Naumburg/Saale, H. Sieling, 1906).

Clark, Robert T., Jr., *Herder: His Life and Thought* (Berkeley and Los Angeles, University of California Press, 1955).

——, "Herder's Concept of 'Kraft' ", *PMLA,* LVII (Sept., 1942), pp. 737-752.

Dobbek, Wilhelm, "Herder und Shakespeare", *Shakespeare Jahrbuch,* XCI (1955), pp. 25-51.

——, "Die Kategorie der Mitte in der Kunstphilosophie J. G. Herders", in *Worte und Werte,* ed. Gustav Erdmann and Alfons Eichstaedt (Berlin, Walter de Gruyter & Co., 1961), pp. 70-78.

Flemming, Herbert, *Johann Gottfried Herder und die Deutung des Lebens* (Berlin, 1939).

Fricke Gehard, "Das Humanitätsideal der Klassischen deutschen Dichtung und die deutsche Gegenwart, II. Herder", *Zeitschrift für Deutschkunde,* XLVIII (1934), pp. 673-690.

Gillies, Alexander, *Herder* (Oxford, Basil Blackwell, 1945).

——, *Herder und Ossian* (Berlin, Junker und Dünnhaupt, 1933).

——, "Herder's Essay on Shakespeare: 'Das Herz der Untersuchung' " *MLR,* XXXII (1937), pp. 262-80.

Guthke, Karl S., "A Note on Herder and Rousseau", *MLQ,* XVIIII (1958), pp. 303-06.

Haym, Rudolf, *Herder,* ed., Wolfgang Harich. 2 vols. (Berlin, Aufbau Verlag, 1954).

294   *A Selected Bibliography*

Isaacsen, Hertha, *Der junge Herder und Shakespeare* (Berlin, E. Ebering, 1930).

Jacoby, Günther, *Herders und Kants Ästhetik* (Leipzig, Dürr, 1907).

Keyser, Erich, "Bekenntnis zu Herder", in *Im Geiste Herders*, ed., E. Keyser (Kitzingen am Main, Holzner-Verlag, 1953), pp. 1-25.

Konrad, Gustav, *Herders Sprachproblem im Zusammenhang der Geistesgeschichte* (Berlin, E. Ebering, 1937).

Kühnemann, Eugen, *Herder*, 2te, neu bearbeitete Auflage, (München, C. H. Beck, 1912).

Lewis, Earl N., "Herder's Theory of the Gifted Individual", *GQ*, XXIX, 3, pp. 131-41.

Litt, Theodor, *Die Befreiung des geschichtlichen Bewusstseins durch J. G. Herder* (Leipzig, W. Seemann, 1942).

Mann, Otto, "Wandlungen des Herderbildes", *Deutschunterricht*, X (1958), pp. 27-48.

Markwardt, Bruno, *Herders Kritische Wälder* (Leipzig, Quelle und Meyer, 1925).

May, Kurt, *Lessings und Herders kunsttheoretische Gedanken in ihrem Zusammenhang* (Berlin, K. Ebering, 1923).

McEachran, Frank, *The Life and Philosophy of Johann Gottfried Herder* (Oxford, Claredon Press, 1939).

Nohl, Hermann, *Herder* (Berlin, Weichert, n.d.).

Peyer, Heinz, *Herders Theorie der Lyrik* (Winterthur, 1955).

Pfeiffer, Johannes, "Die Erneuerung der deutschen Dichtung im Zeitalter Herders", in his *Über das Dichterische und den Dichter* (Hamburg, 1956), pp. 40-57.

Rasch, Wolfdietrich, *Herder - Sein Leben und Werk im Umriss* (Halle/Saale, Niemeyer, 1938).

Schütze, Martin, *The Fundamental Ideas in Herder's Thought*. Serially in *Modern Philology*, XVIII (1920-21), pp. 65-78, pp. 289-303; XIX (1921-22), pp. 113-130, pp. 361-382; XXI (1923), pp. 29-48, pp. 113-132.

——, "Herder's Concept of 'Bild'," *GR*, I (1926), pp. 21-35.

——, "Herder's Psychology," *The Monist* XXXV (Oct., 1925), pp. 507-554.

——, "Johann Gottfried Herder," *Monatshefte für den Deutschen Unterricht*, XXXVI (1944), pp. 257-287.

Shaw, Leroy H., "Henry Home of Kames: Precursor of Herder," *GR*, XXXI (1960), pp. 16-27.

Sommerhalder, Hugo, *Herder in Bückeburg als Deuter der Geschichte* (Frauenfeld und Leipzig, Huber & Co., 1945).

Spranger, Eduard, "J. G. Herder, Ahnung und Erfüllung," in *Vom Geist der Dichtung*, ed., Fritz Martini (Hamburg, 1949), pp. 31-48.

Stadelmann, Rudolf, *Der Historische Sinn Bei Herder* (Halle/Saale, Max Niemeyer, 1928).

Ulrich, Gisela, *Herders Beitrag Zur Deutschkunde*, (Würzburg, Konrad Triltsch Verlag, 1943).

Weber, Gottfried, *Herder und das Drama* (Weimar, A. Duncker, 1922).

Wiese, Benno v., *Herder, Grundzüge seines Weltbildes* (Leipzig, Bibliographisches Institut, 1939).
——, "Der Philosoph auf dem Schiffe," in his *Der Mensch in der Dichtung* (Düsseldorf, A. Bagel, 1958).
Wiora, Walter, "Herders Ideen zur Geschichte der Musik", in *Im Geiste Herders*, ed., E. Keyser (Kitzingen am Main, Holzner-Verlag, 1953), pp. 73-128.
Wolf, Hermann, "Die Genielehre des jungen Herder", *DVJS*, III (1925), pp. 400-430.
Wolff, Hans M., "Der junge Herder und die Entwicklungsidee Rousseaus", *PMLA*, LVII (1942), pp. 753-819.

D. GENERAL WORKS

Auerbach, Erich, *Mimesis*. 2te Auflage (Bern, Francke, 1959).
Babbitt, Irving, *The New Laokoön*. 3rd imprint (Boston and New York, 1910).
Blackall, Eric A., *The Emergence of German as a Literary Language* (Cambridge, University Press, 1959).
Cassirer, Ernst, *The Philosophy of the Enlightenment*, trans. Fritz Koelln and James Pettegrove (Princeton, Princeton University Press, 1951).
Ermatinger, Emil, *Die Deutsche Lyrik seit Herder*, "I. Von Herder bis Goethe" (Leipzig and Berlin, 1925).
Gilbert, Katherine E. and Helmut Kuhn, *A History of Esthetics* (New York, Macmillan, 1939).
Gundolf, Friedrich, *Shakespeare und der deutsche Geist*. 9. Auflage (Godesberg, H. Küpper, 1947).
Hettner, Hermann, *Geschichte der deutschen Literatur im achtzehnten Jahrhundert*, 5te, verbesserte Auflage (Braunschweig, Friedrich Vieweg und Sohn, 1909).
Korff, H. A., *Geist der Goethezeit* (Leipzig, Koehler & Amelang, 1957f).
Lotze, Herman, *Geschichte der Aesthetik in Deutschland* (München, 1868).
Mann, Otto, *Geschichte des deutschen Dramas* (Stuttgart, Kröner, 1960).
Markwardt, Bruno, *Geschichte der deutschen Poetik*, 5 vols. (Berlin, Walter de Gruyter & Co., 1937f).
Nadler, Josef, *Literaturgeschichte der deutschen Stämme und Landschaften*, 2. Auflage (Regensburg, 1923).
Nivelle, Armand, *Les Théories Esthétique en Allemagne de Baumgarten à Kant* (Paris, 1955).
Schasler, Max, *Ästhetik: Grundzüge der Wissenschaft und der Kunst* 2 vols. (Leipzig & Prag, 1886).
Schultz, Franz, *Klassik und Romantik der Deutschen*, 2te Auflage (Stuttgart, Metzler, 1952).
Staiger, Emil, *Die Kunst der Interpretation* (Zürich, Atlantis, 1955).
Strich, Fritz, *Deutsche Klassik und Romantik*, 4te Auflage (Bern, MCMXLIX).

Wellek, René, *A History of Modern Criticism: 1750-1950.* 4 vols. (New Haven, Yale University Press, 1955f).

——, and Austin Warren, *Theory of Literature* (New York, Harcourt, Brace and Company, 1956).

Wiese, Benno v., *Die deutsche Tragödie von Lessing bis Hebbel,* 3te Auflage (Hamburg, Hoffmann und Campe, 1953).

Wimsatt, William K., Jr. and Cleanth Brooks, *Literary Criticism, A Short History* (New York, Alfred A. Knopf, 1957).

Zeller, Eduard, *Geschichte der deutschen Philosophie seit Leibniz* (München, R. Oldenburg, 1873).

Zimmermann, Robert, *Geschichte der Aesthetik als philosophischer Wissenschaft* (Wien, W. Braumüller, 1858).

E. OTHER SOURCES CONSULTED

Berger, Friedrich, *Menschenbild und Menschenbildung* (Stuttgart, Kohlhammer, 1933).

Blockmann, Elizabeth, "Die deutsche Volksdichtungbewegung in Sturm und Drang und Romantik", *DVJS,* I (1923), pp. 419-452.

Böhm, Wilhelm, *Schillers "Briefe Über Die Ästhetische Erziehung Des Menschen"* (Halle/Saale, M. Niemeyer, 1927).

Brett, H. L., *The Third Earl of Shaftesbury* (London, Hutchinson's University Library, 1951).

Butler, E. M., *The Tyranny of Greece Over Germany* (Cambridge, 1935).

Caird, Edward, *The Critical Philosophy of Immanuel Kant* (New York, Macmillan & Co., 1889).

Cassirer, Ernst, *Freiheit und Form* (Berlin, B. Cassirer, 1922).

——, *The Logic of the Humanities,* trans. Clarence Smith Howe (New Haven, Yale University Press, 1961).

——, *The Philosophy of Symbolic Forms,* trans. Ralph Manheim. I. *Language,* II. *Mythical Thought* (New Haven, Yale University Press, 1955).

——, *The Problem of Knowledge,* trans. William H. Woglom and Charles W. Hendel (New Haven, Yale University Press, 1950).

Cysarz, Herbert, *Schiller* (Halle/Saale, M. Niemeyer, 1934).

Dilthey, Wilhelm, *Das Erlebnis und die Dichtung.* 3te Auflage (Leipzig, 1910).

Driver, Tom, *The Sense of History in Greek and Shakespearean Drama* (New York, Columbia University Press, 1960).

Jespersen, Otto, *Language, Its Nature, Development and Origin* (London, 1922).

Knox, Israel, *The Aesthetic Theories of Kant, Hegel, and Schopenhauer.* (New York, Humanities Press, 1958).

Kommerell, Max, *Der Dichter als Führer in der deutschen Klassik* (Berlin, Georg Bondi, 1928).

Köster, Albert, *Die allgemeinen Tendenzen der Geniebewegung im 18. Jahrhundert* (Leipzig, A. Edelmann, 1912).

Leibniz, Gottfried Wilhelm, *The Monadology and Other Philosophical Writings,* trans. and ed. by Robert Latta (London, Oxford University Press, 1951).

Nohl, Hermann, *Die Ästhetische Wirklichkeit.* 2te Auflage (Frankfurt, 1954).

Plato, *The Myths of Plato,* trans. and intro. by J. A. Stewart, ed., G. R. Levy (Carbondale, Southern Illinois University Press, 1960).

Revesz, G., *The Origins and Prehistory of Language,* trans. J. Butler (London, New York, and Toronto, Longmans, Green and Co., 1956).

Sewell, Elizabeth, *The Orphic Voice* (New Haven, Yale University Press, 1960).

Smith, Ronald Gregor, *J. G. Hamann* (New York, Harper and Bro., 1960).

Staiger, Emil, *Goethe,* 3 vols. (Zürich, Atlantis, 1956f).

Wiese, Benno v., *Schiller* (Stuttgart, Metzler, 1959).

Wilhelm, Richard, *Friedrich Justus Riedel und die Ästhetik der Aufklärung* (Heidelberg, C. Winter, 1933).

Will, Frederic, *Intelligible Beauty in Aesthetic Thought from Winckelmann to Victor Cousin* (Tübingen, Niemeyer, 1958).

NAME AND TITLE INDEX

SUBJECT INDEX

aesthetics, 16 f., 69, 98, 110, 132, 133 f., 150 f., 167, 183, 202 f., 258, 281 f.
allegory, 171, 200, 212
Anacreontic, 82

Begebenheit, see event.
Besonnenheit, see reflection.

Christianity, 64 f., 256 f.
creation, 17 f., 275 f., 280
criticism, 71 f., 182 f., 189 f.

education, 283 f.
empathy, 73, 149 f.
Enlightenment, 34, 69, 90 f., 187, 234, 246, 286
epistemology, 146 f., 283.
event (*Begebenheit*), 214 f., 219 f.
evolution, Theory of, 48

fate, 230 f.
feeling (*Gefühl*), 39 f., 72 f., 151 f.
folk poetry, 216, 246 f., 264 f., 280
form, 161 f., 264 f., 287 f.
form and content, 29, 34 f., 83 f., 125, 166 f., 191 f., 223 f., 265 f., 281 f., 289
freedom, 44, 49, 54, 287 f.

Gefühl, see feeling
geistiges Band, see spiritual bond
genius, 90 f., 185 f., 212 f., 222 f., 247 f., 260, 270 f

history, 218 f.
Humanität, 14, 29, 56 f., 69, 77, 96, 150, 161, 171 f., 181, 201, 246 f., 265, 270, 279, 282, 289
humanities (*schöne Wissenschaften*), 98 f.

ideal, 198 f.
imitation, 75 f., 209
immortality, 65 f., 277
individuality, 123 f.
inversion, 87, 244 f.

Kraft, see power

language, 43, 70, 79 f., 150 f., 181 f., 234 f.

mimesis, 75, 133, 177
monad, 31, 43, 271, 282
music, 179 f.
mythology, 110 f.

national literature, 97, 116 f., 252
national spirit (*Nationalgeist*), 95 f., 256

origin, 234 f., 257 f.

perfection, 128 f., 162 f., 171 f.
plastic art, 178 f.
poetics, 79
poetry, 81, 176 f.
power (*Kraft*), 83, 182, 259.
pre-established harmony, 31, 160

STUDIES IN PHILOSOPHY

Out:

1. Nathan Rotenstreich: *Humanism in the Contemporary Era.* 1963. 171 pp.   Gld. 18.—

2. Troy Wilsen Organ: *The Self in Indian Philosophy.* 1964. 184 pp.   Gld. 22.—

3. P. Allan Carlsson: *Butler's Ethics.* 1964. 196 pp.   Gld. 21.—

7. F. Warren Rempel: *The Role of Value in Karl Mannheim's Sociology of Knowledge.* 1965. 125 pp.   Gld. 16.—

8. Ralph Philip Joly: *The Human Person in a Philosophy of Education.* 1965. 147 pp.   Gld. 16.—

9. G. D. Bowne: *The Philosophy of Logic, 1880–1908.* 1966. 157 pp.   Gld. 18.—

MOUTON & CO · PUBLISHERS · THE HAGUE